Turtles, Tortoises and Terrapins

Fritz Jürgen Obst

Turtles, Tortoises and Terrapins

**St. Martin's Press
New York**

To my friend Prof. Mlynarski, Cracow, Poland

Translated from the German by Sylvia Furness

For information, address St. Martin's Press, 175 Fifth Avenue, New York, N.Y. 10010.

Design: Traudl Schneehagen
Drawings: Wolfgang Leuck
Maps: Matthias Weis

Library of Congress Catalog Card Number 85-61662
ISBN 0-312-82362-2   86-3954

First published in the German Democratic Republic by Edition Leipzig in 1986

Second U.S. Edition

10 9 8 7 6 5 4 3 2 1

Contents

Preface

Anyone who publishes a book about turtles today must take a stand on certain questions touching the very existence of one of the most seriously endangered groups of animals in the world. Its future was never so precarious as it is today. Archaic animals, often with a very low reproductive rate, a slow succession of generations and without the ability to react rapidly to a changing environment are not easily able to hold their own in an increasingly urbanized world. They have a particular need of our help and protection. But a vital prerequisite of any such action is knowledge and experience. To impart a modicum of such knowledge to nature lovers is the principal aim of this book. From the abundance of fascinating material, it is difficult to select the small amount that can fit within these pages. I can only hope that it will be sufficient to provide some information on the most important aspects and that it has been chosen in a way that will interest many readers. Much may seem skimped or neglected. The subject of keeping turtles in captivity as pets has been deliberately avoided. In the present situation, they cannot be pets for large numbers of animal lovers. Nevertheless, successful breeding programmes carried out by conscientious animal keepers and by zoos give no small measure of hope for the conservation of threatened species of turtles. Committed conservationists meanwhile are working to preserve the last habitats of many species of turtles. A further purpose of this book is to give an account of the admirable work being done by these people.

Dresden 1983   Fritz Jürgen Obst

Zeus and the tortoise

One of Aesop's fables

When Zeus held his wedding feast, all the animals were invited.
Only the tortoise arrived too late. Since Zeus wanted to
know why, he asked her next day why she was the only one
who did not arrive in time for the banquet. At her answer:
"My house is dear to me, my house is the best", he became
angry and ordained that the tortoise should always have to
carry her house round with her.

In just this way, there are many people who prefer to
dwell simply under their own roof than to live
luxuriously in the houses of their friends.

previous page:

A "Santa Cruz giant" has left
its wallowing place. Mud and
algae cover its body.

Green turtles *(Chelonia mydas)* mating on an island near
the coast.

Eggs of a Green turtle. The eggs measure 45 to 55 mm and have an elastic shell.

Green turtle hatchlings 6 to 9 weeks old are released into the South China Sea a long way from land.

Juvenile Green turtle *(Chelonia mydas)* in shallow water.

11

Female Green turtle *(Chelonia mydas)* returning to the sea.

Female Leatherback laying eggs at night. Identification tags are attached to the fore limb.

The eggs, about the size of tennis balls, are collected at once and taken for supervised incubation.

13

Marine turtle breeding station at Kuchling on Borneo. The photograph shows the fenced enclosures where eggs are hatched and the weather station.

Tracks made by a Leatherback (*Dermochelys coriacea*) on a beach in Eastern Malaysia.

following page:

Suckerfish (*Echeneis* spec.) attached to the plastron of a Hawksbill turtle (*Eretmochelys imbricata*).

A half-grown *Chelonoidis elephantopus nigrita* takes a midday rest in the undergrowth.

Chelonoidis elephantopus hoodensis in copulation at the Darwin Breeding Station.

Seychelles Giant tortoise in the reserve on Prison Island off the coast of Zanzibar.

Seychelles Giant tortoises *(Megalochelys g. gigantea)* on board the research vessel "Valdivia" on its return to Germany in 1900. The large specimen on the left can be seen today in the Staatlichen Museum für Tierkunde (State Museum of Zoology) in Dresden.

Seychelles Giant tortoise *(Megalochelys gigantea)* in its natural biotope on the island of Anse Mais (one of the Aldabra Islands). On the second central lamina, a Madagascar gecko *(Phelsuma abbotti)* searches for insects as the tortoise rests in the shade.

One of the last giants:
*Chelonoidis elephantopus
abingdoni* on Abingdon
Island in the Galapagos
Archipelago.

Galapagos tortoise on
Hood Island *(Chelonoidis
elephantopus hoodensis)*
in a prickly-pear forest.

Breeding successes at the Darwin Station on the Galapagos Archipelago. Baby *Chelonoidis elephantopus nigrita*. On the right, a rare albinotic specimen.

A dead Galapagos Giant tortoise *(Chelonoidis elephantopus becki)* on Albemarle.

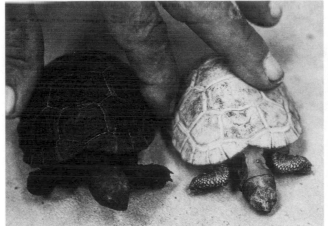

Landscape on James Island in the Galapagos, the home of *Chelonoidis elephantopus darwini*. In the background, feral goats, the most serious food competitors for the giant tortoises.

Crate of Greek tortoises (Testudo hermanni) being exported from Jugoslavia.

Stuffed Hawksbill turtle (Eretmochelys imbricata) as a tourist souvenir on the Seychelles. Wasteful exploitation of this kind has also been resticted recently.

Algerian tortoises (Testudo graeca) in a Moroccan depot awaiting export. Fortunately, the mass export of tortoises has now been brought to an end in Morocco.

following page:

Galapagos Giant tortoises (Chelonoidis elephantopus nigrita) wallowing in the swamps of Indefatigable.

SOS on tropical coasts

Ship in distress! The cry for help sent up by imperilled mariners is as old as the spirit of daring with which they set out across unknown oceans to discover legendary distant shores or even to search for the end of the world.

It is not so very long since the ocean was considered as the symbol of immensity, since its vast extent seemed infinite and the wealth it contained inexhaustible. The belief in unlimited quantities of food held within the sea as "bread" for mankind has long since yielded to the reality of over-exploited fishing grounds, "fishery wars" that have been fought out or are not yet resolved, and the constant search for new fishing areas that lie progressively farther from coasts. Oil pollution following tanker disasters and the death of large numbers of fish near the mouths of large rivers that are used as the sewers of the civilized continents, daily washing vast quantities of chemical waste into the sea, are an urgent reminder to us that the extent to which a huge ecosystem like the sea can be burdened, although very difficult to calculate, is nevertheless not limitless . . . For some time now, reports of the rapid decline in numbers of a wide variety of marine creatures have signalled the disastrous consequences. In addition to the traditional commercial species of fish, all kinds of edible crayfish and table mussels have become increasingly scarce, while seals and whales have disappeared from extensive areas of the oceans. Some species have been depleted almost to the limits of their existence. At one time, massive aggregations of marine turtles were to be found on almost all the warmer coasts. For travellers on sailing ships, the sighting of marine turtles was an everyday occurrence as soon as they reached the more southerly latitudes, from the Mediterranean onwards. In the 19th century when steamship navigation introduced the next stage in the technical development of seafaring, considerably large shoals of swimming turtles still inhabited all tropical oceans. A handsome turtle shell became one of the obligatory souvenirs testifying to voyages to exotic shores. For thousands of years, sea turtles have provided food and raw material to people living along the coasts. The flesh of the Green turtle, the Ridley and the Loggerhead has already enriched the menu for numerous tropical peoples for countless generations, long before European gourmets elevated "real turtle soup" to one of the many courses served at formal dinners. Just as much in demand was tortoise-shell, the beautifully mottled or flammulated scutes of the carapace of the Hawksbill or of the Green turtle. South Sea Islanders were using it to make articles of everyday use and filigree ornaments long before anyone in Europe had thought of the baroque fashion in which artistically worked Spanish tortoise-shell combs would support the upswept coiffures of the ladies. What in the 17th and 18th century was still a luxury demanded by the relatively small stratum of courtly society was to become, with the capitalistic emancipation of the bourgeoisie, an element in the demand for status symbols from a new upper class that was numerically much more powerful. The industrial processing of marine turtles brought about, within a few decades, what before had seemed impossible within thousands of years. The abundance of the creatures rapidly came to an end. In the first half of the present century, stocks of all species declined so sharply that coastal regions which had served as turtle's nesting grounds for what seemed an eternity, were now virtually deserted. On a number of beaches, no turtle ever appeared again.

Alarming reports on the critical situation facing sea turtles awakened the interest of scientists in these hitherto largely neglected animals. Little was known of their life and habits. For instance, nobody really knew whether they return repeatedly to the same nesting beach, whether this is also the place where they were born, how far they travel and in doing so, how they find their way and return home, what is their rate of reproduction and their chance of survival, what age they attain, and much more. It was not even known for certain how many species of marine turtles exist.

Today seven species of sea turtles are recognized:

the Loggerhead *(Caretta caretta)*,
the Flatback *(Chelonia depressa)*,
the Green turtle *(Chelonia mydas)* with an Atlantic subspecies *(Ch. m. mydas)* and a Pacific subspecies *(Ch. m. japonica)*,
the Hawksbill *(Eretmochelys imbricata)*,
the Atlantic Ridley *(Lepidochelys kempi)*,
the Pacific Ridley *(Lepidochelys olivacea)* and
the Leatherback *(Dermochelys coriacea)*.

The first six species have many features in common. They possess typical turtle shells that are oval, somewhat flattened in shape. The size of the various species ranges from 0.60 m to 1.40 m for particularly fine specimens. The shell of all these marine turtles is entirely covered with horny scutes. The head is quite large and cannot be withdrawn into the shell. The extremities have developed into broad, flattened flippers, the paddle action of the front limbs being particularly striking. The limbs are covered by a thick, textured, scaly skin in which individual claws indicate the incorporation of the finger and toe bones. When swimming, turtles move their flippers in a powerful, usually slow movement up and down. Underwater, the turtles seem to "fly" in graceful, weightless motion. The sea turtle's head is also covered with large, clearly discernible scutes. These external similarities are supplemented by common anatomical features and consequently, these four recent genera are combined into a single family, the Marine turtles (Chelonidae). The last species, the Leatherback, differs considerably in form. It is the sole living representative of a separate family of the same name Dermochelydidae. Its shell is streamlined and elongate, with well-defined longitudinal ridges. With a length of up to 2 m, it is considerably larger than the other marine turtles. The weight of this colossus is put at 350 to 500 kg. With such dimensions, the Leatherback far outstrips not only its marine cousins, but also all other modern testudinates. The Leatherback lacks the typical horny scutes on head and limbs. Instead it has a uniformly smooth, thick, leather-like skin covering from which it gets its name. However, the shell of the young Leatherback has a mosaic-like structure resulting from the presence of small bony platelets in the skin. This mosaic "shell", however, soon be-

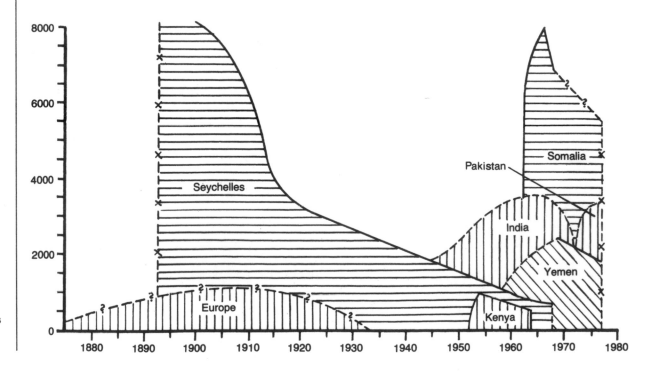

Over-exploitation of sea turtles in the Indian Ocean. Number of Green turtles caught there between 1880 and 1980 by seven countries or groups of countries. (after Frazier, 1981)

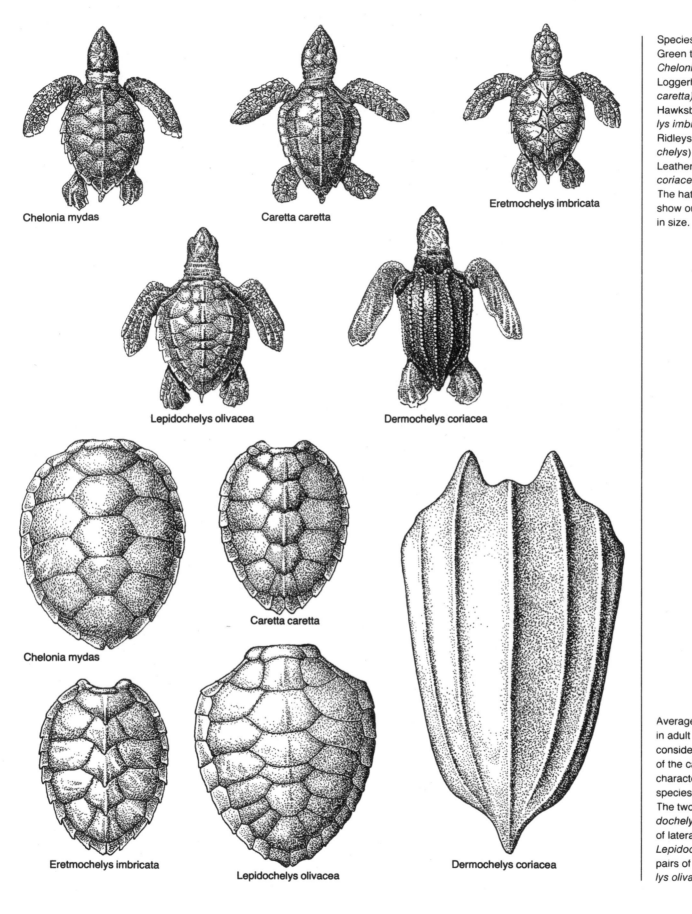

Chelonia mydas

Caretta caretta

Eretmochelys imbricata

Lepidochelys olivacea

Dermochelys coriacea

Chelonia mydas

Caretta caretta

Eretmochelys imbricata

Lepidochelys olivacea

Dermochelys coriacea

Species of marine turtles
Green turtles (genus *Chelonia*)
Loggerhead turtle *(Caretta caretta)*
Hawksbill turtle *(Eretmochelys imbricata)*
Ridleys (genus *Lepidochelys*)
Leatherback *(Dermochelys coriacea)*
The hatchlings of sea turtles show only slight differences in size.

Average length of carapace in adult sea turtles varies considerably. Arrangement of the carapacial shields is characteristic of genus and species.
The two species of *Lepidochelys* differ in the number of laterals:
Lepidochelys kempi has 5 pairs of laterals, *Lepidochelys olivacea* 6–9 pairs.

comes covered by leathery skin, and vestiges of it still remain as minute bones embedded in the leathery skin of the adult animals.

The ability to withdraw head and limbs into the shell has been retained to an even lesser extent by the Leatherback than by other sea turtles. Their limbs carry no claws, in contrast to those of the distantly related species. Differences in head structure are also striking. Both the remarkable hooked bill and the vertically aligned eyes lend it an unmistakable appearance. The differences in skeletal structure between the Leatherback and the other marine turtles are even greater. The typical turtle's

bony shell has been reduced so greatly that In the carapace, only the proneural or nuchal bone and very narrow pleurals remain, and although the plastron has been retained virtually completely in the number and arrangement of the bony elements, it too is only in the form of quite narrow bony straps. Skull structure also deviates in certain aspects from the typical. The Leatherback can rightly be looked upon as something of an outsider among recent turtles.

Help is at hand...

The publication of various writings by the young American zoologist Archie F. Carr jr on the subject of Painted turtles towards the end of the thirties marked the professional debut of the man who, some three decades later, was to earn the reputation of having rescued marine turtles from extinction. His field of study expanded rapidly and by 1942, his attention had turned to marine turtles and various Emydid turtles living in fresh water. By 1952, when his *Handbook of Turtles* appeared, Carr had become a Professor at the University of Florida in Gainesville. It was at this time that his interest concentrated increasingly upon marine turtles. Reports coming from the Caribbean area, where marine turtles were traditionally important to the fishing industry, made it clear that the creatures were endangered. Investigations carried out on the spot by Carr, confirmed the seriousness of the situation. In addition to publishing his findings, he immediately sought a practical solution to the problems. On his initiative, the Caribbean Conservation Corporation ("CCC") was founded, an organization that has taken as its task the conservation of marine turtles in the Caribbean. John H. Phipps, a wealthy nature lover, became President of the corporation and contributed substantially to financing the plans of the "CCC". An early major project was the construction of a turtle conservation station near Tortuguero in Costa Rica. By 1961, 18,500 baby turtles had been hatched there and they were subsequently liberated from a hydroplane at 17 different points in the Caribbean. In parallel with these practical measures of species conservation by the "CCC", Professor Carr directed a wide-ranging programme of research into various aspects of marine turtle biology, in which colleagues

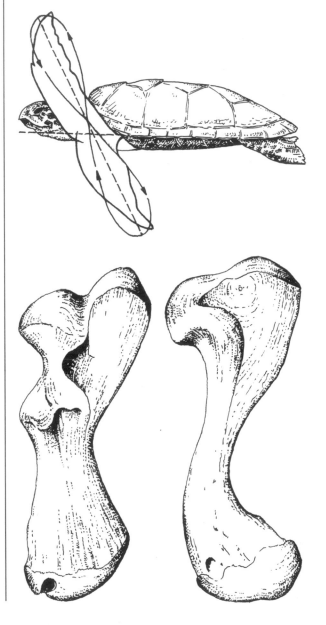

The oar-stroke action of a marine turtle
Whereas freshwater turtles propel themselves mainly by thrusting movements of the hind limbs, sea turtles work with the fore limbs. A number of freshwater river turtles already show indications of a move towards this type of locomotion.

Comparison of the upper arm of a sea turtle (left) with that of a land tortoise (right).
In sea turtles, the bone is straight and squat and has more highly developed articulation making it a more efficient stabilizer for the flipper. (after Walker and Gregory, combined)

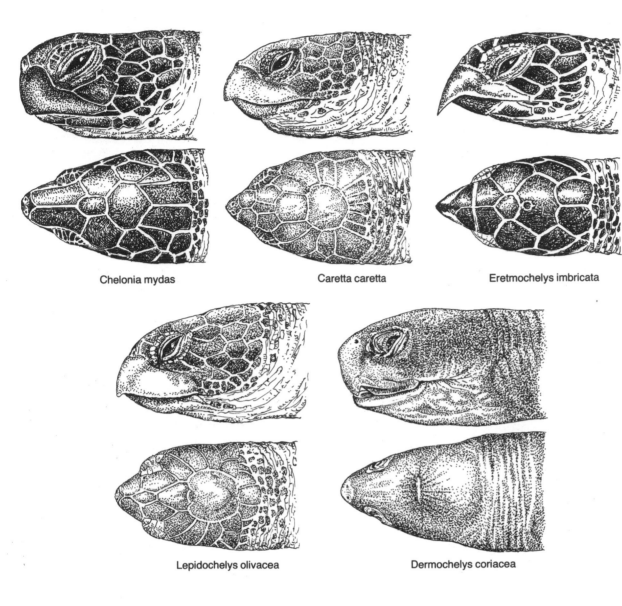

Chelonia mydas

Caretta caretta

Eretmochelys imbricata

Lepidochelys olivacea

Dermochelys coriacea

Marine turtles' heads
The large scales covering the head are species-characteristic, those of the top of the head, the pileus scales, showing particularly striking variations. The head of the Leatherback is quite distinctive in appearance: the upper jaw bears two hooks and there is no covering of scales.

and students of his such as Ehrenfeld, Pritchard, Hirth, Pearsons and many others took part.

Stimulated by this example, zoologists in other parts of the world also devoted their attention to marine turtles. In Australia, Robert Bustard of the Australian National University in Canberra spent a number of years studying the life of marine turtles on Heron Island off the coast of Queensland. Some very exhaustive studies carried out in 1929/30 by the Australian F. W. Moorhouse, one of the pioneers of marine turtle conservation, provided an indispensable basis for Bustard's work on Heron Island.

On Kalimantan in southeast Asia, Tom Harrison, curator of the Sarawak Museum, engaged for many years in research into marine turtles. His stu-

dies prompted Professor John Hendrickson to carry the work further. In the following years, he gave energetic support to the setting-up of a marine turtle conservation area at Trengganu. The speciality of this establishment is the hatching of baby Leatherbacks. Other turtle conservation areas were developed in Surinam, French Guiana, Nicaragua, Belize (formerly British Honduras) and Mexico. The International Union for Conservation of Nature and Natural Resources (I. U. C. N.) took over sponsorship of these establishments.

In addition, the World Wildlife Fund (WWF), as a private organization, has contributed much to the conservation of marine turtles by providing substantial resources for this purpose, although the major activities of this extraordinarily praiseworthy society are directed primarily towards the protection and conservation of endangered land tortoises. Other well-known names are those of certain researchers who studied the problems of turtle conservation in particular regions: J. Frazier in the Seychelles and the Indian Ocean, G. R. Hughes on the eastern and southern coast of Africa, S. Bhaskar on the coasts of India, J. P. Schulz on the situation along the coast of Surinam.

The World Conference on Sea Turtle Conservation held from 26–30 November 1979 in the USA represents a preliminary climax in international cooperation in the preservation of these creatures.

The work of the sea turtle conservation stations in regions in which the stocks of turtles have not yet declined to a minimum can be financed in part by sensibly restricted economic exploitation of these animals. The "Turtle Board" set up by Dr. Harrison on Borneo used this method of self-financing successfully right from the start. The "Turtle Society" took over the administration of three small islands from Kuchling, the capital of Sarawak, situated in northern Borneo. Sarawak in turn belongs to the Federation of Malaysia. The small islands are visited by the Green turtle in particular, for the purpose of egg laying. The sandy beach on the islands which provides the nesting ground or "rookery", measures no more than some 3.0 acres. Within this area, almost 2.2 million turtle eggs were gathered annually in the years before the Second World War. After 1945, the yield declined consistently and by the beginning of the sixties, had fallen

to a million eggs. The Turtle Board marketed between 90 and 98 per cent of this annual yield of eggs, which on Kalimantan are highly prized as food. In this way, the running costs of the station and the wages of more than ten assistants could be covered. The remaining eggs are left to hatch outdoors placed in simulated egg chambers dug out of the sand. Netting enclosures mark the site of the artificial nests and prevent the hatchlings from moving straight into the sea or from falling prey to seabirds. After hatching, the young turtles are looked after for some three months in containers of seawater. They are fed generously on shrimps and fish, so that eventually they can be liberated a good distance from the shore and thus out of reach of the many predaceous fish that lie in wait.

At first glance, it seems questionable whether the number of young released is adequate to justify the taking for human consumption of 90 per cent of the eggs laid. In all probability it is. To start with, under natural conditions, only 5 per cent of hatchlings from a single clutch reach the open sea. And even then, the chances of survival of these animals are so small that probably not more than one female out of a clutch lives to reach sexual maturity. But in controlled breeding, young turtles hatch from about 50 to 60 per cent of the eggs, and of these, getting on for 90 per cent reach a stage at which they can successfully be released. So the chances of survival of the young turtles liberated in this way are probably high enough to equal those of the entire population under natural conditions.

Skeleton of Leatherback
(*Dermochelys coriacea*)
Side view of whole skeleton with secondary shell

Degenerate elements of the primary shell
Whereas the carapace is strongly reminiscent of the shell of a normal sea turtle, all that remains of the plastron are the bony rods.
Individual rudiments of plates occur in the skin as isolated small bones.
(after Bellairs and others, combined)

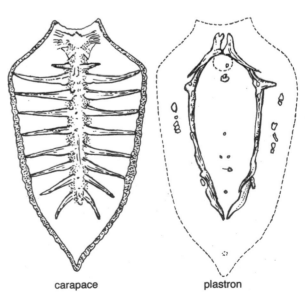

carapace   plastron

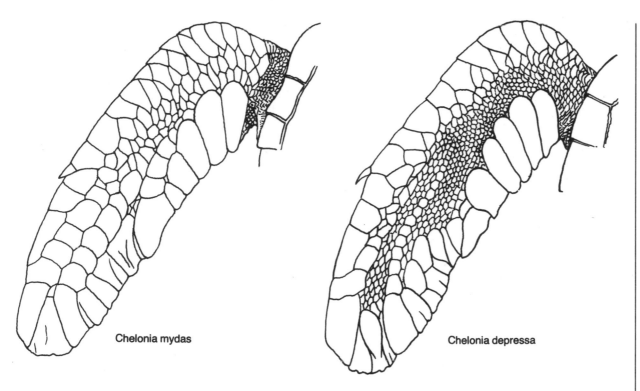

Chelonia mydas

Chelonia depressa

The common Green turtle *(Chelonia mydas)* and the Australian Flatback *(Chelonia depressa)* can be distinguished most easily by the scutellation of the fore flippers. (after various authors, combined)

It remains to be seen whether this calculation proves correct, that is, whether in the long run the turtle populations are able to remain viable with this calculated quota of young.

In this connection, it has to be said that in addition to the thoroughly sound turtle breeding stations, there also exist numbers of other farms which, on closer examination, have revealed themselves to be extremely dubious in their working methods, if not actually "wolves in sheep's clothing". For example, the turtle farm on the Cayman Islands has, at its own declaration, a stock of about 100,000 turtles. But last year, 106 tons of deep-frozen turtle meat was imported from there as a single shipment into the German Federal Republic; since an average yield of meat from each fully grown animal is 6 kg, this represents some 18,000 green turtles, almost a fifth of the total stock of the farm. And as this was undoubtedly not the only turtle meat sold by the firm, it is impossible to believe that an adequate quota of offspring was obtained from their own animals. Indeed, according to data provided by the farm's directors, "amelioration" of the progeny quota by the taking of eggs from natural sites had been necessary in the years 1976–1978.

The decidedly fraudulent nature of the activities of a Mexican "Turtle Farm" that turned out to be virtually a slaughterhouse in disguise, was revealed by some American researchers working on turtles. There, on the Pacific coast, 50,000 female Pacific Ridleys *(Lepidochelys olivacea)* were butchered annually. Most of the animals were caught and killed even before they had laid their eggs. In a deliberate attempt to deceive the public, a small proportion of the eggs that were taken were hatched and the young released.

The export of "tortoise-shell" (a material in fact obtained from marine turtles) from Thailand, Indonesia and other countries of southeast Asia reveals a similar picture. If the large quantities of this highly-prized material that are exported really came from farms, those farms would have to be enterprises on a scale that would far outmeasure the quite imposing grounds and buildings of the Cayman Turtle Farm Ltd., which was mentioned above with a certain degree of scepticism. Considering that one Hawksbill turtle *(Eretmochelys imbricata)* provides about 900 g of tortoise-shell, official government figures for tortoise-shell exports in 1978 of more than 58,000 kg from Thailand and almost 220,000 kg from Indonesia indicate that some 65,000 and 270,000 Hawksbill turtles respectively must have been used for this purpose.

To prevent over-exploitation of this kind, not only are international conventions required such as the "Washington Convention" that controls trade in endangered species of animals (which lists all species of marine turtles), but also satisfactory nature conservation legislation at a national level. Above all, the attitude of the public can be an important force affecting the fate of these creatures. Without a wide circle of customers for tortoise-shell and turtle meat, the mass butchery of turtles will cease to be profitable. In this way, the deliberate actions of people living far from tropical coasts can be an answer to the marine turtle's distress call.

As well as contributing to the protection of the species, conservation stations throughout the world have carried out fundamental research into the life and habits of marine turtles. Tagging is the most important means of observing turtle movement. Usually it is the female coming ashore to lay eggs that is marked with an identification tag made of stainless steel. The disc is attached to one of the hind limbs with riveting tongs during egg laying. It does not hamper the turtle in any way, and fitting it probably causes no more pain than the sort of laceration that might be made by a predaceous fish. Sometimes young turtles that are released are marked on the carapace with a branding stamp. A valuable development has been the practice of attaching microtransmitters, making it possible to observe the migrations of sea turtles.

Life and habits of sea turtles

Adult sea turtles are quite capable of living in the high seas. But the majority of turtles prefer to remain close to the shores in the littoral zone. Only the Leathery turtle or Leatherback is fully pelagic, preferring the open sea. In shallow coastal waters, the water temperatures are sufficient to keep the turtle's body temperature at optimal levels. In the open sea, the turtles seek out large beds of drifting seaweed above which the water is more intensively heated. The sea turtle's heat requirements seem to vary between species. Whereas the Loggerhead and the Leatherback are fairly insensitive to certain fluctuations in temperature, Green turtles and Ridleys prefer constantly warm water. The "most tropical" of the marine turtles is the Hawksbill.

Marine turtles sun themselves in a calm sea by floating motionless on the surface of the water. It is also in this way that the animals fulfil their modest sleep requirements. Adult turtles have relatively few enemies in the ocean. Killer whales occasionally seize turtles, even Leatherbacks. Sometimes large predaceous fishes hunting in shoals appear to attack individual turtles and to take them as prey after a long chase.

All sea turtles eat both animal and plant food. Crustaceans, jellyfishes, mussels, molluscs and echinoderms are more important items of prey than fishes, while algae (seaweeds) make up the vegetable food. At one time, it was generally held that the various species had different feeding habits. Green turtles, for instance, were said to be predominantly or exclusively herbivorous, in contrast to all other sea turtles. Today we know that feeding habits depend much more upon the seasonal and local occurrence of a particular food supply. Turtles usually eat whatever the sea offers in greatest abundance. It has been shown beyond doubt that in addition to their partiality for invertebrates, they are extremely skilled in catching fish.

It is not at all unusual for the shell of a sea turtle to be covered with a whole fauna and flora of marine organisms, such as balanids (sedentary crustaceans), gooseneck barnacles, various leeches and sabellariid worms, polyps and seaweeds. Sometimes they are accompanied by cleaner fishes, particularly near coral reefs. In addition, sucker fishes—the best-known representatives are the genera *Echeneis* and *Remora*—frequently allow themselves to be carried along by sea turtles. The adhesive force of the suction disc situated on the head or in the neck region is so great that many primitive peoples use them successfully to catch turtles. They make a hole through the tail fin and attach a line to the back of the fish. Sucker fishes tied in this way are drawn along behind the boats by the fishermen. When a turtle makes an appearance, some of the fishes are thrown towards it; they immediately attach themselves so firmly to it that the turtle can be pulled in and captured without difficulty.

Green turtle with three remora or suckerfishes *(Echeneis naucrates)* that have attached themselves to the turtle with the belly side turned outwards.

Coastal fishers or cosmopolitans?

One of the most interesting phenomena in the life of sea turtles is undoubtedly their power of orientation combined with their marked migratory instinct. As a result of tagging, it has been shown that Green turtles migrate from the nesting grounds or rookeries in Guayana "only" as far as certain preferred grazing areas (seaweed beds) off the northeast coast of Brazil, whereas Atlantic Ridleys migrate from the same rookery a distance of about 3,800 km to the coast of South America. The maximum distance recorded was for a Leatherback tagged on a beach in Ghana and recovered two years later some 5,900 km from the nesting site. At the turtle grazing areas mentioned above off the Brazilian coast, turtles were also caught which could be identified by their tags as members of the Green turtle population at Ascension Island some 2,000 km away. In general then, it is clear that most marine turtles migrate relatively far from their home shores. On the other hand, it is an established fact that quite a large number of rookeries on all warm coasts can be assigned to individual species. The Atlantic or Kemp's Ridley is an exception. On the one hand, it does not appear to migrate very far,

and it is exceptional for it to leave the Caribbean area. On the other hand, this species apparently uses only a single rookery, the beach between Tampico and Soto la Marina in north-eastern Mexico. However, it took 75 years from the original discovery and scientific description of *Lepidochelys kempi* until Professor Carr and his team succeeded in finding this solitary nesting ground. From the numbers of individuals that congregate there every year, it is possible to estimate the total numbers of this species in existence. On the assumption that the females do not lay eggs every year, the total number of all *Lepidochelys kempi* must be higher than that number, but under no cir-

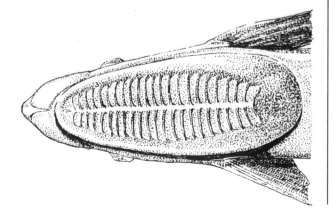

Top of the head of a suckerfish *(Echeneis naucrates)* showing the adhesive disc consisting of two rows of lamellae. This kind of suckerfish frequently allows itself to be carried along by sea turtles.
(after various authors, combined)

33

With the help of a US satellite, American scientists have, over a period of nine months, been following the migration of a marine turtle from the mouth of the Mississippi westwards as far as the coast of Texas. Experts are hoping to get new information on the habits of this endangered species. A transmitter has been fitted to the shell of the reptile that is estimated to weigh some 100 kilograms.

New York (ADN), August 1980

The migrations of marine turtles from Heron Island off the west coast of Australia into various regions (after Bustard, 1970)

Leathery turtles occasionally drift as far as the coasts of Europe.

cumstances more than two or three times higher. Twenty years ago, 40,000 individuals came ashore to nest annually, today it is 5,000 turtles at most. Observation of Green turtles has shown that the females of certain populations come to lay eggs only every three or four years. Whether the males are sexually active every year is not yet clear. In contrast, the Pacific Ridley of the same genus *(Lepidochelys olivacea)* has a whole series of rookeries distributed round the Atlantic and Pacific Oceans.

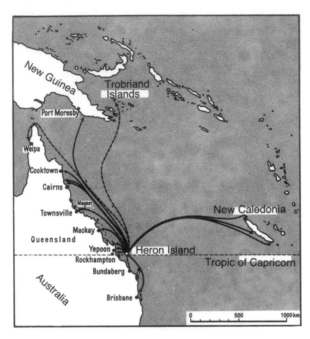

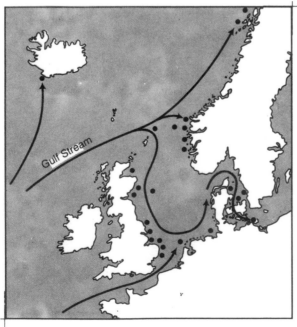

The Caribbean Ridley is one example of a sea turtle that remains within a restricted area. A second is the Australian Green turtle or Flatback turtle *(Chelonia depressa)*. It lives primarily off the northern coast of Australia. Here, however, it is not restricted to a single nesting beach, but visits several, sharing them with other marine turtles. Its closest relation, the common Green turtle *(Chelonia mydas)* nests in company with it. After much research into marine turtles, it has been established that widespread species such as the common Green turtle and the Hawksbill show rather more tenacity to locality than had originally been thought. The populations of both species form two groups respectively that are dispersed on the one hand across the Atlantic and Mediterranean and on the other, the Pacific and Indian Oceans. As a result, they are recognized as geographical subspecies. Only the Loggerhead *(Caretta caretta)* and the Leatherback *(Dermochelys coriacea)* cannot be shown by any special characteristics to belong to particular nesting areas. Assignment of this kind is possible only in the case of marked individuals. Sufficient data on their migratory habits and the extent of their range are not yet available. But already it can safely be stated that the Leatherback, as the most pelagic in habit, also lays claim to the most extensive range both as an individual and as a species. A particularly important factor in the Leatherback's proficiency in global cruising is the stability of its body temperature in comparison with that of other sea turtles. Professor Frair and other American workers have measured the body temperature of Leatherbacks in relatively cold waters off the coast of North America and found them to be up to 18 °C higher than the ambient temperature. The reason is probably the considerable body volume and the production of heat by the muscular action of the strikingly long front limbs. The cooling rate in water is no more than 0.001°C per minute, which also explains the appearance of Leatherback as periodic visitors to northern shores.

Information obtained by tagging also gives some idea of the speed at which sea turtles travel. Along the coasts of Surinam, J. P. Schulz established that the creatures swim a distance of about 11–35 km in a day. A Pacific Ridley *(Lepidochelys olivacea)*, marked with a tag, completed a journey of 1,900 km in only 23 days, that is, an average of 82 km each day. Also very remarkable was the discovery of a

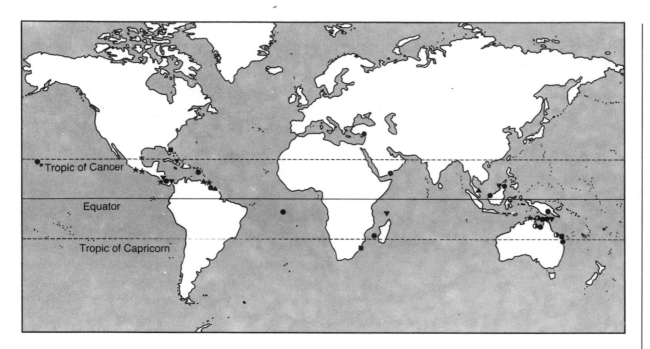

Circumtropical nesting beaches of marine turtles (after Bustard, 1970)

	America	Africa	Asia	Australia and Oceania
● Green turtle	Costa Rica Aves Island Surinam Western Hawaiian Island	Ascension Island Europa Island	Turkey Sharma, Yemen Kalimantan (Sarawak, Sabah)	Crab Island Raine Island Bountiful Island Capricorn Group Bramble
◑ Flatback turtle	—	—	—	Crab Island Bountiful Island Facing and Curtis Islands near Gladstone
▲ Leatherback	Guayana French Guiana	—	Terengganu	—
▼ Hawksbill turtle	Cuba Costa Rica Panama	Cosmoledo Island (Seychelles)	Sabah	eastern Torres Strait
■ Loggerhead turtle	Florida	Tongaland	—	—
★ Pacific Ridley	Guerrero (Mexico) Oaxaca (Mexico) Costa Rica Surinam	—	—	Arnhemland
＊ Atlantic Ridley	Tamaulipas (Mexico)	—	—	—

The Old Man and the Turtles

". . . and nothing showed on the surface of the water but some patches of yellow, sun-bleached Sargasso weed and the purple, formalized, iridescent, gelatinous bladder of a Portuguese man-of-war[1] floating beside the boat . . .

The iridescent bubbles were beautiful. But they were the falsest thing in the sea and the old man loved to see the big sea turtles eating them. The turtles saw them, approached them from the front, then shut their eyes so they were completely cara-paced and ate them with fil-aments and all. The old man loved to see the turtles eat them and he loved to walk on them on the beach after a storm and hear them pop when he stepped on them with the horny soles of his feet. He loved green turtles and hawks-bills with their elegance and speed and their great value and he had a friendly contempt for the huge, stupid logger-heads, yellow in their armour-plating, strange in their love-making,

[1] Portuguese man-of-war: a tropical jelly-fish of the genus *Physalia*, with a poison that can be dangerous even to humans.

and happily eating the Portuguese men-of-war with their eyes shut.

He had no mysticism about turtles although he had gone in turtle boats for many years. He was sorry for them all, even the great trunk-backs that were as long as the skiff and weighed a ton. Most people are heartless about turtles because a turtle's heart will beat for hours after he has been cup up and butchered. But the old man thought, I have such a heart too and my feet and hands are like theirs. He ate the white eggs to give himself strength. He ate them all through May to be strong in September and October for the truly big fish."

(Ernest Hemingway:
The Old Man and the Sea.
London, 1952)

newly-born Loggerhead turtle *(Caretta caretta)* in the Sargasso Sea. The famous seagrass grazing grounds in the Sargasso Sea lie at least 1,000 km from the nearest islands on which the turtles could have their hatching place.

In spite of a good deal of research, much remains to be explained about the impressive navigational capacity of sea turtles. Orientation in animals probably combines a number of factors. Fundamentally, direction finding in turtles is based on a sun compass sense, in addition to which ocean currents provide an important aid to navigation. Undoubtedly communication also plays a part. As the migrating turtles get progressively closer to their destination, they meet up with increasing numbers of other turtles of the same or different species, all swimming in the same direction. The distance between individual turtles and the chance of error thus become progressively less. Only the Leatherback is an exception here, too. It is decidedly a "loner" and joins up only into small groups.

That the turtle's power of orientation and internal clock, although adequate, are less than perfect is, in fact, an advantage to them. On the one hand, navigational errors encourage the use of new nesting beaches, on the other, the wide range of arrival times of the different groups at the rookeries favours the individual's chances of egg-laying. It is easy to imagine how hundreds or thousands of female turtles arriving on the same beach within a short space of time would impede one another. As it is, a certain amount of damage is caused to eggs already concealed in the sand, by the purely instinctive activity of the next female intent upon nesting. The Australian specialist on sea turtles,

Robert Bustard, observed that on the shores of the Great Barrier Reef, this has brought about a natural process of stock regulation, preventing the numbers of offspring exceeding a particular quota. But today, the Great Barrier Reef is probably the only breeding ground of marine turtles in which an automatic mechanism controls population size.

To lay their eggs, turtles emerge from the sea at twilight or during the night and move up the beach to a point above the high tide mark. Using all four limbs, the female excavates a preliminary pit in the soft dune sand, then with the hind flippers alone, digs out a pear-shaped hole some 30 to 70 cm deep, the egg cavity. In doing this, the flippers work alternately. The egg cavity is widened at the base to about 30 to 40 cm by twisting movements of the flipper. Using the back flippers as a slipway, the eggs are deposited carefully, either singly or in groups of up to 3 or 4, at intervals of 8 to 12 seconds. From time to time, there may be pauses of rather longer duration. The total egg laying process takes between 15 and 30 minutes. Finally, the egg chamber is covered over with sand shovelled into place by the hind limbs, and the nesting hollow filled in and flattened by all the limbs. Afterwards, it is almost impossible to locate the actual position of the nest. In nature reserves, one of the most important parts of the night's work for the wardens is to mark the sites immediately with marker-flags, so that next day, the eggs can be recovered for controlled incubation.

The number of eggs per clutch is determined by the size of the female but also depends upon species. A typical nest contains between 90 and 150 eggs. They are uniformly spherical with a diameter

Hawksbill turtle laying eggs
Characteristic tracks indicate the turtle's path across the beach to the nesting place.

of 42 to 54 mm. Denting which occurs frequently in the elastic shell does not harm the embryos. Sometimes a few smaller, infertile eggs are also deposited. In the case of the Leatherback, the percentage of such eggs is surprisingly high: one clutch may contain up to 30 per cent of undeveloped eggs. Most females are ready to lay again after 9 to 15 days. It is normal for 3 to 4 clutches to be produced within 6 to 8 weeks, then the supply is exhausted. But it has been known for a single female to produce up to eight clutches in a season. This could give a maximum of almost 1,000 eggs. But 400 eggs per female and season is probably the norm. After that, the female has an interval of two or four years for recuperation.

The turtles return to the sea immediately after they have concealed the nesting site. They haul themselves across the sand with synchronous movements of the forelimbs and as they move towards the sea, leave behind them broad, regular tracks. From time to time, the exhausted creatures have to pause for rest, and dawn may already be breaking before they regain the safety of the sea.

The males are waiting in shallow water offshore, and mating occurs as soon as the females return. In all species, the females probably far outnumber the males which are unlikely to leave the water during the whole of their life. Copulation can occur at any time of day or night, but is more usual during the hours of daylight. The male is generally the smaller of the two partners, and covering and copulation can last up to 6 hours. Preliminary to mounting, the male often bites at the edge of the female's carapace, which can become quite severely damaged in this way. Further harm can be caused by the male's

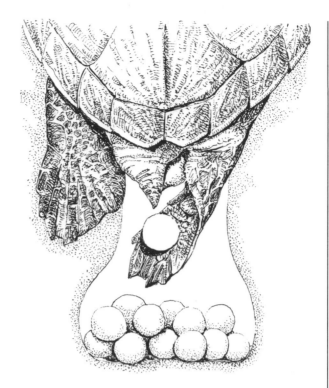

The eggs are laid; as the eggs emerge, looking rather like tennis balls, they are caught by the turtle's hind limbs and deposited at the edge of the egg chamber.

violent efforts to maintain a grip on the shell of the female. Whereas the copulating male is at least from time to time above the water, the female must struggle continually to get to the surface to breathe in air. During coitus, turtles may allow themselves to be carried along by ocean currents. Sometimes individual un-paired males follow a mating pair. Whether they also have a chance of mating is not certain. Like other turtles, female marine turtles are able to store in their genital tract the sperm from the last copulations of the season, to fertilize the eggs of the following season *(amphigonia retardata)*.

The nesting cavity, and within it, the pear-shaped egg chamber are dug out. (after various authors, combined)

Table 1	Egg-laying season for sea turtles in certain districts
Ascension:	December to June
Australia:	October to February
Bermudas:	April to June
Borneo:	peak period July to August, otherwise all year round
Florida:	May to June
Sri Lanka:	peak period June to November, otherwise all year round
West Indies:	May to October, small numbers also all year round in places
Central America:	June to August

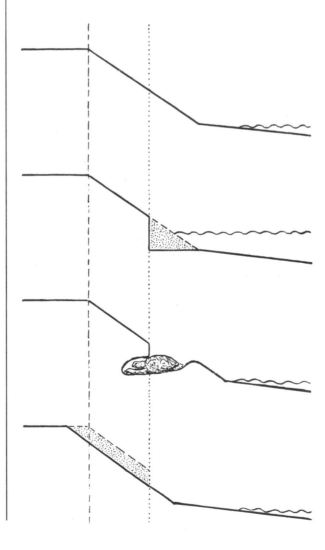

A rare eventuality: nesting marine turtles contribute to shore erosion on a sandy beach in Australia.
(after Bustard, 1970)

Female marine turtles unwilling to mate try to evade the male's attentions by a show of coyness. They press the hind flippers together and avoid swimming freely. If this fails, they turn to the male and confront him face to face. Their final defensive ploy is to dispatch him with a few well-aimed bites.

Mating and egg-laying are the most perilous occasions in the life of a sea turtle. This is when it is most vulnerable to predation. Killer whales, predaceous fishes and man take advantage of the situation. For example, while turtles are laying, research workers can easily carry out checks and even attach tags. But egg pirates also exploit the creature's defencelessness. In Mexico, astonishingly large numbers of coyotes plunder the eggs of the Caribbean Ridleys. Often they devour the eggs as they drop from the turtle's cloaca into the egg chamber. On the coasts of Arabia and East Africa, dogs that gather in troops are the greatest egg thieves. In some cases small females are killed while they are laying, by larger predators such as hyenas and dogs.

The baby turtles hatch after differing periods of incubation that vary according to species and environmental conditions. On the coast of South Africa, Loggerhead's eggs were found to take 67 days to hatch, while under the same conditions, those of Leatherbacks took 72 days. The size of the young also differed considerably: the average length of carapace in *Caretta caretta* was 45 mm, that of *Dermochelys coriacea* 60 mm. The hatchlings leave the egg chamber to emerge from the sand only after darkness has fallen. They make straight for the sea as fast as they can with alternate movements of fore and hind limbs. They establish the shortest way to the sea visually, since even at night, the sea is lighter than its surroundings. David Ehrenfeld, working in America, established that the marine turtle's eye has greater sensitivity to ultraviolet light than the freshwater turtle's eye. The path across the beach is fraught with danger. Numbers of birds pursue the hatchlings, gulls, ravens, various groups of predaceous birds lie in wait for them. Below high tide mark, wading birds and even large crustaceans such as Large Ghost crabs (genus *Ocypoda*) are their natural enemies.

In the water, sharks, sea-perch and other predaceous fishes are already waiting for their meal of turtles. In addition, the baby turtles may become exhausted by the great distance they still have to cover in the sea before they reach the feeding grounds. Resorption of remnants of yolk will keep them going for a few days, after which a compulsory period of fasting begins, combined with a marathon long-distance swim. It is no wonder that large numbers of hatchlings perish on the way.

Many workers believe, with Tom Harrison, that at most, only 1 to 2 hatchlings from a clutch survive to reach maturity. Robert Bustard takes a more critical view, calculating that probably only 2 to 3 in a thousand have this chance.

Young turtles probably take 4 to 6 years to reach sexual maturity; Leatherbacks, once again an exception, twice as long as this. But these calculations are based on optimal growth rates on turtle farms, whereas investigations in the field have shown that turtles are at least 15 to 20 years old before they become sexually mature. Observations made off Hawaii suggest that there, Green turtles are not capable of reproduction until they are 50 years old. Such a rate of maturation naturally makes it difficult to achieve rapid success in the stabilization of marine turtle stocks.

Among many unanswered questions in the sphere of marine turtle biology is that of how turtles in the oceans of the temperate zone survive the winter. Until recently it was assumed that they simply migrated to tropical latitudes. And this, indeed, seems to be true of certain populations. But a few years ago, American zoologists found Green turtles in the Gulf of California that were obviously overwintering on the seabed in a state of torpor, as large numbers of freshwater turtles do in temperate zones. It is reasonable to suppose that sea turtles in the Mediterranean and the Black Sea can get through the winter in the same way.

Another danger that threatens sea turtles is tourism. In the Mediterranean area, for example, particularly along the coast of Spain but also on the Aegean Islands, numerous nesting places have been abandoned. Not only are the animals disturbed on the beaches by the presence of people there, but they also run the risk of being injured, usually fatally, by the propellors of the many pleasure boats which the turtles do not recognize as a danger. Even on the once secluded South Sea Islands, the advance of tourism has made it possible for the enthusiastic amateur to take flash-light photographs of the egg-laying spectacle, in the process of which he undoubtedly frightens off other turtles and tramples the well-camouflaged nests already there.

Modern fishery methods also contribute to the continuing decline in the numbers of turtles. Shrimp trawlers fishing off the coast of North America and along the Gulf Coast spread their trawl nets in precisely those areas in which the Atlantic Ridleys (Lepidochelys kempi) search for their food at depths of up to 20 metres. A considerable number of turtles become entangled in the nets and are drowned.

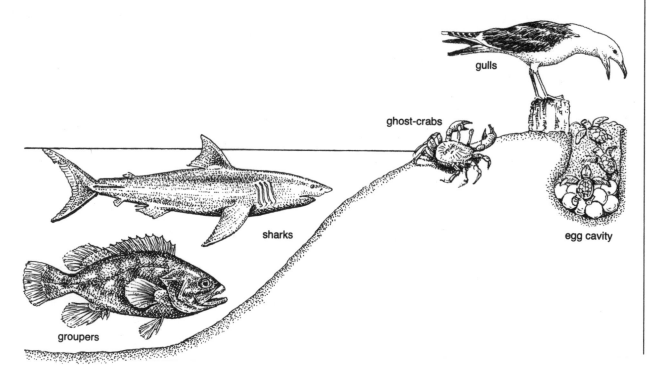

Some predatory enemies of sea turtle hatchlings in the first few days of life: gulls—as representative of many other shore birds, ghost crabs representing larger crustaceans, sharks and sea bass representing predatory fishes, all of which seasonally pursue the baby turtles with great persistence.

gulls

ghost-crabs

egg cavity

sharks

groupers

In spite of all the campaigns that have been launched to save the animals, the SOS call of the sea turtles is still topical today. New dangers are being added to those already familiar, and scarcely a single one has yet been entirely averted...

The islands of the last giants

The Great Age of Discovery brought a flood of sensational reports to Europe. Not only had a New World been discovered and the long-sought sea route to the real India, but much that was marvellous along the way. When the first travellers to the East Indies had passed the Cape of Good Hope and could at last head northwards again, their route carried them past islands large and small that were inhabited by strange and unfamiliar animals. On the small island that was later to bear the name of Saint Maurice (Mauritius), the sailors discovered some creatures straight from the realm of fable: plump birds the size of geese, which although they did not quite fly ready-roasted to the table, nevertheless stood by stupidly trusting, while the uncouth men, hardened by all the dangers and privations of the long sea voyage, slew them in large numbers to provide themselves with a welcome banquet. Such was the fate of the Dodo, a flightless bird distantly related to the pigeon, that once was among the most remarkable of endemic island-dwellers in the entire animal kingdom. It only needed a few years, and there were no dodos left. Just a handful of bones in a few famous museums is all that remains today to bear witness to the former existence of this bird.

But apart from such "delicious poultry" for immediate consumption, the island also provided an incredible wealth of provisions suitable for storage: huge land tortoises a hundred times heavier than

Arrival of the first Dutchmen on the Island of Mauritius in 1598 (in the foreground giant tortoises, in the background dodos). Copper engraving from: Th. de Bry: *Icones insularum ab Hollandis.* Frankfurt, 1601.

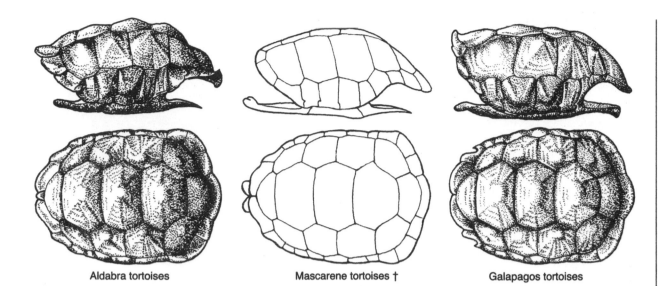

Aldabra tortoises   Mascarene tortoises †   Galapagos tortoises

their small relations in the Mediterranean area, which proved to be equally unsuspecting and easy prey for the hungry ship's crews. Other islands were just as rich in tortoises, even though the curious dodos did not live there. Reunion, Rodriguez, Farquhar, Aldabra and Mahé—everywhere there were huge tortoises, uniformly dark in colour, in their hundreds of thousands. The crews of the sailing ships took them on board and slaughtered them as they were needed. Just a few of the huge shells completed the journey back to the ship's home port.

There, they attracted considerable attention as visible evidence in support of many a sailor's yarn. In 1598, the first Dutch merchantmen reached the Mauritius. They slaughtered dodos and giant tortoises in large numbers, but of their remains, nothing survived. It was not until 1676 that the shell of a giant tortoise almost a metre in length reached Paris from Reunion, where it caused a stir as the "Tortue des Indes". In 1691, François Leguat brought some giant tortoises from Rodriguez to Europe. The Leyden Museum houses a carapace that dates from about this time.

The period during which the giant tortoises could withstand this destructive exploitation soon came to an end on the small islands visited most frequently by the merchant ships. By the middle of the 18th century, stocks on Mauritius were declining rapidly. An attempt was made to remedy the situation by bringing in several shiploads of live tortoises from the distant island of Diego Rodriguez.

Within 18 months, in the years 1759/60, the settlers on Mauritius imported about 30,000 tortoises, and the provision of food supplies to sailing ships—no matter whether they were naval craft, merchant vessels or pirate ships—continued as a lucrative business. But this new supply was eventually exhausted, and it became increasingly difficult to find replacements. By about 1760, giant tortoises on Diego Rodriguez were in such short supply that exports were restricted. In 1790 they were halted completely. Apparently the original testudinate fauna on a second island had been completely wiped out. When investigations were made into the fate of the giant tortoises on Diego Rodriguez in the middle of the 19th century, all that was found was a meagre quantity of shell fragments . . . The situation was much the same on some of the other islands. Soon after the extermination of the Mauritius tortoises, the sands also ran out for those on the nearby island of Reunion, and so the giant tortoises of the Mascarene Archipelago had ceased to exist before any real study of them could be made.

To the north of Madagascar, but somewhat further from the route to the Indies, giant tortoises were living on the Farquhar Islands, the Aldabra Atoll and the Seychelles Archipelago. Not only did they bear a strong resemblance to the Mascarene tortoises, but to a large extent they also shared their fate, as live meat stores to feed mariners of all nations. In the 18th century, the stocks on the Farquhar Islands were finally wiped out, while those

Transportation of land tortoises from islands in the Indian Ocean.
Aldabra tortoises were shipped to the Seychelles, Mascarene Islands, Sri Lanka and St Helena.
Mascarene tortoises within the archipelago of Reunion and Rodriguez were taken to Mauritius.
Madagascan Radiated tortoises were transported as far as Vietnam and the Tonga Islands ("*Testudo hypselonota*" and "Tui malila").

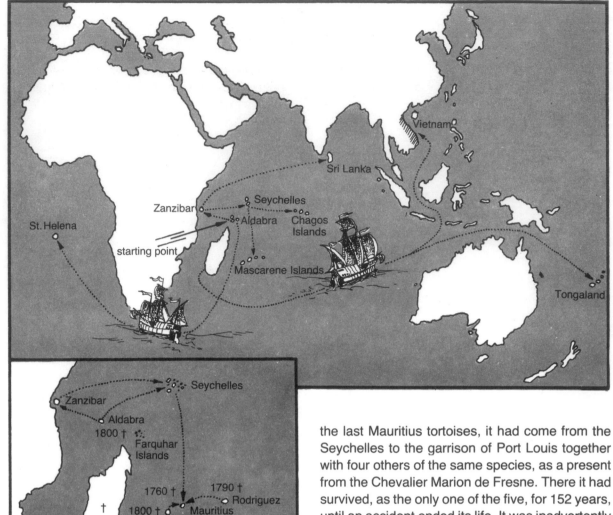

on the Seychelles held out a little longer. But towards the end of the last century, stocks there were so depleted that the only way to save the last remaining Mahé giants was to pen them into enclosures. Fortunately, their descendants are still living there in semicaptivity today, and have become one of the island's tourist attractions. Numbers of giant tortoises are still living on other islands in the Seychelles Archipelago, although all of them are descendants of animals imported from Aldabra. One of the very few tortoises that can be called an original Seychelles giant tortoise lived from 1766 until 1918 as the well-known "Marion's tortoise" on Mauritius. A few years after the inglorious extermination of

the last Mauritius tortoises, it had come from the Seychelles to the garrison of Port Louis together with four others of the same species, as a present from the Chevalier Marion de Fresne. There it had survived, as the only one of the five, for 152 years, until an accident ended its life. It was inadvertently shot as a soldier was cleaning his rifle. Today this famous Methusela of tortoises can be seen in the British Museum in London as a preserved museum specimen.

Another renowned individual is Chun's giant tortoise from Mahé which in 1899 was presented to the German Deepsea Expedition led by the Leipzig Professor of Zoology, Carl Chun. Until then, the dark giant had lived on the small island of Principé not far from Mahé to which it had been "transferred". It is, however, probably not an original Seychelles tortoise but one of the first individuals brought to Mahé from Aldabra. With a carapace measuring 106 cm (as a straight-line distance), the creature far exceeds the others of the same species on the expedition ship "Valvidia" (Fig. 22). Today it is one of the prepared specimens in the *Staatliches Museum für Tierkunde* (State Museum of Zoology) in Dresden.

Table 2   Giant tortoises on islands in the Indian Ocean

Island or island group	Species of tortoise	Subsequent history of population
Seychelles Archipelago	*Megalochelys sumeirei †*	probable remnant still in captivity on Mahé; museum specimen of "Marion's tortoise" in British Museum, original population exterminated in middle of 19th century
	Megalochelys gigantea	imported tortoises from Aldabra living in wild and on farms on the remaining islands
Aldabra	*Megalochelys gigantea*	In original habitat, still some 30 – 100,000 individuals; introduced population on Zanzibar (Prison Island), Seychelles, Chagos Islands, Sri Lanka and other islands
Farquhar	*Megalochelys gouffei †*	became extinct towards end of 18th century
Madagascar	*Megalochelys grandidieri †*	only as Ice Age fossil (Pleistocene), already exterminated by island's first inhabitants
Mauritius	*Cylindraspis indica † (= C. vosmaeri, C. inepta, C. sauzieri)*	both species exterminated about middle of 18th century, later *Megalochelys sumeirei †* and *Megalochelys gigantea* were introduced there
	Cylindraspis grayi †	
Reunion	*Cylindraspis borbonica †*	exterminated towards end of 18th century
Diego Rodriguez	*Cylindraspis peltastes †*	both species exterminated at about middle of 18th century
	Cylindraspis vosmaeri †	

The only population of giant tortoises in the Indian Ocean in existence today, much depleted but still fairly numerous and in its original form, is that on Aldabra. In the years round 1960, its numbers were put at well over 30,000 individuals. In 1971, P. Grubb estimated that about 100,000 Aldabra tortoises are still in existence. The majority of them are living in the wild, the rest in modest but adequate farm-like conditions. Obviously Aldabra lay too far off the direct sea route to India.

The transfer of giant tortoises by ship was not restricted to that melancholy example of trade between Mauritius and Diego Rodriguez alone. Thousands of tortoises were "deported" from the Seychelles and Aldabra in what became a veritable animal migration. A number of Aldabra tortoises were taken to Zanzibar. On Prison Island off the coast of Zanzibar, a group of well over 100 individuals is still thriving and multiplying today under the strict protection of the authorities.

Round about 1850, stocks on Aldabra were suffering seriously from over-exploitation, so in 1874, on the initiative of some famous English naturalists —at their head Charles Darwin, and among their number Georg Albert Günther, the renowned custodian of the reptile collection in the British Museum—the export of these animals on a large scale was begun. The Military Governor of Mauritius arranged for many of them to be shipped to the Seychelles. These animals are the ancestors of most of the small populations of giant tortoises living there today. A number of the animals came back to Mauritius. But Aldabra giant tortoises were also taken by British officers and government officials to other islands that had never before been the home of giant tortoises. In 1776 the first specimen came to St. Helena, where it lived until 1877. Napoleon saw it during his exile there. After the Emperor's death, another specimen was added and it lived there until 1918. Today an Aldabra tortoise by the name of "Jonathan" lives on St. Helena, having "gone into exile" there as recently as 1882.

The largest Aldabra tortoise ever recorded lived for many years as a "foreigner" on Egmont Island in the Chagos Archipelago. It weighed 560 pounds and its carapace was 55 inches long when it made its last journey to the British Museum in about 1900. Towards the end of the 18th century, Aldabra tortoises were transported as far as Ceylon. Later more were added to the original ones so that today, a small artificial colony of Aldabra tortoises exists there as well.

Galapagos—
Islands of Tortoises

A few thousand kilometres from the tortoise islands in the Indian Ocean, Spanish mariners in 1535 discovered an archipelago of volcanic islands situated just under 1,000 kilometres off the west coast of South America. The islands were no less strange and wonderful than those of the East Indies. On their shores also lived "tame" birds, such as penguins and flightless cormorants, which however could not compare in flavour with the dodos of the Mauritius. On the other hand, they lived among more remarkable companions. The cliffs of the islands were inhabited by thousands of lizards of curious appearance, which also seemed entirely unafraid of humans. But on being approached too closely, they jumped into the sea. These marine iguanas are the only modern lizards that, as harmless vegetarians, habitually entered the sea.

Closely related to these remarkable animals are some large ground-dwelling lizards, the land iguanas, that live on the dry mainland parts of the islands. They feed mainly on the fruit and vegetation of the prickly pear. Both endemic giant lizards belong to the family of Leguans (Iguanidae). But once again, the most striking animals on the mainland were the dark-coloured giant tortoises. And it was from them that the island group got its name, Galapagos.

The Galapagos Archipelago consists of five "large", ten middle-sized and a large number of small islands, comprising an area of 7,800 km^2. The giant tortoises lived on eleven of the islands. The creatures were so incredibly abundant on many of the islands that it was possible to walk on their backs over long distances without ever touching the lava ground beneath. From the coastal strip, well-defined trails polished smooth by the passage of many thousands of tortoises extended inland towards the volcanic uplands. Most of the large craters had become extinct long ago, tropical shrubs flourished on their slopes while fresh water, so welcome on Galapagos, collected on their level central floors. Extensive swampy areas rich in ground vegetation extended across these uplands. Here, the brownish-black giants wallowed in the mud, here they found an abundance of food. In the hot, dry lava soils of the coastal region and of the mountain slopes, they had to make do with cactus plants and scrub.

Long after the last hour had struck for the Mascarene tortoises, the Galapagos tortoises were still living entirely undisturbed in these obscure islands at the end of the world. But the idyll of the Galapagos islands was not to last for ever. In the 19th century, seal hunters put in at the islands in pursuit of valuable skins, for there is also an endemic species of seal on Galapagos. They found that the giant tortoises were a welcome supply of fresh meat, so Galapagos tortoises in their turn became living food stores. But worse was to come. After the sealhunters came the whalers, and floating abattoirs with great boilers in which blubber was processed, sailed the formerly peaceful expanses of

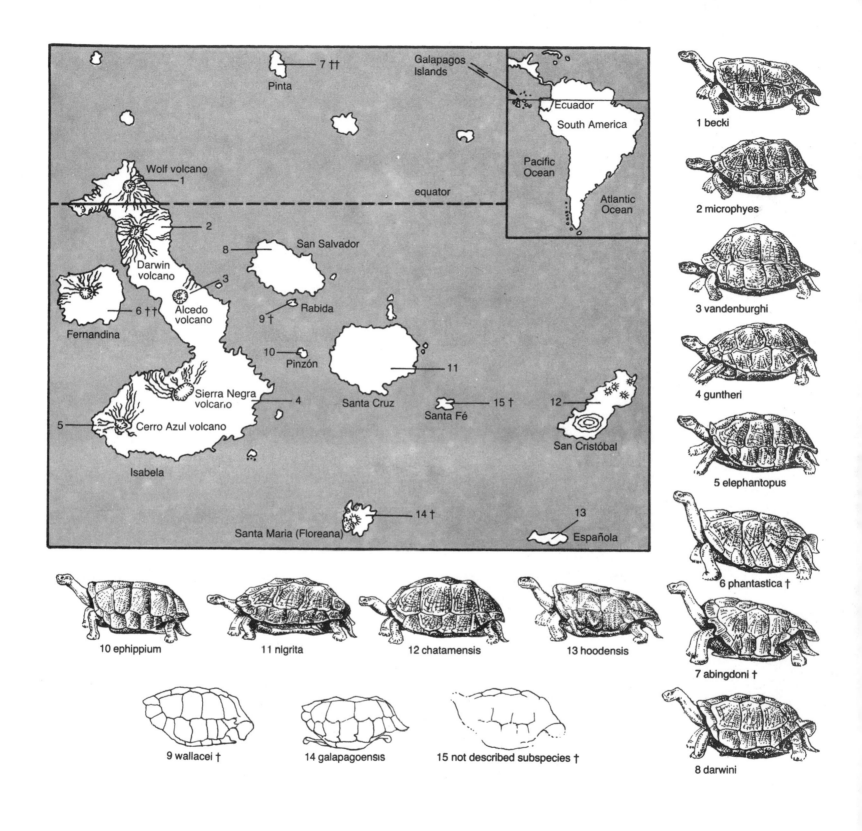

7 †† Pinta

Galapagos Islands

Ecuador
South America

Pacific Ocean

Atlantic Ocean

equator

Wolf volcano — 1

— 2

Darwin volcano

San Salvador 8

— 3

Alcedo volcano

Rabida 9 †

Fernandina 6 ††

10 Pinzón

— 11

Sierra Negra volcano — 4

Santa Cruz

15 † Santa Fé

12 San Cristóbal

Cerro Azul volcano 5

Isabela

14 † Santa Maria (Floreana)

13 Española

1 becki

2 microphyes

3 vandenburghi

4 guntheri

5 elephantopus

6 phantastica †

7 abingdoni †

8 darwini

10 ephippium

11 nigrita

12 chatamensis

13 hoodensis

9 wallacei †

14 galapagoensis

15 not described subspecies †

The Galapagos Archipelago and its Giant tortoises—classified as subspecies of *Chelonoidis elephantopus*.

Table 3   Current situation of Galapagos Giant Tortoises (Chelonoidis elephantopus)

name of island Spanish = English	subspecies † = extinct †* = nearly extinct	size of population
Isabela = Albemarle	in north, near Wolf volcano: *Ch. e. becki* in north, near Darwin volcano: *Ch. e. microphyes* in central part of island near Alcedo volcano: *Ch. e. vandenburghi* in south-east of island, in the Sierra Negra: *Ch. e. guentheri* in south-west of island, Cerro Azuel: *Ch. e. elephantopus*	approx. 1,000–2,000 individuals in original habitat approx. 500–1,000 individuals in original habitat approx. 3,000–5,000 individuals in original habitat approx. 300–500 individuals in original habitat approx. 400–600 individuals in original habitat
Fernandina = Narborough	*Ch. e. phantastica †**	probably almost exterminated in its original habitat by volcanic activity in 19th century. Last specimen (elderly ♂) is living in the Darwin Station, Indefati- gable
Pinta = Abingdon	*Ch. e. abingdoni †**	probably extinct in original habitat, one elderly ♂ in the Darwin Station on Indefatigable, hope of further finds may be justified
San Salvador = James	*Ch. e. darwini*	approx. 500–700 individuals in original habitat
Rabida = Jervis	*Ch. e. wallacei †*	completely extinct. Its classification as a subspecies is controversial; descrip- tion possibly based on mistaken alloca- tion to site of finding, possibly no tortoise population ever existed on Rabida
Pinzon = Duncan	*Ch. e. ephippium*	about 150–200 specimens found in original habitat, but unable to increase because of large number of rats. Successful egg-hatching and rearing programme in the Darwin Station, 100 young tortoises already released on Duncan.
Santa Cruz = Indefatigable	*Ch. e. nigrita*	approx. 2,000–3,000 individuals in origi- nal habitat
San Cristobal = Chatham	*Ch. e. chathamensis*	approx. 500–700 individuals in original habitat

name of island Spanish = English	subspecies † = extinct †* = nearly extinct	size of population
Española = Hood	*Ch. e. hoodensis*	The last 10 females and 1 male were brought to the Darwin Station on Indefatigable, where 25 young had been bred successfully by 1970/71. Release into natural habitat will be possible soon.
Floreana = Charles	*Ch. e. galapagoensis* †	entirely extinct, the only complete mounted specimen of this subspecies is on exhibition in British Museum, London
Santa Fé = Barrington	undescribed subspecies †	entirely extinct. Reliable historical sources indicate existence of giant tortoises on Barrington. Specimens of *Ch. e. nigrita* introduced from Indefatigable have been living there since 1956.

the Pacific in ever-increasing numbers. Today we know that within the space of a few decades, whales, the largest mammals in the world, were almost exterminated by the industrial nations, and all for the sake of a few years' supply of cheap oil. The whalers emulated the seal hunters. Their visits to the Galapagos Islands to stock up with tortoise meat became increasingly frequent. Soon they hit upon the calamitous idea of extracting oil from tortoises as well, since whales were becoming scarce...

Within about 30 years, some 200,000 Galapagos tortoises were slaughtered in this way, on the evidence of the whalers' log books alone, and these are far from being complete and accurate. It has been estimated that since the discovery of the Galapagos Archipelago, almost ten million individuals have been turned to profit in this way.

At the beginning of the present century, the critical situation facing the stocks of giant tortoises on the Galapagos was already giving cause for general concern. An expedition to study the animals, organized in 1906 by the Californian Academy of Sciences and later analyzed by John van Denburgh, was able to establish the presence of modest stocks still living on a number of the islands, though by no means on all. The fate of the tortoises on some islands was not clear. Fortunately the members of the expedition collected whatever they could find on all the islands in the way of useful skeleton remains left behind by whalers and sealers. In this way, the most extensive collection of material for the study of Galapagos tortoises found its way to the USA. Regrettably, the tortoises on the small island of Barrington had already become extinct without any reliable remains having been found.

The interest of zoologists and nature conservationists in the fate of the Galapagos tortoises has grown enormously in the last few decades, and today it is possible to take stock of the situation. Out of some 16 tortoise populations that once inhabited the islands, two have certainly become extinct. Whereas all the remains of the Barrington tortoises are lost, a taxidermal specimen of a Charles Island tortoise is still in the British Museum. The continued existence of two other populations, that on Abingdon and that on Narborough, hangs by a thread. Of the two populations, only one or two surviving individuals have been found, too few to start a programme of breeding. A fifth population, that of

Hood Island, was rescued at the eleventh hour. Ten tortoises, nine females and one male, were found; sufficient to ensure the continuation of the race. The numbers of individuals in the remaining populations vary between 100 and 5,000, and so at the moment, they are not critically endangered. But their survival will be ensured only if it proves possible to preserve or restore natural conditions on the islands.

Since Charles Darwin visited the Galapagos Archipelago in the Beagle in 1835, and found inspiration for his theory of evolution by natural selection, the island, as a unique site for the study of evolutionary processes in living organisms, has constantly drawn scientists of all nationalities, including William Beebe, Irenäus Eibl-Eibesfeldt and numerous film documentarists. But the significant turning point in the fate of the tortoises was the founding in 1964 of the Darwin Memorial Research Station (Estación Biológia Charles Darwin) on Indefatigable Island and the establishment of the Archipelago as the national park of Ecuador. The most urgent task was the reduction or total destruction of feral mammals—dogs, cats, pigs and goats—as well as of rats and mice, with which the tortoises are unable to compete successfully. In 1958, three goats (a billy and two nannies) were released on Abingdon. Within a few years, their numbers had reached 30,000 individuals. The National Park authorities have already shot 18,000, but only their complete eradication can save the island's natural life. On Hood Island as well, the major task of nature conservation is the elimination of goats by shooting. While Albemarle, the largest island, is overrun by packs of dogs.

Preservation of species by captive breeding

The idea of a last-minute rescue of critically endangered species of animals by a controlled programme of breeding is an old one, of which there are many famous examples: Père David's deer, the wisent or European bison and Przewalski's horse serve as the classic models for such endeavours.

Even before the Darwin Research Station was set up on Indefatigable Island, some American scientific associations and zoos were carrying out experimental research into selective breeding with Galapagos tortoises. In 1928, on the initiative of the New York Zoological Society, about 200 tortoises were collected on South Albemarle Island and were distributed to zoos or breeding stations on Hawaii, the Bermudas, in California, Texas, New Orleans, Arizona and Florida. The zoo of San Diego, California, and the Zoological Society of that town have done sterling work and achieved the first breeding successes. At the same time, the societies named above, together with the World Wildlife Foundation have supported the development of the Darwin Memorial Station.

The work of the station concentrates on two aspects. On the one hand, the last remaining specimens of certain populations are cared for, so that with optimal feeding and health supervision, they may be encouraged to breed. In this way, the last eleven tortoises on Hood Island have already been increased to a stock of more than 50 individuals. On the other hand, tortoise eggs are collected from the natural laying sites, taken to Indefatigable Island and there hatched in incubators. The baby tortoises are then reared under optimal conditions. Such a project has greatly strengthened the Duncan Island population, which had been stagnating for the whole of this century. Of particular interest are a number of albinotic young Galapagos tortoises bred in the Darwin Station (p. 22).

So far, the breeding of Aldabra tortoises has been successful only on some of the Seychelles Islands. René Honegger, who carried out investigations for the World Wildlife Foundation in 1963/64 into the situation of endemic vertebrates on the Seychelles, reports examples of successful breeding both in the Mahé Botanical Gardens and on certain other islands. But he concedes that regular breeding success occurs only in a few private tortoise enclosures, where adequate supplies of bananas, banana leaves and other green fodder is supplied to the animals. Although Aldabra giant tortoises are kept in zoos all over the world, only Taronga Zoo in Sydney, Australia has so far achieved successful breeding results. The Zoological Garden in Zurich, under the supervision of its distinguished Curator of Reptiles, René Honegger, has created at great expense an admirably-planned enclosure for giant tortoises, combining outdoor and glass-covered areas, so one may hope that reports of success there will follow.

previous page:

The Angonoca *(Asterochelys yniphora)* from western Madagascar, the rarest and most highly endangered species of land tortoises in the world.

The Flat-backed tortoise *(Pyxis planicauda)*, one of the rarest land tortoises in Western Madagascar.

Australia's rarest tortoise: *Pseudemydura umbrina* from the region round Perth, Western Australia.

Vietnamese Box turtle *(Cuora galbinifrons)*, one of the rarest terrestrial emydid turtles. It was described by René Bourret as recently as 1939.

Eastern Painted turtle *(Chrysemys picta picta)* from the northeast of the USA. One of the most beautifully coloured emydid turtles.

Western or Pacific Pond turtle *(Clemmys marmorata)* from the west coast of North America. An emydid turtle that is entirely or semi aquatic and also inhabits brackish waters.

Giant Musk turtle *(Staurotypus triporcatus)* from Mexico with a carapace length of almost 40 cm is the largest representative of the family of Staurotypidae from Mexico.

Barbour's Map turtle *(Graptemys barbouri)*, one of the rarest species of the genus, from southeastern USA.

Black-knobbed Map turtle *(Graptemys nigrinoda)* from Alabama and Mississippi, one of the rarest of the Map turtles.

Wood turtle *(Clemmys insculpta)*, a rare and endangered species from the northeastern states of America and Canada.

Florida Red-bellied turtle (*Chrysemys rubriventris nelsoni*). The most southerly subspecies of Red-bellied turtle, widely distributed in eastern USA.

Long-necked Chicken turtle (*Deirochelys reticularis*) basking in the author's outdoor terrarium.

Diamondback terrapin (*Malaclemys terrapin*). Inhabitant of brackish water and salt marshes along the eastern coast of North America.

following page:

The American or Common Box turtle (*Terrapene carolinensis*) is well known in America.

Female of Callagur turtle *(Callagur borneoensis)* on the coast of Malaysia. This giant turtle lives not only in freshwater, but also in the brackish waters of river mouths and protected bays. While egg-laying these turtles can be found at night in the dunes.

Male of Callagur turtle *(Callagur borneoensis)* in plain coloration out of mating.

While mating the male of the Callagur turtle shows significant colours both of the skin and the shell.

Shell closure in a cryptodire, the Four-toed tortoise or Horsfield's tortoise *(Agrionemys horsfieldi)*. The limbs provide full protection to the retracted head.

Shell closure in a side-necked turtle (pleurodire), the Flat-shelled turtle *(Platemys platycephala)*. The head can merely be placed to the side.

Common Musk turtle, known as the "Stinkpot" *(Sternotherus odoratus)*.

White-lipped Mud turtle *(Kinosternon leucostomum)*.

"Peacock's eye turtle" *(Chrysemys scripta callirostris)*

Portrait of an Antillian Slider *(Chrysemys terrapen)*. The elongate claws of the forelimbs are a sexual characteristic of the males.

An Australian Snake-necked turtle, the Oblong tortoise *(Chelodina oblonga)* emerging from mud.

John Cann and his assistant with a Plateless River turtle or Papuan turtle or Pignose turtle *(Carettochelys insculpta)* that they have caught in northern Australia.

Young Papuan turtle *(Carettochelys insculpta)*. The proboscis is clearly visible.

The Fitzroy River turtle *(Rheodytes leucops)* was discovered as recently as 1977 and described scientifically in 1980 by John Cann and Prof. Legler. Elderly male specimen.

Young *Rheodytes leucops*

Adult Plateless River turtle *(Carettochelys insculpta)*. The powerful, paddle-shaped forelimbs are a striking feature.

Giant or Broad-shell Snake-necked turtle *(Chelodina expansa)* from eastern Australia.

Australian Common Snake-neck *(Chelodina longicollis)*

following page:

The New Guinea Painted tortoise *Emydura australis subglobosa*, a Side-necked turtle from West-Irian and Papua New Guinea, considerable numbers of which are regularly bred by turtle enthusiasts.

63

Giant tortoises—their origins and relational links

Ever since Darwin's studies on the Galapagos, the question of the origin of the giant tortoises on the islands in the ocean has been a frequent subject of scientific hypothesis. Darwin's assumption that all the populations of the Archipelago can be traced back to a common primitive form is today shared by all scientists. Their close relationship to the land tortoises of South America is confirmed by numerous studies of comparative anatomy and by modern work in biochemistry. In addition, palaeontological evidence gives considerable support to this view. It can be assumed that the ancestors of these giant tortoises were smaller and were transported on pieces of driftwood—perhaps in the wake of major geological catastrophes on the South American mainland—to the Archipelago. Right from the start, the populations of the individual islands were totally isolated from one another. Even on Albemarle, the largest island, the lava fields between the volcanoes effectively ensured the isolation of the various groups. Thus it was possible for the different genetic traits to take effect which have led to the specific shaping of the individual populations. Nevertheless, many common features have also developed independently of one another. For instance, saddle-backed tortoises developed on different islands. As they get older, the anterior part of the carapace flattens or even curves forwards and upwards. As a result, the tortoises are able to stretch their long neck upwards—a very useful accomplishment when feeding on high-growing stems of prickly pear. But at the same time, the gap left at the front of the carapace is so wide that even when the limbs are drawn in, the large opening in the shell cannot be closed. Such tortoises would fall easy victim to predatory birds and beasts. But significantly, both are absent from the Galapagos Islands. For this reason alone, giant tortoises of this kind, that have relinquished part of the protective function of their carapace, were able to evolve.

The relationship between the separate populations on the Galapagos Islands is still so close that nowadays, they are all considered as geographical races of a single species. At the beginning of this century, the individual island forms were still often regarded as independent species. In any case, variability among members of each population of Galapagos giant tortoises *(Chelonoidis elephantopus)* is so great that even the experts can rarely identify the creatures with certainty if they have no information on their origin.

For the Aldabra tortoises *(Megalochelys gigantea)*, the division into subspecies that had generally been made hitherto, has turned out to be impossible to sustain. The features of the various forms are much more readily explained as characteristics of particular age groups, particularly since, in contrast to the Galapagos Islands, no effective geographical barrier exists between the tortoise populations of the north and south of the island.

An interesting criterion of the taxonomical status of tortoises is their crossbreeding capacity. So far, nothing has been heard about hybridization experiments in breeding stations, where, of course, efforts are concentrated primarily upon maintaining genetically pure populations. But it may be that the crossbreeding of the last remaining tortoises on Narborough and Abingdon with other tortoises would be the only chance of retaining genetic material from these animals. The success or failure of such experiments could also have significant bearing on the taxonomical assessment of the Galapagos tortoises.

Undoubtedly two disparate groups of giant tortoises had evolved on the islands of the Indian Ocean, each of which must be accorded its own generic status—*Megalochelys* and *Cylindraspis*. It is assumed that these genera were also able to evolve giant form because of the absence of competitors and enemies. According to a different theory, these giant tortoises are seen as relics of species that were originally much more widely distributed and which, for the same reasons, were able to survive only on the islands. Numerous findings of fossil land tortoises from the Eocene and Pleistocene support this assumption. Possibly the giant land tortoises of various genera that were common in the lignite forests succumbed to the competition and enmity of mammals, although the existence of two recent giant tortoises on the mainland bears witness to their capacity for survival. These are the Spurred tortoise *(Geochelone sulcata)* from the arid zone of Central Africa and the Burmese Brown tortoise *(Manouria emys)* from the tropical forests of Indochina and the Greater Sunda Islands of Kalimantan (Borneo) and Sumatra. But *Manouria emys* could, with some justification, be considered as an

Table 4 Morphological characteristics of giant tortoises on the tropical islands of the Indo-Pacific

Aldabra tortoises (genus *Megalochelys*)	Mascarene tortoises (genus *Cylindraspis*)	Galapagos tortoises (genus *Chelonoidis*)
nuchal lamina present gulars normal in form carapace generally evenly domed and high; "saddle-back" in old individuals rather rare; the sub-fossil *M. grandidieri* even was strikingly flat	nuchal lamina absent gulars elongate and often bifurcate carapace evenly domed, not too high	nuchal lamina absent gulars normal in form carapace evenly domed usually only in young animals, high "saddle back" very frequent in old animals

isolated relict of the giant land tortoises of the genus *Manouria* that were widespread in the lignite forest and are also found in Central Europe today.

One thing is beyond doubt, the island giants of the Pacific and of the Indian Ocean are descended from different ancestors. Their similarity is not the result of common ancestry, but is rather to be interpreted as the result of their having evolved under similar conditions.

The practice of transporting the giant tortoises of the Indian Ocean between the individual islands by sailors has made it very difficult subsequently to determine the original situation. Mauritius alone, for instance, repeatedly imported tortoises from Rodriguez, Reunion and the Seychelles and later from Aldabra as well. In the past, single old museum specimens, often consisting of only a carapace, with inexact or even incorrect indication of origin were used in the description of new species. The enormous variations in carapace form that are the result of differences in age and sex were all too frequently overlooked, and the specimens were simply given new names. The consequence was a good deal of confusion. In the 1870s, G. A. Günther attempted to clarify the original distribution of the giant tortoises of the Mascarene and Galapagos Islands, using material in the British Museum. In spite of this work and of subsequent revisions carried out by various specialists, the status of the giant tortoises, of the Indian Ocean in particular, remained unclear in many details. The most recent survey was made in 1980 by Roger Bour from the collections in the Museum of Natural History in Paris.

Tortoises in department stores and supermarkets

Land tortoises are among the earliest animals to have been kept in captivity as pets in Europe. In the Middle Ages, a tortoise brought back home from a pilgrimage would occasionally be kept—and this often for centuries—in the garden of a monastery or castle. At the beginning of this century, when there was an upsurge in the fashion for domestic pets, tortoises were regularly on sale in petshops. But after the Second World War, there was an incredible increase in animal imports which inevitably affected the countries of origin. According to official statistics, more than a million Mediterranean Spur-thighed tortoises (*Testudo graeca*) were imported into Great Britain between 1967 and 1971 from Morocco alone. If one considers this enormous number in relation to figures given by a British herpetologist, Dr. Lambert, when he estimates the total stock of *Testudo graeca* in Morocco to be about five million individuals, the extent of the damage done to the tortoise population becomes clear. Some years later, the export of tortoises from Morocco was prohibited by law. The remaining stocks probably amount to just under half the original population.

In 1971, Jugoslavia exported some 400,000 Hermann's or Greek tortoises (*Testudo hermanni*). Here again, it will never be possible to compensate for the depletion in stocks that this immense export caused, because a land tortoise takes 10 to 15 years to reach maturity, and lays only about 20 eggs a year.

What are the prospects for these tortoises that are put on the market? Unsuitable, even cruel treatment during shipment damages the animals so much that usually they are already weakened by the time they reach the customer. And who buys the tortoises? Because they are modestly priced, 99 per cent of them are not bought by terrarium keepers but by customers who simply want the animal as a plaything. Incorrect treatment kills 98 per cent of all imported tortoises within their first year. Well authenticated examples of individual longevity in European tortoises that have survived for 70 years in Stuttgart, 59 years in Dresden or even 120 years in the garden of Lambeth Palace in London do not, unfortunately, alleviate the melancholy balance sheet. The only answer can be an end to mass imports, while continuing to permit the import, subject to a strict quota, of quite small numbers of individuals, collected and transported with care, to be looked after by seriously interested enthusiasts or to take part in a programme of breeding.

Unless all Mediterranean countries agree quite soon to act in this way, the European tortoise may soon share the fate of its more exotic cousins. All species of land tortoises alive today are so critically endangered that they feature on Lists 1 and 2 of the Washington Convention on the Preservation of Species.

The situation is rather different with the American Painted turtles (genera *Chrysemys* and *Pseudemys*) which also turn up year after year in the USA and Europe for sale as "department store pets". Most of them, however, come from farms and are not taken from natural habitats. The small, brightly-coloured baby Emydid or Pond turtles (known as terrapins in Britain) prove irresistible to millions of aquarium owners. But few of the customers know that Painted turtles should properly be housed in an aqua-terrarium and not in an aquarium. They also fail to realize that with correct care, they grow rapidly and as fully grown adults, can achieve a carapace length of 15 to 40 cm, making them somewhat unsuitable for the average indoor tank.

"Fortunately" however, the highly-sensitive baby terrapins share the fate of the land tortoises: 99 per cent of them die within two years. Nor is the fate of those turtles that have grown too large and become a problem to their owners usually a happy one. Zoo officials throughout the whole of Europe are almost swamped by offers of such animals. And the frequent discovery of Painted turtles that have been released into European waters tells its own lamentable story.

The world's rarest tortoises

The rarest tortoise in the world lives on Madagascar. A small region at the centre of the island's west coast in the vicinity of Cape Sada is the home of *Asterochelys yniphora*, known as the Angonoka in Malagasy. Careful estimates put the number of the total population at about 20 individuals. The range of the species is only a few square kilometres on the Bay of Soalala. Clearing of the land by burning and grazing by animals are destroying the last habitat of these remarkable tortoises (p. 49), that are closely related to the Malagasy Radiated tortoise *(Asterochelys radiata)*. In recent years, scientists from Madagascar, France, the USA and the German Federal Republic have studied the situation of these tortoises in their almost inaccessible habitat. Government permission was given for four specimens to be taken to the Honolulu Zoo on Hawaii. There, under the direction of James Juvik, who has contributed substantially to research into the ecology of *Asterochelys yniphora*, attempts will be made to breed them. Meanwhile the WWF, working in the field, is making every effort to preserve for posterity the last Angonokas in their original habitat.

About 700 km south of the Angonoka's habitat is that of *Pyxis planicauda*. Its correct systematic classification as a species related to the Spider tortoise *(Pyxis arachnoides)* is one of the more recent results obtained by chelonology, the study of turtles and tortoises. But as yet, little is known with certainty about the conditions under which the species lives in its very restricted range (the vicinity of the town of Morondava).

Undoubtedly, *Pyxis planicauda* is also one of the most critically endangered of the tortoises, and nobody can tell whether it will survive into the next century.

In the southern parts of the continent of Africa there are several more seriously endangered species of land tortoises, the biology and ecology of which will be considered later. However, the situa-

Zoologisches Museum (Berlin Museum of Zoology). Inquiries made by the zoo staff revealed that this animal had probably been found close to Hanoi, the Vietnamese capital, a long way from site of the first finding of *Testudo hypselonota* BOURRET 1941. The custodian of the Berlin reptile collection at that time was Dr. Heinz Wermuth, one of the leading experts on recent turtles and the author of numerous publications in this sphere. The question of its provenance gave him no rest. What was the significance of *Testudo hypselonota*, why was it so rare? Clarification came in 1965. The Vietnamese "highbacked tortoise", *Testudo hypselonota*, is identical with the Madagascan Radiated tortoise *Asterochelys radiata*! A thorough morphological comparison of the "two species" supported this view. And a plausible explanation was soon available for the final unanswered question of how the Radiated tortoise could have come to Indochina. In all probability, some French colonial administrators or officers had been stationed on Madagascar before their period of service in Indochina, and while there, had adopted as a pet one of the popular and attractive Sokakes, as the Madagascans call the Radiated tortoises. Because the family became so fond of the pretty creature, it had been taken with them on the new posting and allowed to live in semi-captivity in the house and garden. Nevertheless, at least the first specimen of Cho-lon had escaped from its owners, the second had perhaps been deprived of its master by war, and become self-sufficient. Natural conditions in Vietnam would be perfectly congenial to the Radiated tortoise, so it could easily live and thrive there.

tion of some of these species, such as the Geometric tortoise *(Psammobates geometrica)*, gives some cause for cautious optimism about their chances of survival.

Among freshwater tortoises as well, there are many species whose future seems in doubt. In southwestern Australia, the Western Swamp tortoise *(Pseudemydura umbrina)* (p.50), the rarest tortoise of Australia, lives in the vicinity of Perth, where it is restricted to an area known as the Bullsbrook Estate.

With a carapace only 12.5 cm long, it is also Australia's smallest tortoise. Drainage of the swamp area to turn it into pasture land is rapidly destroying this tortoise's habitat. Not a moment too soon, a protected area was established for it,and at about the same time, the first tortoise was successfully bred in captivity.

There are some other rare freshwater species about which very little is known. For some of them, prospects do not appear good. Included here are the two East Asian Morenia species, *Morenia ocellata* from Burma and *Morenia petersi* from Bangladesh, the huge Painted Batagurs *(Callagur borneoensis)* from Indochina and the Greater Sunda Islands, as well as the large Soft-shelled turtles *(Trionyx euphraticus)* in the Euphrates, and the North African and Southwest Asian populations of Nile Soft-shelled turtles *(Trionyx triunguis)*. At present, one can only hope that the world's recent turtle fauna will not become poorer by any one of its mere 220 species. Marine turtle specialists working to this end have been joined recently by an international group of scientists that devotes itself particularly to land tortoises. In October 1981, it held its first International Conference in Oxford.

The turtle fauna of the world

The number of species within the order of modern turtles is small. Only 220 species are living in the world today. If the fact is taken into account that certain widely distributed species inhabit their large range as different geographical races (or better, subspecies), the total rises to 340 distinguishable forms. This, compared with the extraordinary abundance of species and forms in the groups saurians and snakes, is a modest number. Within the heterogenous class of reptiles, crocodiles and tuataras can claim even fewer species; only 22 and one single species respectively are extant. These figures indicate that the last three reptilian groups mentioned are remnants of phylogenetically old groups, whereas the saurians and snakes that comprise the order of Squamata are only just now at the zenith of their evolution, that is, they represent the youngest branch of reptiles.

Examination of the world's turtle fauna reveals a series of fundamental features that they share with all other reptiles and even with other vertebrate groups. Abundance of form is related directly to climatic conditions; it is greatest in the tropics and decreases steadily towards the poles. In addition, there is a significant parallel in the fact that in their distribution quite large relational groups within the order of turtles are linked to particular continents.

Regions of the world where turtles abound

So great is the dependence of turtles upon climate, that the majority of species occur only between the tropics. The areas with the greatest wealth of turtles lie within this tropical belt. Exceptions to this basic rule are the turtle fauna of North America, with its many species, and the distinctive turtle fauna of Australia, that has many fewer species. In North America, 12 species of turtle extend to about 45°N, whereas at the same latitude in Europe and Asia, there are nowhere more than one to a maximum of four species of turtle. This is primarily the result of the different physical structure of these areas. Because of the east-west disposition of all the major mountain ranges in Europe and Asia, animals with little migratory capacity which were at the same time heat-loving, were rarely able, after the glacial periods, to surmount the barrier that the mountains represented. This is seen most clearly in Central Asia. While only one or at most two species of turtle still live north of the Himalaya complex and all its foothills, Peninsula India and Indochina house a considerable abundance of species: Peninsula India including Sri Lanka 23, Indochina including the Sunda Islands, Southern China and the Philippines as many as 40 species. Among them are only six that occur in both Peninsula India and Indochina. On the other hand, a great many of them are endemics, that is, species living exclusively within a strictly defined geographical area.

In North America, the north-south configuration of the mountain ranges has created much more favourable climatic conditions. In addition, after the retreat of the diluvial ice masses, the turtles were able to immigrate without the hindrance of geographical barriers. It was predominantly Emydid or Pond turtles (family Emydidae), that took advantage of this situation, and have since produced a striking abundance of species in the south-east of North America. Apart from the Emydid turtles, the family of Mud and Musk turtles (Kinosternidae), as an endemic group, represents an important part of the turtle fauna of North and Central America. As a result, these two areas are among the regions of the world with the greatest abundance of turtles. North and Central America each have more than 30 species. In tropical South America, on the other hand, the turtle fauna, although interesting, has considerably fewer species.

Turtles as characteristic animals of continents

The distribution of the various turtle groups across the faunal regions of the world presents an interesting picture. If one considers first the range of the two suborders Cryptodira (that retract the neck in a vertical plane) and Pleurodira (Side-necked turtles that retract the neck in a horizontal plane) which together make up the entirety of modern turtles (Order Testudines), their distribution can be seen to be in broad agreement with the distribution patterns of other organisms. The range of Side-necked turtles seems to conform with geographical regions that are rich in archaic animals retaining a number of more primitive features. Australia gives a very clear example of this. The family of Snake-necked turtles (Chelidae) belonging to the suborder of Side-necked turtles, characterizes the Australian turtle fauna in an unmistakable way. More than half of all the genera and species of the Chelidae are endemic to the region of Australia. The remaining ones occur exclusively in South America. This coincides broadly with the distribution, for example, of marsupials among the mammals. The second family of Side-necked turtles consists of the Pelomedusid turtles (Pelomedusidae). Although this group is absent in Australia, it occurs together with Snake-necked turtles in South America. The South American Pelomedusids represent only about a third of their family, the majority living in Africa. African Pelomedusidae (genera *Pelusios* and *Pelomedusa*) are inhabitants of small bodies of water, and in terms of their ecological classification, are really mud turtles. The South American Pelomedusids, on the other hand, are river turtles of considerable size (genera *Podocnemis* and *Peltocephalus*), living exclusively in the Amazon and Orinoco river systems. In the African region, only the Malagasy species *Erymnochelys madagascariensis* corresponds to this group. For a long time, this species existing in isolation was combined with its South American related species in the genus *Podocnemis*. Among turtles, it is the only example of the remarkable links existing between the reptilian fauna of Madagascar and America (the sole occurrence of boid snakes and iguanas in the Ethiopian region is in Madagascar). So the Malagasy species is further evidence of the

special position Madagascar holds within its zoogeographical region. The pattern of distribution of these animals can logically be considered as evidence of the primitive nature of the group, since undoubtedly the areas have relict status as a result of early geological isolation of the regions. The missing groups, on the other hand, can in terms of spread, be considered as phylogenetically younger. The Cryptodira, with the exception of the completely aquatic New Guinea Plateless River turtle *(Carettochelys)* obviously "could not get as far as" Australia.

In areas in which Pleurodira and Cryptodira both occur in large numbers, the distribution of the species between the two suborders is noteworthy. In South America, the Pleurodira provide 14 species, the Cryptodira only 8 species of the chelonian fauna of the subcontinent. In Africa, on the other hand, there are only 9 Pleurodira but as many as 22 species of Cryptodira. These figures exactly reflect the ratio of more primitive to more recent animal groups in the sequence Australia—South America—Africa.

A closer examination of the distribution of the Cryptodira also reveals some very significant facts. Within the group of Cryptodira with the greatest number of species, namely the Emydid turtles (family Emydidae), the two centres with the greatest diversity stand out clearly: they are Southeast Asia, particularly Indochina and the south of North America. McDowell, a turtle specialist, recognized that the two centres are at the same time the focal point of two evolutionary branches of the family. He considered the Asiatic (Oriental) Emydid turtles as a separate subfamily, the Batagurinae, while assigning the American (Nearctic) turtles to the subfamily Emydinae. This classification can be justified by a number of anatomical pecularities of both shell and skull. But curiously enough, a small number of Emydid turtles proves to be an exception to the distribution scheme of the two subfamilies. The European Pond turtle or terrapin *(Emys orbicularis)*, one of the most familiar and widely distributed testudinids in the world, belongs to the subfamily Emydinae as the sole emydid turtle of the Old World. It can therefore be considered as a Nearctic, American element within the Palaearctic turtle fauna. In contrast, there are six species of turtles of the genus *Rhinoclemmys* belonging to the Batagurinae that live in Central and South

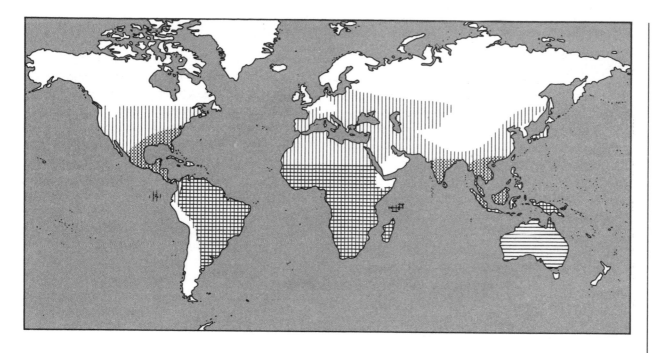

America. Thus they represent an Oriental element in the turtle fauna of the neotropical part of America.

Just as remarkable is the distribution of land tortoises (family Testudinidae), the second large group of the Cryptodira. Because of their morphological and biological similarity, most tortoises were, until recently, considered by zoologists as a single, world-wide genus, Testudo. From a zoogeographical point of view, this would imply that they must be extraordinarily conservative and archaic creatures. But in fact, this uniformity conceals a good deal of parallel specialization rather than a very close common genealogy. This was first recognized in the case of the North American Gopher tortoises *(Gopherus)*, whereas for the remaining "testudos", differentiation of this kind was acknowledged only much later. The view was given initial impetus by the Americans Loveridge and Williams, working a few decades ago. Today, acceptance of a large number of genera is general.

Land tortoises have completely conquered the continent of Africa. The Ethiopian region (that is, the whole of tropical Africa south of the Sahara) is the centre of the greatest diversity in land tortoises. Here, the most striking examples of specialization in this family have evolved: three species of Hinged tortoises *(Kinixys)*, the curious Pancake tortoise *(Malacochersus)* and the variously adapt-

ed desert tortoises of the genera *Homopus*, *Psammobates* and *Chersina*. But of course, "normal" tortoises are also widespread in Africa (genus *Geochelone*). The number of tortoise species increases progressively towards the south, to reach its highest point in Cape Province with seven species. Africa is indeed the "Continent of Tortoises".

Another large and at the same time highly specialized group within the Cryptodira is the family of Soft-shelled turtles (Trionychidae). Of the Cryptodira, they are the members most perfectly adapted to an aquatic way of life. The family has evolved its greatest diversity in the Oriental region, with four genera and about twelve species. This centre of diversity seems likely to be close to the group's original home. This, at any rate, is indicated by the range of the family of Plateless River turtles (Carettochelydidae) in New Guinea, that is, outside the oriental region but in very close proximity to it. This family consists of a single species *Carettochelys insculpta*. It is the most primitive of the Soft-shelled turtles, and indicates the way in which the Trionychidae may have derived from Cryptodira of "normal" form.

But Soft-shelled turtles also live in Africa. Members of the genera *Cycloderma* and *Cyclanorbis* are widespread in tropical central Africa, with four species, which have a counterpart only in the "Soft terrapin" of India and Ceylon, *Lissemys*. The

Africa—continent of
land tortoises

 1 species:
G *Testudo*

 2 species:
G *Testudo*,
Geochelone

 3 species:
Gn *Kinixys*,
Malacochersus,
Geochelone

 4 species:
Gn *Kinixys*,
Geochelone

 5 species:
Gn *Kinixys*,
Geochelone,
Psammobates,
Homopus
Madagascar:
Gn *Asterochelys*
and *Pyxis*, as
well as a *Kinixys*
species, proba-
bly carried in

 6 species:
Gn *Kinixys*,
Geochelone,
Psammobates,
Homopus

 7 species:
Gn *Kinixys*
Geochelone,
Psammobates,
Homopus,
Chersina

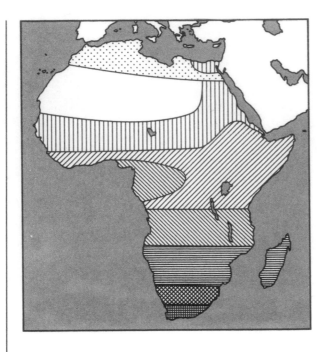

three genera together make up the subfamily of Cyclanorbinae. Their Oriental-Ethiopian scheme of distribution is one of zoogeography's textbook cases. The remaining Soft-shelled turtles make up the subfamily Trionychinae, a group with a strong expansionist drive, which extends from the oriental region westwards as far as the Palaearctic *(Trionyx euphraticus!)*, and similarly, in the east, borders upon the Palaearctic with *Trionyx sinensis*. In North America, that is, in the Nearctic, there are four more species of Soft-shelled turtles of the genus *Trionyx*. As "young" turtles in evolutionary terms, the Soft-shelled turtles have not reached the neotropical part of America, nor have any fossils of Soft-shelled turtles been found so far in the Neotropics.

Turtles have shown an astonishing capacity for exploiting a very wide range of habitats on the mainland. In addition, certain species have become cosmopolitan inhabitants of warm and temperate seas. Yet today, there are certain large areas that appear to offer suitable conditions, but remain without a single species of turtle.

Some unusual forms

In various parts of the world, there are a few turtles that present considerable difficulties to the zoologist attempting to assign them to a place in the taxonomic system. In body structure, they exhibit a number of characters absent in other modern turtles. Only a comparison with species of turtles long since extinct gives clues to the origin and so to the genealogical relationships between these animals.

Science has long been familiar with the two North American Snapping turtles (family Chelydridae). The Common Snapping turtle or Snapper *(Chelydra serpentina)* is found in the east of North America from southern Canada to the north of South America. Remarkable features are its flat, broad carapace and the much reduced, cruciform plastron. The enormous head with the conspicuously hooked beak and dangerously powerful jaws give it a striking appearance. Notable too is its unusually long tail that is heavily tuberculated along the stem. With a maximum carapace length of almost 50 cm, the Snapper is one of the largest American water turtles. The species most closely related to it, the Alligator Snapping turtle *(Macroclemys temmincki)* is considerably larger, with a maximum shell length of 66 cm and the splendid top weight of almost 100 kg. With these extraordinary dimensions, it is the largest American species and at the same time, one of the largest freshwater turtles in the world; yet it is not this alone that makes it a special case among modern turtles. Its similarity to *Chelydra* is relatively great. In particular, the tail of both species is very similar, being rather crocodilian in appearance (hence the popular name of this species). However, the Alligator Snapper has a much larger skull, which it is unable to retract beneath the carapace. Its hooked bill curves even more conspicuously downwards and was responsible for the animal's German vernacular name of "vulture turtle". The shell of the Alligator Snapper is also very similar to that of the Snapping turtle. But on its carapace, the Alligator Snapping turtle has, on either side, an extra row of marginal laminae (supramarginals) occurring as a border between the ordinary marginals and the laterals. This type of structure is unique among modern turtles. It can be explained as a feature that is phylogenetically very ancient and indicates that Snapping turtles represent an archaic branch of turtles. Distribution of the Alligator Snapping turtle is restricted to the south-eastern part of North America. But from fossil finds, it is clear that in "quite recent" geological times, in the Oligocene and the Pleistocene, Snapping turtles also lived in Europe and Asia. Here they became extinct with the arrival of the first glacial period, so their American descendants are the sole surviving representatives of a very ancient family that was once widely distributed. Because they are restricted to North and Central America, the modern Snapping turtles are an endemic species and in terms of their genealogy, relics of a great, long-extinct tribe.

In a broader sense, the family of Mud and Musk turtles (Kinosternidae), that is also endemic to America, is related to the family of Snapping turtles. This is also true of the curious Tabasco turtle *(Dermatemys mawi)* of Central America. This river turtle can be up to 40 cm long and lives in a small area extending from eastern Mexico southwards to Guatemala and Honduras. *Dermatemys* is also the sole relict of a family with many species that existed from the Cretaceous to the Tertiary and was also widely distributed in Asia and Europe. The modern Tabasco turtle is easily recognized by a complete row of additional plastral laminae situated between the normal abdominals and the marginals.

Finally there is a very curious endemic turtle living on the Indochina Peninsula, which in many respects, is reminiscent of the North American Snapping turtles. This is the Big-headed turtle (or Casked terrapin), *Platysternon megacephalum*. This strange creature has not only a very large, beaked head which cannot be retracted into the shell, similar to that of the Alligator Snapping turtle, but like the latter, a very flat shell and a strikingly long tail.

The upper side of the tail is covered with large flat scales, very like the tubercles of the Snapping turtles. A feature of the plastron is the presence of additional rows of inframarginals on either side. Such laminae incidentally also occur on the plastron of Snapping turtles and of most the Mud and Musk turtles.

In addition, there is a series of anatomical features of shell and skull structure in which these curious endemics correspond. Sufficient to justify the view that the remarkable Big-headed turtle also belongs to the wider relationship of that primitive group of chelonians, which in the view of the Polish palaeontologist, Professor Mlynarski, a well-known expert on fossil and modern turtles, makes up a superfamily of "Snapping-turtle-related species". Apart from the nominate family and the families of Tabasco turtles, Mud and Musk turtles and Big-headed turtles, there are two other families in this group both of which became extinct in the Cretaceous. Looked at from a zoogeographical point of view, Mlynarski's views on the relationship between Asiatic Big-headed turtles and the Chelydridae of America and species related to them, are equally persuasive. Crocodiles present a parallel example of isolated relict occurrence of a primitive species of crocodile in Asia, related species of which are still living as a self-contained group only in America; this is the Chinese Alligator. Its range is comparatively close to that of the Big-headed turtles in the lower reaches of the Yangtze Kiang. The other Asiatic crocodiles living to the south of this region belong to the family of True Crocodiles, among which the Chinese Alligator is just as much an isolated stranger as is the Big-headed turtle among the many species of Emydid turtles in Indochina.

The Phylogeny of turtles

Fossil turtles are not particularly rare in larger palaeontological museums. Turtle fossils have been found, sometimes in large quantities, at many well-known finding places of faunas from far back in geological time. The reasons are not far to seek. There is scarcely any other vertebrate which, size for size, can provide such a large mass of bone for fossilization (or petrifaction). As a result, the shell and the bulky, compact skull have been preserved in fossil form far more frequently than have the skeletons of other vertebrates of the same size. Accordingly, the relatively frequent occurrence of turtle fossils can be explained simply by the greater chance of petrification that exists for the body of a dead turtle, and not as the result of any enormous abundance of turtles in earlier geological epochs. It is very probable that even in earlier fauna, turtles existed neither in a larger variety of species nor in significantly larger numbers of individuals than they do today in those few tropical regions of the earth in which nature has remained unspoiled.

The Triassic turtle, *Proganochelys dux*
Notable features are the flat shell and the scaly tubercles on the neck and tail of this land tortoise.
(after various authors, combined)

The Triassic turtles of Halberstadt

The earliest turtle finds come from the lower formations of the Mesozoic, from the Triassic. In the years before the First World War, well-preserved remains of a turtle with a shell over half a metre long were discovered in layers of the Upper Middle Triassic, known as the Halberstadt Keuper, at a well-known fossil site near Halberstadt in the Harz foreland. Between 1916 and 1918, the palaeontologist O. Jaekel published his findings on this fossil. He called the creature *Triassochelys dux*, the Triassic turtle. Even at first glance, it is obvious that *Triassochelys* is a true chelonian. Its shell has a remarkably squat appearance, and is decidedly broader than long. The horny scutes of the carapace already have typical chelonian form. A striking feature is an additional row of supramarginals between the disc and the marginal laminae. The hind edge of the carapace is distinctly cut away in the tail region, and the side parts above it end in distinct points. *Triassochelys* has a comparatively long neck (with eight vertebrae, that is, one more than modern turtles) which bore spiny protuberances along the back and on the sides. These spines were supported by massive bony processes from the cervical vertebrae. Obviously this made retraction of the neck impossible, either in a vertical or horizontal plane: *Triassochelys*, then, was neither one of the Cryptodira nor one of the Pleurodira. The tail of *Triassochelys* probably also had similar spinous processes. But it was in features of the skull that it differed most markedly from modern chelonians. On the roof of the mouth (on gums and vomer) there were large numbers of small, uneven teeth that undoubtedly were still functional in crushing food. Jaekel found rudiments of teeth even on the jawbone. The *Triassochelys* skull also exhibits a well-developed nasal bone. The turtles lost this bone in the course of later evolution. Further details of skull anatomy, such as the structure of the middle ear with a lateral aperture, distinguish the Triassic turtles from all later related forms. The axial skeleton, thoracic girdle and pelvis also exhibit a number of unique features. For example, the number of dorsal vertebrae is eleven, one more than in other chelonia. In addition to the coracoid and scapula in the thoracic girdle, there is a third bone, the cleithrum, which is absent in all later chelonia. *Triassochelys* was furnished with powerful limbs that enabled it to walk and scrape at the ground. They probably lived on land and were also found on marshy ground. It is to this circumstance that we owe the preservation of tracks made by Triassic turtles. In the Upper Bunter Sandstone at Hildburghausen in Thuringia, fossilized tracks were found that unquestionably indicate Triassic tortoises. Geologically, these tracks are somewhat older than the fossil finds at Halberstadt, and are, at present, the earliest evidence of chelonians that we have. A number of chelonian fossils from the Württemberg Keuper that were found and described as early as the 1880s, were very similar to the turtles of the Halberstadt Keuper.

These animals, that were given the name *Proganochelys*, must also have been large Triassic land tortoises. The picture of the earliest chelonians was rounding itself off, but two fundamental questions remained unanswered—that of the origin of chelonia and that of the subsequent path followed in their evolution. A survey of all existing fossil turtles shows that it is probably easier to find a satisfactory answer to the second of these questions. Triassic turtles are an evolutionary branch

that probably became extinct at the end of the Mesozoic, that is, in the Cretaceous. No transitions to modern turtle form are to be observed in Triassic turtles. It must rather be assumed that the turtles of today split off from common unknown ancestors at an equally early time as the Triassic turtles. Which poses the other question, on the origins of turtles. Triassic turtles are the oldest true chelonians, not chelonian ancestors. At this point, the chain of evidence for the evolution of these creatures is broken, and for the time being, we must turn to conjecture in our search for the origin of the turtle.

Chelonian origins and relationships

On the track of false claimants

For a long time, a small fossil saurian, *Eunotosaurus africanus*, remains of which were found in strata of the Upper Permian in South Africa, was considered to be a probable ancestor of modern turtles. The skeleton exhibits several interesting features which persuaded the palaeontologist Watson in 1914 to recognize in this creature the long sought ancestor of the turtle. In particular, the expanded, leaf-shaped ribs of *Eunotosaurus* suggested themselves as the origin of the typical turtle carapace. But later investigations into turtle embryology and comparative anatomy showed that the chelonian carapace could not possibly have had its origin in the extension of the ribs. Today, workers are unanimous in the view that small bony nodules embedded in the skin developed into the bony

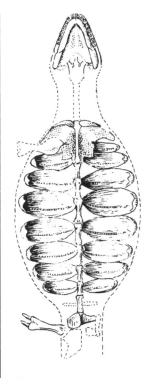

Turtle imposters
The "pseudo-turtle" *Eunotosaurus* from the Permian. The fossil is drawn lying on its back; thus the ribs, which in contrast to those of turtles, spread out broadly, and the extensive dentition on the jaws can be seen clearly. These animals lived on land.

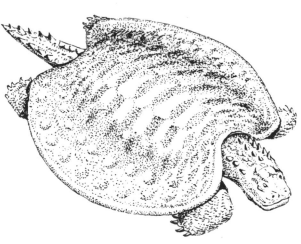

The "plate-toothed" saurian *Placochelys*, a turtle-like marine saurian of the Triassic. It bears a strong resemblance to the sea turtles.

The "plate-toothed" saurian *Henodus*, another turtle-like marine saurian of the Triassic. Again there is some similarity to sea turtles. (after various authors, combined)

75

plates of the turtle carapace. The ribs below simply became fused to the dermal plates. In the process, they regressed strongly, as the narrow, strap-like, residual ribs in the skeleton of the modern turtle shows. On no account, then, could they have enlarged to become a carapace. Recent studies of all geological finds of *Eunotosaurus* have made it increasingly clear that this remarkable saurian must be considered as a doppelgänger or pretender, and not as an ancestor of the turtle. Professor Oskar Kuhn, a renowned expert on fossil reptiles, gave them the appropriate colloquial name of "pseudo-turtles". This small group of reptiles soon became extinct and did not enter into competition with true turtles.

From the Triassic, another group of saurians is known to have lived in the shallow tropical ocean, much in the manner of sea turtles. These marine saurians were extraordinarily similar to marine turtles in external appearance. Their body was covered by an elongate shell, the surface of which was composed of irregular horny plates. The limbs, that had developed into powerful paddles, were also strongly reminiscent of turtle flippers. Even the head resembled that of the turtle in its external appearance. But anatomically there are many important differences. The large, flat teeth along the rami of the lower jaw and on the roof of the mouth are particularly striking. This unusual dentition has earned them their scientific name of Placodontia or plaster-toothed saurians. Apparently they lived on a diet of hard-shelled sea creatures, molluscs, crustaceans or even corals. The true character of the Placodontia as an independent reptilian branch, in which turtle-like characteristics represent only convergent development, was soon recognized. One more imposter had been unmasked, but the search for an ancestor was far from over.

The probable ancestors

Today, most scientists look for the origin of the turtle among groups of saurians that are themselves very primitive reptiles from the earliest epochs of terrestrial vertebrates. Some specialists even go so far as to postulate the direct descent of turtles from primitive amphibians. This last view is based primarily on similarities in the structure of the nasal cavity in turtles and in modern caudates. Another widely-held view that turtle ancestors can be traced back to original cotylosaurs or "stem rep-

tiles" of the Upper Carboniferous is based primarily on fundamental similarities of skull structure in Testudines and Cotylosauria. Both show the typical anapsid type of structure with an absence of temporal vacuities (openings in the side of the skull). Opinions differ again as to whether the anapsid structure of the turtle skull is a primary feature and therefore identical to the cotylosaurians, or else has been acquired secondarily in the course of evolution. Among cotylosaurs, both the unwieldy, sprawling Pareiasauria and the group of the Romeriidae from the Upper Carboniferous could be considered as possible ancestors.

The primeval nature of turtles also explains the extraordinary complexity of their relationships to the other recent reptilian groups. From a phylogenetic point of view, consequences arise that cannot easily be reconciled with the familiar, straight-forward picture of the hierarchy between the various classes of vertebrates, but which rather demand some constructive rethinking. First of all, it is essential to realize that an isolated examination of "fossil" and "modern" animals can provide no information about the relationship of the one to the other. The modern animal world can best be understood analogously as tips of a huge iceberg standing out in apparent isolation, while the links that connect them have to be sought far down beneath the visible horizon. Turtles are certainly the most ancient land vertebrates on earth to have survived to the present day. They can justifiably be described as an integrated group of diverse "living fossils". It is more usual for relicts of extinct animal groups to occur only as single species existing in complete isolation within a modern fauna.

According to the zoologist Willi Hennig, relationships between species or groups of organisms are defined as sister-group relationships, when their evolution can be traced back to a certain point in the chain of common ancestors, at which point their separate evolution as appositional sister groups or species must have started. Today, turtles stand in just such a sister-group relationship to all other terrestrial vertebrates. But the only common feature that still links them is egg structure. All terrestrial vertebrates have what are called amniotic eggs, and are therefore described as Amniota. Because of the amnion, a firm membrane inside the egg enveloping the embryo, they became independent of water in their embryonic development, in contrast to amphibians and fishes. Whereas many large groups of Amniota—today they are usually all simply grouped under the term "reptiles" —became extinct towards the end of the Mesozoic, other groups experienced a vast upsurge after the disappearance of serious competitors. The death of the Saurians in the Upper Cretaceous signalled the hour of the mammals and the sauromorphic amniota. The latter group consisted among others of the Rhynchocephalians, the squamates, the crocodiles and the birds. Whereas the Rhynchocephalians became extinct except for a single modern species, the Squamata underwent a very varied evolution to become the lizards and snakes of today. From another large related system of the Amniota, the Archosauria (Ancient Saurians), only two groups managed to cross the threshold into the Neozoic era. These are birds and crocodiles, which, curiously enough, once again confront one another as sister groups. All other groups of Archosaurians, for example, the highly disparate dinosaurs and pterodactyls, disappeared completely with the death of the Saurians.

Cryptodira and Pleurodira

What has been said about the complicated relationships between vertebrates in general is, of course, valid in particular in any consideration of the evolution and systematic classification of turtles. Any attempt to separate the recent and the fossil fauna leads to unexpected difficulties in understanding. However, a rare advantage that chelonology (the specialist study of turtles) enjoys over many other disciplines of vertebrate research, is that the numerous fossil finds make it possible to build up a remarkably comprehensive mosaic picture of the evolutionary history of these animals, although one that is nevertheless incomplete.

The discovery of the Triassic turtles posed the question of their relationship to the two major groups of turtles, the Cryptodira and the Pleurodira. The two groups differ in a whole series of characteristics (see Table 5), the primary criterion being the plane of retraction of the neck into the shell: Cryptodira, vertical retraction; Pleurodira or Sidenecked turtles, lateral retraction. It was as recently as 1975 that the chelonologist Eugene Gaffney of the American Museum of Natural History in New York first succeeded in producing a satisfactory explanation of the relationship between the Trias-

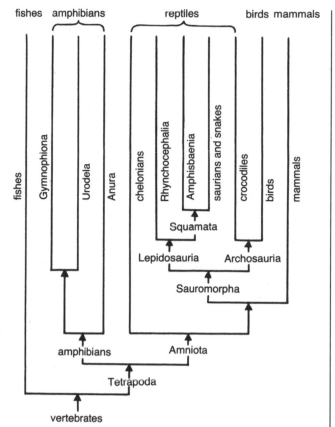

sic turtles and the Cryptodira and Pleurodira. His investigations concentrated mainly on cranial morphology. He showed that, in contrast to all other turtles, Triassic turtles (Proganochelydia) had a gap in the palate between the pterygoids, and a lateral opening to the middle ear. Therefore Gaffney placed them in a sister-group relationship to the rest of the turtles, which he defined as Casichelydia. These again subdivide into Cryptodira and Pleurodira. Not only does this explain the special position of the Proganochelydia, which represent a branch of turtle evolution that became extinct again very early, but it also shows it to be more probable that the splitting of the Casichelydia took place at a very early stage at the beginning of turtle evolution. Consequently it can hardly be claimed that either one of the two groups is older than the other, although certainly they were successful to different degrees in the later course of their phylogenetical history.

The Cryptodira developed a great wealth of forms. They produced the highly specialized land

The position of turtles among present-day vertebrates

The top line presents a summary of the five traditionally accepted classes of vertebrates. The fact that they do not always coincide with the relationships in the phylogenetic system as described by Hennig is particularly clear in the case of "Reptiles". It can be seen that, for example, crocodiles and birds can be traced back to a common starting point, that is, both are Archosaurians. Archosaurians and Lepidosaurians make up the group of the Sauromorpha. This can be considered as a sister-group of the Mammals. In turn, Sauromorpha and Mammals stand in a sister-group relationship to Turtles. It is only at this stage that they can be seen as a probable sister-group to the Amphibia, since both of them are Amniota (animals with an amniotic egg). As Tetrapoda (vertebrates with four feet), this pair of sister-groups in turn stands in opposition to "Fishes" as apodal vertebrates (no feet). The diagram is highly simplified, in that all extinct vertebrate groups have been omitted, and it is precisely these groups that would the more clearly reveal the complicated interrelationships that exist.

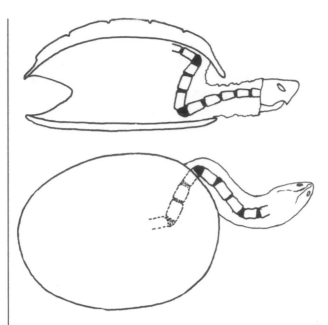

Movement potential in the neck vertebrae of Cryptodires (above) and Pleurodires (below).
In both cases, the enormous mobility is provided by neck vertebrae with different modes of articulation.
(after various authors, combined)

tortoises, freshwater turtles and marine turtles. The Soft-shelled turtles (Trionychidae), that embody an extraordinarily high degree of specialization for life in fresh water, can with some justification be called the ultimate in chelonian evolution. Not all groups of Cryptodira survived the geological epochs equally well. Some became extinct, others persisted until the present only as modest remnants. This is particularly clear in the case of marine turtles which, in the Cretaceous period comprised five variously specialized families with large numbers of species. Of these, only two families with a total of seven species still exist today. Other Cryptodira groups, such as Emydid turtles (Freshwater or Pond turtles, terrapins—family Emydidae) developed their greatest diversity only very recently, and indeed, some groups have not yet reached the final stages of evolution. This is particularly true of the "most modern" group, the North American subfamily of Emydinae. It is at the same time proof of the vitality of the turtles as a group of animals phylogenetically extremely ancient.

The Side-necked turtles (Pleurodira) were less successful in their evolution. Obviously, they had a distinct preference for an exclusively freshwater habitat. Only the Proterochersidae, a family from the Upper Triassic, the Württemberg Keuper, may perhaps have been a pleurodiral land tortoise. The allocation of this fossil family to the Pleurodira is however, still uncertain, since until now, only remains of carapace and not of skull have been

Table 5   Distinctions between Cryptodira (1) and Pleurodira (2)

Mobility of head and neck
1) Head can generally be retracted under shell, with inversion of the neck skin. This presupposes lateral processes on the cervical vertebrae that are only slightly developed. Once the head is retracted, the front opening of the carapace can be closed almost completely by the fore limbs.
2) Head can be retracted laterally only, skin of neck cannot be invaginated. Lateral processes of the cervical vertebrae are well-developed. Forelimbs cannot protect head and neck.

Arrangement of external laminae of shell
1) Plastron generally covered by six symmetrical pairs of laminae. Only the front pair (gulars) may be fused into a single scute. Certain groups have a leathery skin instead of the horny plates.
2) Plastron always has six symmetrical pairs of laminae and an additional horny plate (intergular lamina). Horny scutes never replaced by leathery skin.

Condition of pelvic girdle
1) Pelvis lies free of the shell casing, but is anchored within the shell by firm connective tissue.
2) Pelvis is fused to plastron.

Skull structure
1) The pterygoid bone of the skull reinforces the cranium; insertion of the trochlea-masseter muscle ends at the ear cavity.
2) Quadrate bone (quadratum) reinforces the cranium; insertion of trochlea-masseter muscle is by way of the process of the pterygoid bone.

found. In our system it is allocated to the Triassic turtles (Proganochelia). The earliest unquestionable Pleurodira turtles, the family of Platychelidae, found in the famous turtle sites of the Upper Jura at Solothurn in Switzerland, were already amphibiously living in fresh water like their modern relations. Today's Sidenecked turtles (Pleurodira), the families of the Pelomedusid turtles (Pelomedusidae) and the Snake-necked turtles (Chelidae) are known to us from finds dating back only to the Upper Cretaceous and the Tertiary. Although they can still be found in fossil form in Europe and Asia, their current geographical distribution is restricted to regions rich in relicts of ancient primitive animal groups. Modern Pleurodira reach their greatest diversity in Australia, while their numbers are much fewer in South America and South Africa.

Some remarkable turtles in geological history

Pictures of life in epochs lying far back in geological time exert a strong fascination on anyone interested in natural history and not only on the palaeontologist. It would be impossible here to depict the entire evolutionary processes of the different chelonian faunas that have inhabited the earth since the Triassic, interesting though that would be. We shall content ourselves with a glance at a few remarkable examples of turtle faunas.

Marine turtles in the Jurassic and Cretaceous oceans

The Cretaceous was not only the age of the most impressive of the Giant Saurians, but was also the heyday of marine turtles. The sea turtles of the Cretaceous were adapted in different ways to life in the ocean. A striking feature is the reduction of the bony mass of the shell, such as can also be seen in modern sea turtles. Large numbers of gaps (fontanels) developed in the bone layers of the shell. A strut-like structure between the reduced bony elements maintained the shell's firmness. The covering of horny scutes was usually retained in its entirety, so that externally, there was no indication of the lightening of the structure. Reduction of the bony layer of the shell reached its peak in the extinct family of Protostegidae. These creatures lived from the Upper Cretaceous to the Oligocene in ocean regions to the north of present-day North America. The largest marine turtle ever to have existed came from this group: *Archelon ischyros* from the Upper Cretaceous of Dakota and Colorado (p. 94). The carapace of this "ocean giant" measured about three metres in length, and the span of the paddle-like forelimbs some five metres.

Certain other families of marine turtles that have also become extinct, had large protuberances along the spine. In particular, the family of Toxo-

chelyidae from the Upper Cretaceous to the Tertiary in North America includes species of this kind. The plastron of Toxochelyidae is reduced to a cruciform bony plate. In this, they resemble both marine turtles of the family Cheloniidae and Snapping turtles (Chelydridae) of today.

The most enigmatic of all marine turtles are the Leathery turtles or Leatherbacks (family Dermochelydidae). They probably evolved in the Cretaceous or earlier, but are known to us in fossil form only from Eocene deposits. Leatherbacks are not only the sea turtles in which the bony layer of the shell has been reduced almost totally to rudiments, but also those turtles which, in the course of evolution, must have alternated several times in their choice of habitat between littoral and pelagic regions of the ocean. Reduction of the shell took place when ancestors of the present Leatherbacks first became inhabitants of the deep sea. After some time, the creature's preference for the coastal regions of the oceans re-established itself, and for this, a sturdy shell proves more useful. But the reduced original shell was not able to develop once again into an efficient organ.

Instead, new dermal bones developed, producing a bony shell of mosaic-like structure. The development of this secondary epithelial shell can be seen most clearly in the "Leathery turtle" *Psephophorus polygonus* that lived in the North African-European ocean of the Eocene epoch. With their mosaic carapace, these turtles must have resembled the Triassic Placodonts very closely. But the mosaic shell did not remain a permanent feature. The Leathery turtles once again moved from a littoral to a pelagic habitat, and like their ancestors, were able to dispense with the mosaic shell. In the adult true Leatherback *(Dermochelys)*, all that now remains of the secondary carapace is seven longitudinal ridges, giving the leathery skin a better support. But in the first months of life, the young still bear a distinct mosaic structure extending across the entire shell. Later it is replaced progressively by the uniform skin, which has a parallel in the skin of Soft-shelled turtles.

For a long time, Leathery turtles were considered to be a special case among turtles, and some workers even placed them in a category separate from all other turtles, as representatives of "Shell-less turtles" or Athecae. Since then, however, the Belgian palaeontologist Dollo has shed light upon the fluctuating history of leathery turtles, and even more importantly, in comparative studies of cranial characteristics, has shown them to be related to the other marine turtles. From the phenomenon of the two-fold development of the shell of the leathery turtle from different rudimentary forms, Dollo formulated the principle of the irreversibility of evolutionary processes in organisms.

Giant tortoises of the Tertiary

What the end of the Mesozoic had been for marine turtles, the climate and environment of the Tertiary (the Lignite Age) made possible for land tortoises (Testudinidae). Some of them were able to develop into gigantic forms that lived in a variety of habitats on different continents. In what is today Central Europe, there were land tortoises of the genus *Ma-*

nouria, which in their appearance and in their preference for damp forest regions, were very similar to modern representatives of the genus living on the Indochina Peninsula. Giant land tortoises of this kind with a carapace measuring 120 cm in length, were found in the Geisel Valley near Halle. A striking feature of these huge creatures was that, like their recent cousins, they had extremely thick bony plates in the shell. The land tortoises of the lignite forest lived in association with terrestrial Emydid turtles (*Geoemyda* and related genera) similar to those still found in Southeast Asia. Bodies of water there housed numerous Soft-shelled turtles (Trionychidae) and Snapping turtles (Chelydridae) that are no longer found in Europe.

The largest land tortoise known so far was found in Pleistocene deposits in India and on some of the

Hypothetical evolution of the Leatherback
a) The original form, a normal marine turtle, lived in the coastal zone (littoral).
b) A change of habitat—preference for the open sea, the pelagic zone—permits a reduction in the bony shell and horny covering.
c) Return to the littoral zone means that a shell is again necessary. In place of the reduced shell, a secondary mosaic shell develops.
d) The second move into the pelagic zone permits a renewed reduction in the shell: the mosaic shell is also reduced, leaving a leathery skin covering.

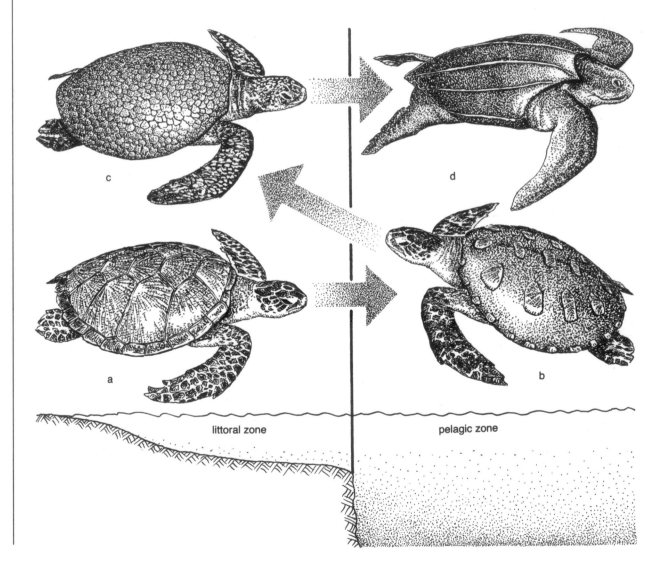

littoral zone

pelagic zone

Greater Sunda Islands. It was described as *Colossochelys atlas* by Falconer and Cautley as early as 1837. Since then, the species has been assigned to the genus *Geochelone, Megalochelys* or the genus *Cylindraspis*. This indicates that the tortoise is quite closely related to the giant tortoises still living on the islands of the Indian Ocean or which have recently become extinct there. *Megalochelys atlas* had a carapace up to 2.5 metres long. The evenly curved, broad carapace had a thickened edge. A striking feature of the plastron is the greatly extended, pronged gulars. In this, it greatly resembles the extinct Mascarene turtles *(Cylindraspis)*. Very similar giant land tortoises were found in excavations on the Greek island of Samos. From calculations based on limb fragments that have been found, it appears that the species *Geochelone schafferi* that lived there in the Pleistocene must also have measured about 2.5 m in carapace length. Remains of giant tortoises have also been found in cave sediments of Pleistocene origin on the island of Malta. Once again the carapace of the original animal must have been at least 2 m long. But the material is so incomplete that no reliable diagnosis of genus can be made. But undoubtedly they were closely related to the genera *Geochelone* and *Megalochelys*. The recent species of giant tortoises from Aldabra and the Galapagos Archipelago cut quite a modest figure in comparison with these extinct species. . . .

Towards a systematic classification of turtles

The will to create order is fundamental to science, and so, ever since Linné's classification of animals, there have been numerous attempts to set up a lucid system of classification for turtles as well. The systematic organization of this small group of reptiles—220 species occurring in some 340 geographical forms—nevertheless meets with a variety of difficulties. Observations already made on geographical distribution and phylogenetical history have given some idea of these problems. In the last three decades alone, systems of chelonian classification have been set up by Romer 1956, Williams 1950, Wermuth and Mertens 1961 and 1977, Mlynarski 1969 and 1976, Parsons 1968,

Zangerl 1969, Ckhikvadze 1970, Gaffney 1975 and others. On the one hand, they reflect the current state of chelonian research, on the other, subjective opinions held by the authors.

In addition to the major systems that have been devised, checklists of turtles also play an important practical role. These lists catalogue all those species and subspecies of turtles that are recognized by the authors of the lists. They offer rapid guideline assistance on existing forms. In this century, checklists have been published by Siebenrock 1903, Mertens, L. Müller and Rust 1934, Wermuth and Mertens 1955, 1961 and 1977 and Pritchard 1979. Surprisingly enough, differences in the lists arise not merely from new re-groupings of known turtle species in order to express more clearly relationships existing between them, but fortunately also through the discovery of new species and subspecies hitherto unknown (see "List of recent turtles", Appendix).

The following system is based primarily on the views of Mlynarski (1976) and Gaffney (1975). Extinct species are indicated by a cross preceding the name. They are listed only up to family level, while recent groups are sometimes further subdivided into subfamilies and generic groups (tribes). As far as the systematic rankings of the various groups are concerned, the classic categories of Order, Family, Genus, Species are inadequate to express the actual situations. Here again, the use of intermediate terms is unfortunately inevitable, since they cannot be replaced appropriately and unambiguously by a common term. At first glance, this may appear confusing, at a second however, it makes many connections clear.

The amount of work that has been carried out on finer classification below the level of family varies strikingly. Whereas Pond turtles (fam. Emydidae), for example, have already been assigned to generic groups that are recognized by most specialists, subdivision of Land tortoises (fam. Testudinidae) has not yet been concluded. Undoubtedly, groupings will reveal themselves there as well. For instance, the genera *Kinixys–Pyxis–Malacochersus* are closely associated, as are the genera *Geochelone–Asterochelys–Megalochelys–Chelonoidis*. In the individual Cryptodira families there are groupings that are not yet reflected within the system. This shows how many questions on relationships between turtles still remain unanswered.

Order Testudines (= turtles)
Suborder 1 † Proganochelydia (Triassic turtles)
    Family 1 † Proganochelyidae (Triassic)
    Family 2 † Proterochersidae (Triassic)
    Family 3 ? † Kallokibotiidae (Cretaceous)
Suborder 2 Casichelydia (true turtles)
  Order group 1 Cryptodira
   Subgroup 1 † Paracryptodira (Original cryptodires)
    Superfamily 1 † Baenoidea
    Family 1 † Glyptosidae (Jurassic)
    Family 2 † Baenidae (Cretaceous–Eocene)
    Family 3 † Neurankylidae (Cretaceous)
    Family 4 ? † Meiolaniidae (Giant horned tortoises) (Cretaceous ?–Pleistocene)
   Subgroup 2 Eucryptodira (Modern cryptodires)
    Superfamily 1 Chelonioidea (marine turtle relationship)
    Family 1 † Thalassemydidae (Jurassic)
    Family 2 † Protostegidae (Cretaceous)
    Family 3 † Toxochelyidae (Cretaceous–Eocene)
    Family 4 Cheloniidae (Cretaceous–recent)
      Subfamily 1 Cheloniinae (recent marine turtles)
      Subfamily 2 † Eochelyinae (Eocene–Oligocene)
      Subfamily 3 Carettinae (Cretaceous–recent)
    Family 5 Dermochelydidae (Leathery turtles) (Eocene–recent)
    Superfamily 2 Chelydroidea (Snapping turtle relationship)
    Family 1 † Plesiochelyidae (Jurassic)
    Family 2 † Macrobaenidae (Cretaceous)
    Family 3 Dermatemydidae (Tabasco turtles) (Jurassic–recent)
      Subfamily 1 † Adocinae (Cretaceous)
      Subfamily 2 Dermatemydinae (Jurassic–recent)
    Family 4 Kinosternidae (Mud and musk turtles) (Oligocene–recent)
    Family 5 Staurotypidae (Oligocene–recent)
    Family 6 Chelydridae (Snapping turtles) (Palaeocene–recent)
    Family 7 Platysternidae (Big-headed turtles) (?–recent)
    Superfamily 3 Trionychoideae (Soft-shelled turtle relationship)
    Family 1 Carettochelydidae (Papuan turtles) (Cretaceous–recent)
      Subfamily 1 † Anosteirinae (Cretaceous–Miocene)
      Subfamily 2 Carettochelyinae (Miocene–recent)
    Family 2 Trionychidae (Soft-shelled turtles) (Jurassic–recent)
      Subfamily 1 Cyclanorbinae (Miocene–recent)
      Subfamily 2 Trionychinae (Common Soft-shelled turtles)
    Superfamily 4 Testudinoidea (Land tortoise relationship)
    Family 1 Testudinidae (Land tortoises) (Eocene–recent)
    Family 2 Emydidae (Pond turtles or terrapins) (Eocene–recent)
      Subfamily 1 Batagurinae (Eocene ?–recent)
       Tribe 1 Geomydini (Eocene–recent)
       Tribe 2 † Sakyini (Pliocene–Pleistocene)
       Tribe 3 † Ptychogastrini (Miocene)
       Tribe 4 Batagurini (Eocene ?–recent)
      Subfamily 2 Emydinae (Eocene ?–recent)
       Tribe 1 Nectemydina (Eocene ?–recent)
       Tribe 2 Emydina (Eocene ?–recent)
  Order group 2 Pleurodira (Side-necked turtles)
    Family 1 † Platychelyidae (Jurassic)
    Family 2 Pelomedusidae (Cretaceous–recent)
    Family 3 † Eusarkiidae (Eocene–Miocene)
    Family 4 Chelidae (Oligocene–recent)
      Subfamily 1 Chelinae (Pliocene ?–recent)
      Subfamily 2 Pseudemydurinae (?–recent)

Biotope turtle

In steppe, desert and savanna

Arid regions in the temperate and warm zones of the world offer favourable living conditions for land tortoises. It is not surprising, then, that the reptile fauna of the steppe and desert belt and of the savannas of the Old World and the New usually includes land tortoises. Only in Australia are they absent. To a great extent, species of land tortoise have even taken over the role of characteristic animals of such landscapes. One need think only of Gopher tortoises (genus *Gopherus*) of the arid regions of south-eastern USA and Mexico, of Leopard tortoises *(Geochelone pardalis)* of the savannas of East and South-east Africa, of European Land tortoises (genus *Testudo*) in the thickets, stone-pine forests or desert-like arid zones of the Mediterranean region, all of which make their mark on the overall biological picture of these areas, just as strongly as the larger animals in the same biotopes. The giant tortoises of the Galapagos Archipelago or of the Seychelles have even become some of the best-known animals on those islands.

The climatic conditions of arid regions everywhere are very similar, and the tortoises living there have adapted to these conditions in very similar ways. A typical climatic feature of arid districts is the extreme fluctuation of temperature over 24 hours. In the morning, the sun soon raises the temperature to levels that are uncomfortable even for reptiles. At midday, the heat is so great, particularly on the ground, that even the most sun-loving of reptiles can no longer bear it. But at night, there is very considerable cooling. Even in the hottest deserts, the hours before sunrise are cripplingly cold. So the land tortoises of arid regions have organized their day accordingly. They are early risers, warming themselves in the first rays of the sun, so that they can get on with their "day's work" before it becomes too hot. The main tasks are gathering food and looking for a partner. This first phase of activity gradually comes to an end and the tortoises seek out a shady place beneath bushes, clumps of grass or large stones. Some species of land tortoises like to bury themselves for their midday rest with the whole body covered by loose soil. In the afternoon, when the extreme heat has passed, there is usually a second active phase. But it is shorter and less intense than the morning's activity. Most tortoises in arid regions go to sleep early, as soon as the sun begins to set. In general, tortoises remain faithful to a chosen habitat—for weeks at a time, an entire summer or several years—and always seek out the same protected sleeping place. There they quickly dig themselves in and spend the night.

Land tortoises have undergone a whole series of different adaptations to life in arid regions. In areas where months of drought alternate with a shorter spell of rain and rapid vegetation, they have adapted their annual rhythm to these conditions. One example of this is the small Spider tortoise *(Pyxis arachnoides)* from the desert-like regions of south-western Madagascar. During the long drought, they dig themselves a shell's depth into loose ground among shrubs, dried tufts of grass and similar protected places. There they remain for weeks at a time, taking no food, until finally the first rains tempt them from their hiding places. Then the Spider tortoises suddenly appear in large numbers where previously none was to be seen. First they drink their fill and later eat abundantly of the plants that within a few days of the rain starting, have germinated, sprouted and pushed up out of the ground. With this "new life" at the start of the rainy season, the mating drive is aroused in Spider tortoises, as indeed in all seasonally active land tortoises.

Bell's Hinged tortoise *(Kinixys belliana)* also occurs on Madagascar, but only in the extreme northern, desert-like parts of the island, where it lives a similar kind of life. The species also has a wide range on the African mainland. From Senegal and Angola in the west to Ethiopia and Botswana in the east of the continent, it inhabits a wide variety of arid landscapes. These tortoises also spend the period of drought buried in the ground. To survive this period, which in many parts can last for months, they store considerable quantities of water in their body. As a water reservoir, they use their large anal sacs. Completely filled, these take up most of the space inside the tortoise's abdominal cavity. They are also responsible for the considerable weight of the tortoise during aestivation, sometimes giving the false impression that the creature is very well nourished.

The ability to store water is shared to different degrees by all land tortoises living in arid regions. The large Leopard tortoise (Geochelone pardalis), one of the characteristic animals of the East African savanna, has this capacity just as does the Argentinian land tortoise (Chelonoidis chilensis) that also inhabits a broad spectrum of different arid landscapes from the dry forests of South America to the pampas lands. The habits of all these species strongly resemble those of the European land tortoises (genus Testudo), whose daily routine was described above. Anyone finding and lifting a tortoise that is resting buried in the ground may well be given a convincing illustration of its capacity to store water. As a defence mechanism, the animal will spontaneously evacuate the contents of the bowel together with part of the stored water.

Land tortoises in arid regions are frequently food specialists. South African land tortoises (genus Psammobates) that live in desert-like regions, have adapted to a diet of various succulents and scrub vegetation from the highly specialized flora of southern Africa with its many endemic species. The same is true of Psammobates oculifera and Psammobates tentoria (the South African Tent tortoise), while the third species of the genus prefers a rather damper habitat: Psammobates geometrica (the Geometric tortoise) lives only in a very small region of Cape Province. There, on humous soils in a hilly area, various acidy grasses grow which constitute its main food. It is only in recent decades, when its extinction seemed imminent, that the habits of this extremely rare Geometric tortoise, with its very attractive pattern and colouring, has been the subject of detailed study. Investigations carried out by the zoologist Reinhold Rau have revealed not only its specific environmental and dietary requirements, but also the very low rate of reproduction of this species. Like the other Psammobates species, it rarely lays more than one egg in a season. Fortunately, it was possible for naturalists to apply their findings quickly to save this seriously endangered species of tortoise.

Other tortoises in the arid zones of South Africa have become specialists of hilly regions. The small, rather flat tortoises of the genus Homopus live mainly in the rocky "kopjes" of South Africa. Here they find a varied diet of succulents and an adequate choice of hiding places. Within the species, there are different degrees of specialization. A notable feature linked with this, is the differing reproduction rate of the animals. Whereas Homopus boulengeri and Homopus signatus lay a single, relatively large egg per season, Homopus areolatus produces a clutch of 2 to 5 eggs. The former species live almost exclusively in the hills, whereas Homopus areolatus sometimes selects a habitat in the planes. But not enough is known yet about the ecology of this genus. There is an acute danger that the four species of Homopus will be exterminated by alterations to their habitat and by overcollecting before they have been studied thoroughly. One can only hope that effective conservation measures will succeed in preventing this interesting species of endemic land tortoise from becoming extinct.

Tortoises that live in burrows

The land tortoise's ability to dig is developed to varying extents. There are many species that dig themselves a burrow-like refuge. In the deserts and steppes of central Asia, Horsfield's tortoise (Agrionemys horsfieldi) is just such a burrow-dweller. It prefers loamy ground. On the hilly terrain of the steppes, individual shrubs or clumps of grass are useful starting points from which this steppe tortoise digs itself a burrow in which to live, worked either horizontally into the slope or inclining slightly downwards. Depending upon the hardness of the soil, the tortoise may penetrate to a depth of 80 to 200 cm before widening the passage to make a small chamber just large enough to allow it to turn round. Construction of the burrow is possible only when the spring rains have made the soil workable. Later on, the loam and clay harden into solid crusts and make excavation impossible, even for the strong claws on the forelimbs, which are of a depressed spatula shape and relatively long. Instead of the usual five claws on the front feet, *Agrionemys horsfieldi* has only four, but they are much more powerful than those of most other land tortoises.

For a steppe tortoise, a burrow of this kind remains the habitual retreat for at least the whole of one summer, and is visited probably every midday and certainly every evening. In populous tortoise colonies, large numbers of burrows often lie in close proximity on favoured slopes. There, tortoises occasionally visit holes other than their own. In this case, several of them may remain together in one burrow overnight. During the hottest part of the summer, the tortoises often leave their refuges only in the morning for an hour or two. In areas of extreme aridity, they remain resting in the underground chamber for several weeks, when all the plants on which they feed have dried up. During the cold season, the burrows serve as frost-free winter quarters.

Tortoises occasionally have to deal with other animals that contest their right to the laboriously excavated retreat. The porcupine in particular likes to enlarge a tortoise's burrow to make a home of its own, and certain aggressive species of wasps may also take up residence there. Other animals of various groups, such as many small mammals, lizards, snakes and arthropods make peaceable fellow inhabitants and scarcely inconvenience their host at all.

South of the Sahara in Africa's arid belt, the imposing Spurred tortoise *(Geochelone sulcata)* has a way of life similar to that of the steppe tortoise. It digs a deep burrow, the entrance to which is often very well camouflaged, lying hidden under thorn bushes. Here, this land tortoise with conspicuously flattened carapace successfully survives the long periods of drought in the Sahel zone.

The best known of all the burrow dwelling chelonians are the American Gopher tortoises (genus *Gopherus*). Four species inhabit the southern United States and northern Mexico. Gopher tortoises also have a relatively flat carapace, although it is more elongate than that of other cave tortoises. Just as remarkable are the powerful front limbs with which they excavate their deep caves. Like all burrowing land tortoises, Gopher tortoises have broad, strong nails on their front limbs as digging tools. The burrows that Gopher tortoises build at a slight angle into the ground, sometimes extend for a distance of three to six metres before opening out into a spacious chamber. The longest burrows found so far measured over 14 metres. If the terrain is favourable, the Gopher tortoises like to construct their caves in the sides of hills and dunes with south-eastern exposure. Sandy soils are preferred. In comparison with other excavating tortoises, Gopher tortoises have altered

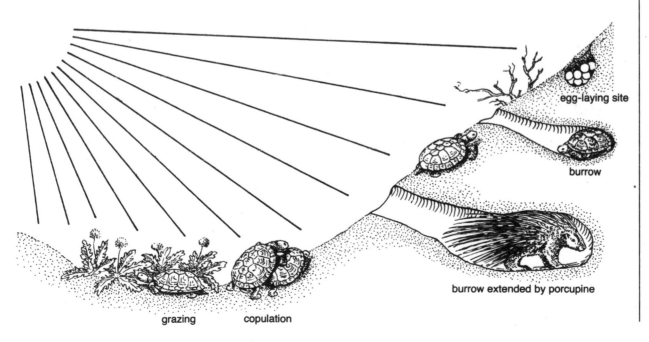

egg-laying site

burrow

burrow extended by porcupine

grazing   copulation

The biotope of Horsfield's tortoise *(Agrionemys horsfieldi)* in Central Asia.
The slopes of steppe-land hills, preferably with an eastern or south-eastern exposure, are the site of burrows in which the tortoises live. Larger mammals (porcupine, fox) like to extend tortoise burrows to make their own lairs. Egg-laying sites of tortoises are usually situated on higher, sunny slopes. The steppe valleys with their herbaceous vegetation serve as grazing grounds. Here, turtles come together for mating.

Common co-inhabitants in the burrows of Horsfield's tortoises:
small mammals, e.g. ground squirrels and marmots
lizards, e.g. agamids and desert runners snakes, e.g. Tartar sand boas, desert colubrids or Levantine vipers numerous arthropods: scorpions, wasps, beetles

the rhythm of their activities. To the land tortoise's habit of early rising, they have added that of nocturnal revelry. The farther south the Gophers live, the more extended is the period of rest in the middle of the day. In the hot desert regions of the southern United States and in the north of Mexico, the tortoises spend the entire day concealed in their burrows after a quite short period of early morning activity. As twilight falls, they appear suddenly on the surface and remain active during the first warmer half of the night. In seeking out their favourite food, the prickly pear (genus *Opuntia*), their acute sense of smell is often more useful to them than their eyes. As it begins to turn cold, the tortoises return to their dens. The habits of these tortoises that are so well adapted to life in an extremely dry climate, have been studied by a number of workers, so we have a good deal of detailed information. Observations that have been made repeatedly confirm the Gopher's impressive sense of direction and loyalty to a locality.

The many animals that regularly share the Gopher burrows became as familiar as the Gopher tortoises themselves. Apart from temporary co-inhabitants, there are animals that prefer to take over burrows abandoned by tortoises. Among mammals, these include raccoons, skunks, foxes, rabbits, opposums, mice and rats, while birds are represented by quail and gopher owls.

There are many reptiles that regularly take refuge in tortoise burrows. Two of the largest North American colubrids, the Eastern Indigo snake *(Drymarchion corais)* and the Black Racer *(Coluber constrictor)* as well as the largest species of rattlesnake in the USA, the Eastern Diamondback rattlesnake *(Crotalus adamanteus)* are regularly found in the holes of Gopher tortoises. As well as a safe retreat, they also find easy prey there, since they readily overcome almost all mammals that live in Gopher burrows, from mice to rabbits, and even young racoons and foxes. The same fate may well befall the various lizards such as the Brown skink *(Eumeces laticeps)*, the Eastern fence lizard *(Sceloporus undulatus)* or the Six-lined Racerunner *(Cnemidophorus sexlineatus)* that often settle in Gopher burrows. Even frogs and toads will live there, particularly the Gopher frog *(Rana capito)*. Other "Gopher animals" include the Spadefoot toad *(Scaphiophus holbrooki)* and certain species of True Toads (genus *Bufo*).

The presence of Diamondback rattlesnakes has often proved fatal to Gopher tortoises. When snake catchers smoke out the snakes, the tortoises do not emerge, but die underground. This indefensible method is still practised, even though all *Gopherus* species are under strict legal protection in the USA and Mexico.

Because of their way of life, Gopher tortoises have become the pioneers of a specialized consequential fauna. Their burrows are an outstanding example of a zoogenous habitat with a symbiotic association of many different kinds of animals linked in a wide variety of ways. This is also demonstrated by the many lower organisms living in Gopher burrows. Many are commensals, others co-residents. Among more than 40 species of insects and spiders that have been found in Gopher burrows, are many species that live either as scavengers or dung eaters (coprophagans) or else as parasites on excrement, the remnants of prey, the corpses of dead inhabitants or even on the blood of the host and his other guests.

In the mountains that rise up from the broad expanses of the East African savanna in Kenya and Tanzania, there is another cave-dwelling tortoise that differs in many respects from the species discussed so far. It is one of the most bizarre of all chelonians, *Malacochersus tornieri*, aptly known as the Pancake tortoise. When the first individuals of this species were discovered, the 15 cm long tortoises with their greatly flattened shape and soft, flexible shell were assumed to be pathologically deformed. But it soon became clear that Pancake tortoises are an example of the extreme specialization of a land tortoise to life in rock caves. Their habitat is in rocky ridges or mountain massifs that rise from the savanna to a height sometimes of only 30 to 50 metres but occasionally to more than 2,000 metres. The greatest height at which Pancake tortoises have been found is about 1,800 metres, but beyond this, it becomes too inhospitably cold even for this very resistant tortoise. Because of its extremely depressed shape and relatively long legs, *Malacochersus* is a skilful climber and a faster mover than other land tortoises. For a safe retreat, it depends entirely upon stony crevices and hollows in rocks, since its forelimbs are not modified into typical fossorial feet—a burrowing tortoise, then, that can scarcely dig. But it has the ability to anchor itself firmly into rock crevices. It resists any attempt to extract it by wedging itself into the fissure in two ways. Firstly it presses its flexible shell tight against the rock, secondly it braces all its limbs and even its head against the roof and floor of its rock

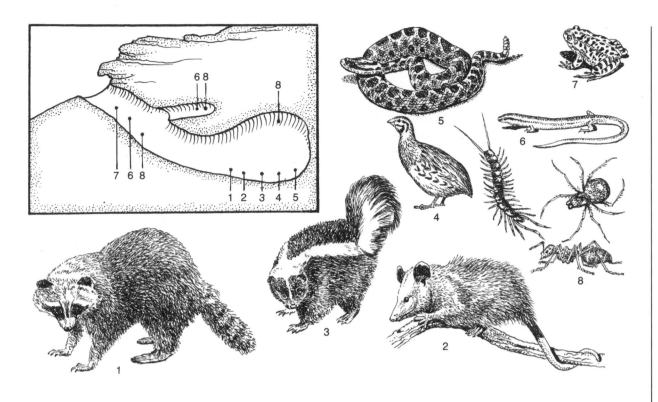

cave. It is an unusual feature among tortoises for the limbs, and in particular the head, to be extended instead of retracted in face of danger. Sometimes when they are being extracted tail-first from their burrow, Horsfield's and Gopher tortoises also resist by stretching their forelimbs widely. But the head always remains retracted as part of the normal defensive reaction of land tortoises. The pattern of activity of the Pancake tortoise is very similar to that of the Gopher tortoise. At higher, cooler altitudes, they live a normal "land tortoise day". They even distinguish themselves by starting to feed as soon as the temperature reaches 12 to 15°C, in order to be able to consume sufficient quantities of the sparsely growing succulents. To obtain maximum warmth, they lie in an oddly tilted position so that the sun strikes the carapace at the optimum angle of incidence. The tortoises living in rocky ridges at lower levels, on the other hand, are active for a short time only in the early morning when it is still cool, and remain inside their retreats during the hot part of the day. They compensate for this by a longer spell of activity in the evening, which can last into the hours of darkness. Once again, an excellent sense of smell enables them to find their food even in the dark.

Today, the Pancake tortoise is one of the critically endangered species. The serious reduction in their numbers has been caused neither by natural enemies nor by environmental changes, but by excessive inroads made into the rather small, isolated populations by commercial collectors. In recent decades, Pancake tortoises have been greatly in demand as terrarium animals. Not only are they biologically interesting but also easy to keep in captivity and of a suitable size. Because of the low rate of reproduction (with rarely more than two eggs per clutch), the size of a population of Pancake tortoises remains relatively stable only as long as it is not affected by harmful influences. A single collecting project undertaken by a "clever" operator is enough to bring it close to extinction. A number of isolated populations has already been destroyed in this way. Effective protection of the remaining stocks of this remarkable tortoise is imperative.

In tropical and temperate forests

Among land tortoises of the family Testudinidae, there is a large number of species whose ecological classification proves difficult, because they have adapted remarkably well to very diverse habitats. Other species, however, are committed strictly to quite specific environmental conditions, from which they never deviate. Recognition of this fact is important not only for a general understanding of the biology of these animals, but perhaps even more so for their successful rearing in a terrarium. One of the best known tortoises with considerable fluidity in its environmental demands is the Starred tortoise *(Geochelone elegans)* from India and Sri Lanka. Unfortunately for tortoise enthusiasts (and for the Starred tortoises they keep in captivity), this adaptability is not typical of every individual within the species, but is a group character that applies only to all members of certain populations of Starred tortoises. In India and Sri Lanka, for example, there are Starred tortoises that live in typical arid country with extreme daily temperature gradients, and the enormous contrasts of alternating dry and rainy seasons. Yet other populations of the same species inhabit river forests in tropical grassland or even rain forests, where there is considerably higher humidity, slighter fluctuations of daily temperature and much more subtle seasonal differences. Moreover, in such biotopes, water is always readily available to the animals for drinking and bathing.

Environmental conditions differ yet again for Starred tortoises living on the coast. In the dunes where they have settled, prevailing climatic conditions correspond in part to those of desert-like, arid zones, but on the other hand, the proximity of the ocean causes higher humidity, strong winds and less extreme fluctuations in day and night temperatures.

Starred tortoises also extend into the mountains. The climate in mountain forests and savannas differs in many ways from that of similar areas in the lowlands. Tortoises living there have become accustomed to all these conditions. Adaptation is the result of processes that have taken place over thousands of years. The members of such a population are to a large extent committed to these conditions, and are rarely able to readjust rapidly. If they are suddenly placed in a different biotope, even one in which climatic conditions still lie within boundaries that correspond to the ecological range of adaptability of the species, they will usually fail to survive. In nature, pressures exerted by environmental changes are rarely sudden, but take effect very gradually. But human intervention in the form, for example, of agricultural and forestry exploitation involving irrigation and drainage schemes, can strike swiftly. Most members of an ecologically committed population fall victim to rapid changes of this kind.

An ecological situation similar to that of Starred tortoises is also found in two South American species of land tortoise, *Chelonoides carbonaria* (the Coal tortoise or Red-footed tortoise) and *Chelonoides denticulata* (the Forest or Wood or Yellow-footed tortoise). In the case of these land tortoises as well, there are populations that inhabit low-lying, hot, damp tropical forests, drier grassland river forests and savanna-like arid regions, or even wooded mountain areas at different altitudes. This broad adaptability has made it possible for both species to cover a very extensive range. Ecological relationships between the species, like phylogenetic relationships, have not yet been adequately researched. There are regions in which the two species occur not only sympatrically but also under the same environmental conditions. But in other regions, they occur separately, for example in Surinam. There, only *Chelonoides carbonaria* inhabits the dry, savanna-like forests, while *Chelonoides denticulata* lives in the tropical forests. And although *Chelonoides carbonaria* also occurs there, it is in much smaller numbers. And there are areas in which only one of the two species occurs. Walter Auffenberg, an American zoologist and palaeontologist who studied the animals for a number of years, believes that the two species must have separated from common ancestors only in the Pleiocene or Pleistocene. It was at that time that savanna and grassland developed round the Amazon lowlands. While *Chelonoides denticulata* occupied the tropical rain forest, *Chelonoides carbonaria* took over the drier regions. Following this differentiation, the "young" species expanded into new biotopes and as a result, the effects of diverging specialization were to some extent cancelled out in many regions.

previous page:

Yellow-head Box turtle
(Cuora flavomarginata) from
southern China.

Bornean River turtle *(Orlitia
borneensis)*, one of the
largest river turtles of Southeast Asia.

Starred tortoise *(Geochelone
elegans)* in a landscape of
dunes in Sri Lanka.

Big-headed turtle (*Platyster-non megacephalum*)

Spengler's terrapin (Geo-emyda spengleri) from Vietnam. The species is characterized by its terrestrial mode of life and the sexual difference in eye colour (♂: yellow-orange, ♀: whitish).

Frog-headed turtle (Phrynops hilari). The two chin barbels are a striking feature.

The Flat-shelled turtle (Platemys p. platycephala) lives in water in the primeval forests of northern South America. The indentation along the middle of the carapace and the light and dark markings are characteristic of the species.

Skeleton of the giant sea turtle *Archelon ischyros*, seen from the plastron side. The right hind limb of the fossil is lost.
Length of the turtle: 3.5 m arm span: almost 5 m (Peabody Museum, Yale, USA)

One of the commonest marine turtles in the Jurassic ocean, *Plesiochelys solodurensis*, found in Solothurn, Switzerland.

Exhibition of the famous fossil turtles of Solothurn, Switzerland.

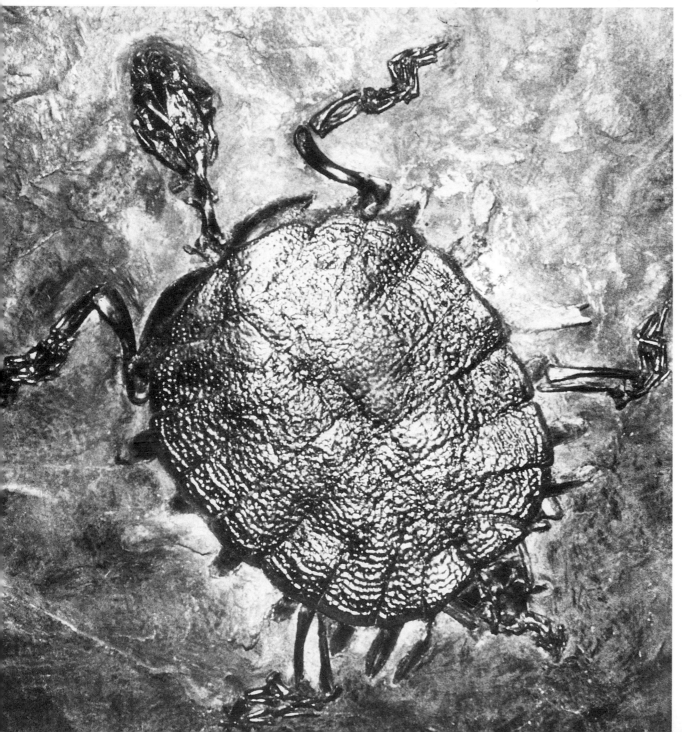

Fossil Soft-shelled turtle (Trionyx messelianus) from the tropical Tertiary of Central Europe, recovered from oil shale at Messel near Darmstadt. (Senckenberg Museum, Frankfurt/Main)

Yellow-spotted Amazon turtle or Terekay turtle *(Podocnemis unifilis)*, one of the highly endangered species of large river turtle from northern South America.

Matamata *(Chelus fimbriatus)*. Note the snorkel-like snout, the small button eyes, the "pseudo eyes" and the shaggy lobes of skin.

following page:

The Keelback terrapin *(Pyxidea mouhoti)* from India, a "pond turtle" with a terrestrial habit.

Biotope of Pancake tortoises: rocks in the savanna country of East Africa.

Skeleton of a Pancake or Crevice tortoise *(Malacochersus tornieri)*. The numerous apertures that developed in the process of secondary shell reduction are a characteristic feature. Some of the bones of the shell are paper-thin. (Staatl. Museum für Tierkunde, Dresden)

following page:

Pancake tortoise *(Malacochersus tornieri)* in a terrarium, in front of its home.

This Pancake tortoise has wedged itself firmly between slabs of stone.

A Pancake tortoise being observed in its hiding place.

following page:

Four-toed tortoise (Agrionemys horsfieldi) in the desert region of Amu Darya.

Entry to a burrow. In front of it lies the shell of a hatched tortoise.

Desert valley in South Tadzhikistan, USSR. On the slopes are the burrows of the steppe tortoises.

Biotope of the Big-headed
turtle *(Platysternon megacephalum)* and the Indochinese
Impressed tortoise *(Manouria impressa)* in Thailand
near Pa Daeng.

Bald-cyprus bog forest in
South Carolina, USA. A
characteristic habitat of the
Spotted turtle *(Clemmys
guttata)* and the Painted turtle
(Chrysemys picta).

The Indochinese Impressed tortoise, *Manouria impressa*, a flat-shelled land tortoise very fond of water.

Spotted turtle *(Clemmys guttata)*, male. One of the smallest pond turtles with a carapace length of only 13 cm.

following page:

Mexican Gopher tortoise *(Gopherus flavomarginatus)*

Land tortoises
that like to go swimming
and Pond turtles
that live on dry land

Among land tortoises (family Testudinidae) in the tropics there are some species or even genera that, as inhabitants of the rain forest, have become very fond of water, and even to some extent live as amphibians. The entire range of ecological specialization that land tortoises can show is to be found among African Hinged tortoises (genus *Kinixys*). Mention has already been made of the East African Bell's Hinged tortoise *(Kinixys belliana)*, as a characteristic inhabitant of arid regions that is able to survive successfully in extremely hot and dry regions. The Central African Hinged tortoise *(Kinixys homeana)*, on the other hand, is an inhabitant of the tropical forest. Its adaptability is also considerable, and it finds the tropical river forests adequate to satisfy its moisture requirements. But it prefers the margins and clearings of rain forests. Plantations within these areas make an equally acceptable habitat. Not only do the tortoises enjoy swimming in the shallow pools that form daily during the rainy season, but they also obtain their food there. Their diet includes marsh plants and the fruits from them, water insects, crustaceans and worms, the spawn and tadpoles of frogs and toads and much more. The commitment to temporary or permanent bodies of water is much more marked in *Kinixys erosa* (the West African Common tortoise, also known as the Forest or Schweigger's Hinged tortoise), that is at the same time the largest of the species. Towards the end of the rainy season, the Forest Hinged tortoises find a particularly abundant food supply in the gradually dwindling, temporary pools. Amphibian larvae and young frogs concentrated into a small space become easy prey, and even fishes frequently end their short life between the jaws of just a land tortoise. The fishes found in temporary bodies of water of this kind, known as seasonal fishes, belong to the Cyprinodonts. These small, often brightly-coloured fishes are able to "over-leap" the dry season, because only the spawn survives. Then the development of the young fishes to sexual maturity takes place within a few weeks, so their continued existence is assured, even if enemies make a clean sweep of them at the end of the season. The seasonal rhythm of the tropics has, in this way, made it possible for a land tortoise to become a facultative, although enthusiastic fish eater.

In Southeast Asia, a genus of land tortoise with only two species shows an equally strong commitment to water in its biotope. The Burmese Brown tortoise *(Manouria emys)* and the Indochina land tortoise *(Manouria impressa)* are forest tortoises, predominantly active in the evening and at night, which often enjoy bathing in warm, shallow water for hours or even days at a time. The scientists Schlegel and Müller who discovered the Brown tortoise, were already quite familiar in 1844 with the amphibian habit of this the largest of Asiatic land tortoises, as can be surmised from their choice of "emys" for the specific name, borrowed from the European Pond tortoise, *Emys orbicularis*. *Manouria emys* has a carapace length of up to 60 cm and weighs some 35 kg. These dimensions make it a true "Giant tortoise", but it differs from the distantly related species on the Seychelles and the Galapagos Archipelago in having a much lower carapace. The considerably smaller *Manouria impressa* has a similarly flattened shell, that is attractively coloured yellowish-brown to orange. So far, little is known about its habits, but its urge for bathing seems less marked. It lives on the moist ground of mountain forests, where standing water is somewhat rare, but humidity very high. It is interesting that both species prefer a much greater proportion of animal food, in addition to vegetable food consisting of leaves and fruit, than is the case with the land tortoise in arid regions.

In forests in tropical and subtropical regions, several species from the family of Pond turtles or terrapins (Emydidae) live a life very similar to that of many land tortoises. An example of this is a large group of terrapins that for a long time was considered as a single genus within the Emydids, and grouped together under the term *Geoemyda*. But anatomical and zoogeographical findings show that the similarity between members of the group is probably the result of parallel evolution starting out from different origins. So it would undoubtedly be more correct to consider the various *Geoemyda* turtles as genera in their own right.

Geoemyda spengleri lives in the mountain forests of Vietnam and other countries in Indochina, on some of the islands of the Sunda Archipelago and even on the Japanese Riu-Kiu Islands. This

The Great River Ganges

"At its rising from wells the Ganges, the river of India, is 20 fathoms deep and 80 stades wide, for it is still flowing with its own native waters unmixed with any other. But as it flows on and other rivers fall into it and join their water with it, it reaches a depth of 60 fathoms, and widens and overflows to an extent of four hundred stades. And it contains islands larger than Lesbos and Cyrnus, and breeds monstrous fishes, and from their fat men manufacture oil. There are also in the river turtles whose shell is as large as a jar holding as much as 20 amphorae . . ."

Claudius Aelianus:
On the Characteristics of Animals.

small "pond turtle" (only 14 cm long) has become an inhabitant of the tropical rain forest, and to a great extent, has broken away from the biotope of water typical of its family. Its way of life differs hardly at all from that of the land tortoises of Indochina that were mentioned earlier. As a refuge, it makes use of the roots of shrubs, tree stumps and holes in the ground on the forest floor. To sun itself, it seeks out clearings among trees. In its search for food in the half-light of the dense forest, its sense of smell plays an important part in finding fallen fruit and other edible parts of plants. The species is typical of a basically aquatic, predatory chelonian that has partially transferred to vegetable food. The animal portion of its diet is made up of various creatures living on the forest floor, such as molluscs, different kinds of worms, insects, spiders as well as small vertebrates such as frogs and possibly small skinks and burrowing snakes.

In other genera of Pond turtles, individual species are known that have shown some adaptations to terrestrial life. For instance, among Asiatic Box turtles of the genus *Cuora*, there are two species in Southeast Asia that have become secondary "land tortoises". The rare *Cuora galbinifrons* from Vietnam and southern China lives in the tropical forest, while *Cuora flavomarginata* of southern China prefers the marshy regions of the tropical lowlands. All these Pond turtles that have adopted a primarily terrestrial way of life, have forfeited something of their ability to swim. In certain populations within the species, the process has advanced to the point at which the creatures drown if they are suddenly introduced to the disaccustomed element. In compensation, they have developed the ability to burrow and dig, and like land tortoises, will often burrow down into loose soil to survive periods of heat or cold.

A master in the art of concealment, a "pond turtle" that often remains hidden in the soil for weeks at a time, is the Indian species *Pyxidea mouhoti*. With a maximum length of 20 cm, this tortoise has a high carapace that is very flattened above the spine between two prominent lateral keels. For a long time, it was considered to be extremely rare, and was hardly ever represented in museum collections. The situation changed a few years ago when for the first time, animal catchers in Thailand found these curious turtles in quite large numbers. Their expedition had set out at the start of the monsoon rains, a time normally avoided for such undertakings on account of rapid deterioration in communications on the ground, particularly in mountainous regions. But it proved worthwhile. The turtles had left their underground hiding places and, in the rain, were on the search for food—for snails, worms, insects, fungi and fruits. The opportunity for mating was also seized. Every evening, the animals burrow down into the soil, and in dry periods, appear only in the early, moist, cool hours of the morning. During the hotter months, they remain buried for weeks at a time, living on their stored bodily reserves, like the land tortoises of arid regions.

An ecological counterpart of the tropical *Pyxidea* is found in the North American Box turtles (genus *Terrapene*). The Common Box turtle *(Terrapene carolina)*, that is widespread in the east and southeast of the United States is ecologically much more adaptable than the highly specialized *Pyxidea*, but wherever habitat and climate allow, leads a very similar life. It prefers open, mixed forest with a relatively hot and dry summer, but with cool winters. Box turtles are also aquatic turtles that are well on the way to becoming terrestrial, indeed certain populations settle a long way from permanent bodies of water. In such habitats, *Terrapene carolina* is content with the heavy downpours of rain that are common in the spring. At this time, the turtles leave the hiding place they have dug out for themselves in the humous soils of the forest and go looking for food and a mate. Their prey consists of snails, small species of salamander, small frogs and earthworms. In addition, berries, fungi and herbaceous plants or flowers are a welcome supplement. When it becomes drier in the summer, the Box turtles emerge only in the morning to wander through vegetation that is still wet with dew. Prolonged drought at high summer eventually forces them to remain buried, sometimes for several weeks, and they become active again only with the rains of autumn. In the northernmost parts of their range, the second period of activity can be very brief, and it is soon time to prepare for hibernation. Where Box turtles live in wetter habitats such as in the proximity of bodies of standing water, they often lead an aquatic existence typical of the family. They prove to be tolerable swimmers and good divers. These skills are distinctly population-dependent, and vary from individual to individual.

The genus *Terrapene* includes other species that live in even drier habitats, such as the attractively marked and coloured Ornate Box turtles *(Terrapene ornata)* from the central and southern United States, or else species that are highly dependent upon seasonal conditions and independent of water, such as the Mexican Nelson's Box turtles *(Terrapene nelsoni)*, which to some extent represent "land tortoises" in the desert-like uplands of Sonora, Sinaloa and Nayarit. In the river valleys of Coahuila, Mexico, there is one representative of the genus that has remained aquatic; this is *Terrapene coahuila* from the low ground of the Cuatro Ciénegas Basin. A geographical subspecies of *Terrapene carolina* has chosen the grasslands and briar thickets in the north-west of the Yucatan Peninsula for its habitat, where it lives a more terrestrial existence than many members of the same species in the east of the United States of America.

The habitats of Pond turtles

Fresh water is a vital element for the majority of recent turtles, for example, for Snapping turtles (Chelydridae), Mud and Musk turtles (Kinosternidae), Soft-shelled turtles (Trionychidae), Side-necked turtles (Pelomedusidae) and Snake-necked turtles (Chelidae). Added to these are three further small families, each of which is represented in the recent turtle fauna by a single species only: Big-headed turtles (Platysternidae), Tabasco turtles (Dermatemydidae) and New Guinea Plateless River turtles (Carettochelydidae).

It can also be claimed that there is no form of standing or flowing water in the world's temperate and tropical zone without its own, specially adapted freshwater turtles. Of course, by no means all these ecological types of turtle occur on every continent in the relevant types of waters. On the contrary, a whole series of highly specialized turtles is restricted to a quite small range. Biotopes in other parts of the world that seem equally "favourable" are not inhabited by these or any similar turtles. The reasons for this fact often lie in the history of the evolution and expansion of the turtles, in other cases, however, there seems to be no explanation.

Turtles in small bodies of water

Even in the temperate zone, there are Emydid turtles or terrapins (Emydidae) that live in small bodies of water of widely differing kinds. A typical representative of a moderately non-specialized, ecologically very adaptable Emydid turtle is the European Pond tortoise *(Emys orbicularis)*. The existence of a particular type of body of water is less vital in its choice of biotope than are climatic factors that will provide a sufficiently long and hot summer to ensure the successful hatching of its eggs. *Emys orbicularis* lives both in quite small accumulations of standing water and in the pools and ditches of North African oases, in flowing streams and in potholes in small rivers in the Mediterranean zone that dry up in the summer, and equally in bogs and fen-woods in central and eastern Europe. But in the same area, it also colonizes the reed-covered or partially open banks of large bodies of standing water from ponds to inland seas of vast dimensions. But it always remains close to the shore and does not venture too far into the open water. The European Pond tortoise can also be found on well-filled, moderately large rivers and canals.

Most Emydid turtles are strictly amphibious. They need the water as much as they do the land. The prime function of this alternation between wet and dry elements is the regulation of body temperature. This is particularly vital in the temperate zone, where the water temperature is often insufficiently high to allow the turtles to maintain optimum body temperature over long periods spent in the water. Basking is the best compensation. The turtles in a habitat often make communal use of a favourable basking site—an overhanging rocky shore, a tree trunk drifting on the water, a dry, warm stretch of river bank. The turtles, which may well be representatives of various species, often lie densely packed together. They even climb over one another to gain the topmost position from which to expose the whole body to the sun's warmth.

All amphibious turtles try to place their body at a favourable angle to the sun's rays, and stretch out their limbs and head as far as possible. They often keep their eyes shut while basking, to protect them from excessive light and from becoming dry. This is not without dangers, for numerous enemies, particularly birds of prey, take this opportunity to attack. As a result, a communal protective flight reaction has developed that involves the entire company of basking turtles, irrespective of species. If a moving shadow falls across one of the turtles, if one of them notices a vibration in the ground or if one of those not "sleeping" sees danger threatening, it immediately plunges into the water. A chain reaction is set off through the entire company and all the basking turtles rush to the water and dive down into it. This explains the preference for basking sites that offer rapid access to the water.

The less specialized freshwater turtles live in a very wide variety of types of waters, which often include small bodies of water such as pools, ditches, mud-filled hollows. But there are many Emydid turtles that positively prefer small bodies of water of this kind. The chosen habitat of one of America's rarest turtles, Muhlenberg's turtle *(Clemmys muhlenbergi)* is in bogs and marshes of the mountainous regions in north-eastern USA. In this marshy countryside, the very small turtle (carapace length only about 11 cm) has scarcely any competition from other species of turtles. It is extremely well adapted to the particular climatic conditions of its habitat (relatively low temperatures, high humidity). Since it is small in size, a female *Clemmys muhlenbergi* produces only 2 to 3 eggs per clutch. But where natural conditions have remained undisturbed, this low rate of reproduction is sufficient to ensure the survival of the species within its range. That even slight intervention can alter the situation drastically is shown by the fate of this species. In programmes of land improvement and fertilization, many of its biotopes in the densely populated areas of the north-east United States have been taken over for agricultural use. It is not possible for these highly-specialized animals to adapt themselves to such changes. First the annual numbers of young decline and finally the stronger, older animals gradually die. Emigration of adult turtles from the altered biotopes also contributes to the decline, since it is extremely rare for migrating turtles actually to reach a new habitat that suits them. In considering the protection of this species, we are again forced to the same conclusion as with the seriously threatened land tortoises: the only effective measures of protection for animals that are closely associated with particular biotopes lies in maintaining that environment unaltered. Apart from this, strict conservation legislation for individual species and in particular, a ban on the commercial catching of the animals are effective aids to maintaining

stocks. Beyond this, the example of Muhlenberg's turtles shows once again that regrettably, the controlled breeding of a species in captivity is probably the only certain way of ensuring that it survives the crisis in its existence caused by human intervention. This species has been bred successfully both in America and in Europe. The North American genus *Clemmys* contains two more species that live semi-aquatically and prefer to inhabit small bodies of water. One of them is the Spotted turtle, *Clemmys guttata*. This species is very closely related to Muhlenberg's turtle, and very similar to it in size and shape. The Spotted turtle's range also lies in eastern North America, but is considerably more extensive than that of the previous species. *Clemmys guttata* is also less restricted in its choice of habitat, being found in pools and ponds, ditches and fenwoods. In the south of its range, it even lives in quite gloomy cypress marsh-woods. It shares these biotopes with other water turtles; the more open waters, for example, primarily with the Eastern Painted turtle *(Chrysemys picta)*, one of the many members of the genus of Painted turtles. The Eastern Painted turtle is also relatively uncommitted ecologically, and in contrast to most of its related species, frequently lives in small bodies of water. In the darker fenwoods and overgrown ditches, Mud and Musk turtles of the genera *Kinosternon* and *Sternotherus* are the usual companions of the Spotted turtles. The largest species of the genus *Clemmys* is the Wood turtle, *Clemmys insculpta*, that has a carapace length of up to 25 cm. On the whole it lives up to its name: its habitats are mixed woodlands with damp areas, but by no means always with small bodies of running water. It shares these areas with the Common Box turtle *(Terrapene carolina)*, whose largely terrestrial life habits have already been mentioned. The most important ecological differences between it and Box turtles are its better adaptability to lower temperatures and its stronger commitment to bodies of water. And the Wood turtle does not bury itself as readily or as thoroughly as does the Box turtle.

There are also water turtles in many tropical regions that prefer small bodies of water. In tropical Africa, amphibious water turtles are represented primarily by two genera of Sidenecked turtles *(Pelusios* and *Pelomedusa)*. Various species of *Pelusios* live in the rain forest and grassland river forest zone of Africa, but certain others, such as *Pelusios* subniger and *Pelusios subrufa*, for example, extend their range far into the savanna and steppe belt. In the tropical forest, the Pelomedusan turtles inhabit various standing or slowly flowing bodies of water. But often, quite small pools and streamlets prove an adequate habitat. In arid countryside, on the other hand, there are usually only temporary accumulations of water as habitats for turtles. When the rainy season comes to an end, the turtles must either bury themselves in the mud at the bottom of the pool and hibernate in a dry state until the next rains come, or else they can migrate.

Turtle associations in larger bodies of water

Larger bodies of water of very diverse forms such as ponds, lakes, rivers and even canals in the temperate and tropical zones often have a quite large turtle fauna in which the species hold themselves apart to a considerable extent by preferences for quite specific places, by differently timed spells of activity, by disparate feeding habits and other features of their behaviour. In this way, the various specialized turtles occupy different ecological niches, so that the living space available to them is divided up and used to the optimum. At the same time, competition between species of turtles is substantially reduced. If the supply of food in a biotope permits it, species with similar food demands that are thus in competition with one another, can nevertheless co-exist successfully. This is illustrated very well throughout the whole of North America by the wide variety of species that make up the turtle fauna there. It is clear, moreover, that the more favourable climatic conditions in the south of the subcontinent bring a rise in the number of species.

Independent of faunal zones, the freshwater turtle associations can be summarized in simplified form in the following ecological groups.
– Semi-terrestrial inhabitants of river-bank regions
They live, at least temporarily, at some distance from water, either in damp, river-bank regions such as in reedy and grassy vegetation or else in areas of fenwoods. An important feature of this group is that they also seek and take food while they are out of water. Many are occasionally or permanently crepuscular or nocturnal. Many species are only moderately good or poor swimmers and therefore prefer regions of shallow water. This group in-

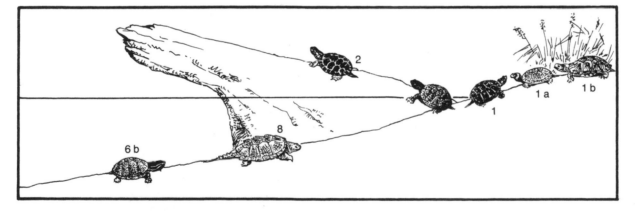

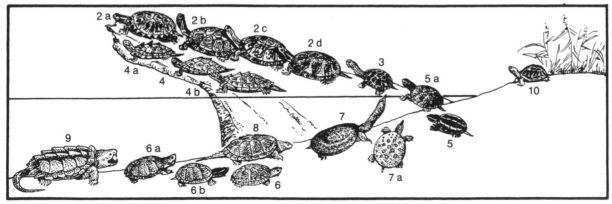

Increase in the diversity of turtle fauna and occupation of ecological niches in North America
above: northeastern USA underwater habitats are only sparsely occupied and in part, not at all. A number of pond turtles live a semiterrestrial life in order to benefit from the more favourable conditions of temperature in habitats on land
below: southeastern USA
The underwater habitats are occupied by a wealth of species. Apart from the box turtles, all pond turtles live amphibiously, since the basking sites always guarantee adequate warmth. The higher water temperatures provide optimal living conditions for aquatic and to some extent crepuscular aquatic turtles.

1 *Clemmys guttata*
1a *Clemmys muhlenbergi*
1b *Clemmys insculpta*
2 *Chrysemys picta*
2a *Chrysemys scripta*
2b *Chrysemys concinna*
2c *Chrysemys floridana*
2d *Chrysemys rubriventris nelsoni*
3 *Deirochelys reticularia*
4 *Graptemys barbouri*
4a *Graptemys nigrinoda*
4b *Graptemys pulchra*
5 *Kinosternon bauri*
5a *Kinosternon subrubrum*
6 *Sternotherus carinatus*
6a *Sternotherus minor*
6b *Sternotherus odoratus*
7 *Trionyx ferox*
7a *Trionyx spiniferus*
8 *Chelydra serpentina*
9 *Macroclemys temmincki*
10 *Terrapene carolina*
(modified after Bruce Bury, 1979)

Turtle biotopes in Southeast Asia

As a result of the extensive north-south alignment and the considerable elevation of the Southeast Asian sub-continent, there is an in-crease both in the diversity and size of the turtles in the southern and low-lying re-gions. The turtles assigned here to the four types of landscape are not, of course, invariably found all together.

a) tropical mountain forest
b) monsoon forest at mod-erate altitudes
c) lowland rain forest
d) river delta with zones of brackish water and dunes near the sea.

to a)
1 Bigheaded turtle *(Platy-sternon megacephalum)*
2 Spengler's terrapin *(Geoemyda spengleri)*
3 Vietnamese Box turtle *(Cuora galbinifrons)*
4 Purple-bellied terrapin *(Notochelys platynota)*
5 Indian Keelbacked ter-rapin *(Pyxidea mouhoti)*
6 Southeast Asian land tortoise *(Manouria impressa)*
7 *Heosemys spinosa*
8 *Heosemys grandis*

to b)
9 Yellow-headed land tortoise *(Indotestudo elongata)*
10 Malayan pond turtle *(Cyclemys dentata)*
11 Yellow-head *(Cuora flavomarginata)*
12 Three-lined Box turtle *(Cuora trifasciata)*
13 Burmese Brown tortoise *(Manouria emys)*
14 Malayan Pond turtle *(Malayemys subtrijuga)*

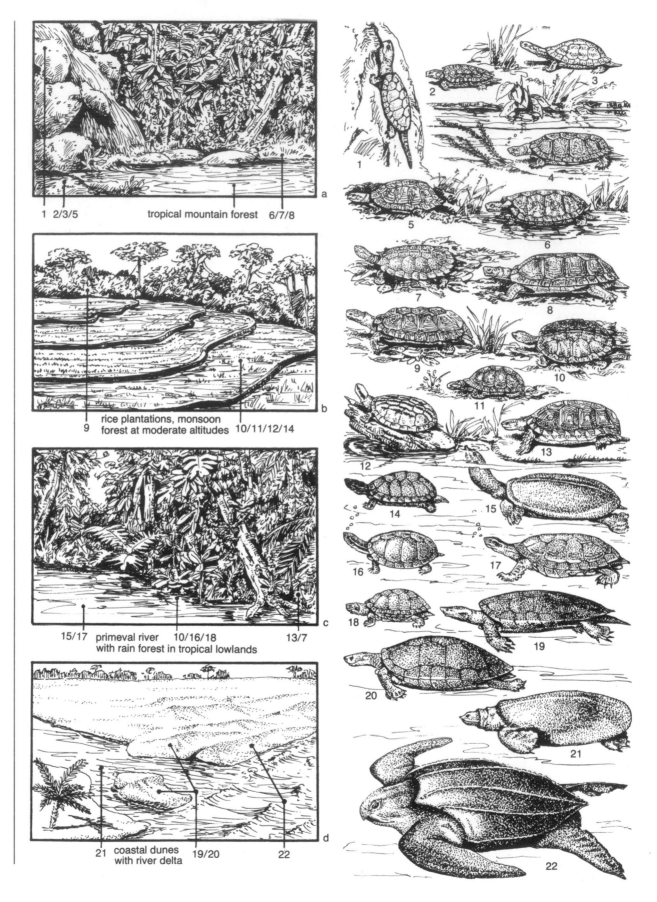

a 1 2/3/5   tropical mountain forest   6/7/8

b 9   rice plantations, monsoon forest at moderate altitudes   10/11/12/14

c 15/17   primeval river with rain forest in tropical lowlands   10/16/18   13/7

d 21   coastal dunes with river delta   19/20   22

110

cludes, for example, representatives of the following genera: American Pond turtles (Clemmys), Blanding's turtles (Emydoidea), True Box turtles (Terrapene), Old World water turtles (Mauremys), Asiatic Box turtles (Cuora), Malayan Pond turtles (Malayemys) and Chinemys, Rhinoclemmys, Heosemys and Melanochelys.

– Amphibious inhabitants of river-bank regions
These turtles only lay their eggs at a distance from water, but otherwise live close to the bank. They are predominantly diurnal. They come on land regularly for thermal regulation (basking), rather less for feeding. Many species feed exclusively in water. In order to sun themselves, they prefer exposed places with flight-access to deep water. All species are good swimmers. This group includes a few species belonging to various genera mentioned in Group 1, such as Mauremys, Clemmys (C. marmorata), Cuora, Rhinoclemmys and Melanochelys. Characteristic members of this group are representatives of the genera of European Pond turtles (Emys), Painted turtles (Chrysemys), Chicken turtles (Deirochelys), Map turtles (Graptemys), Chinese Striped turtles (Ocadia), Malayan turtles (Cyclemys), Pelomedusid turtles (Pelusios, Pelomedusa), and from among the Soft-shelled turtles, the genus Lissemys.

– Aquatic inhabitants of river-bank regions
This group contains a number of river turtles that also leave the water only to lay eggs. In contrast to Group 2, they do not require daily basking, although they still like to engage in it. Often they simply bask at the surface of the water, without going on land. Many species are predominantly crepuscular or nocturnal. Feeding takes place entirely in the water. Many species seek out underwater caves close to the banks. Some typical representatives are Mud turtles (Kinosternon and Claudius), Musk turtles (Sternotherus), Snapping turtles (Chelydra), Staurotypus, Alligator Snappers (Macroclemys), Temple turtles (Hieremys), Siebenrockiella and representatives of Chinemys (cf. Group 1). In addition, many Soft-shelled turtles belong to this group, such as the North American Trionyx species, the South American Frog-headed turtles (Phrynops), Snake-necked turtles (Hydromedusa and Chelodina), Australian Elseya turtles (Elseya) as representatives of the Pleurodira.

– Aquatic turtles of the open water (river turtles)
These turtles are excellent swimmers and divers that can cover extensive areas of great rivers and lakes. Most of them still come on to land regularly to bask, but the very large species of Soft-shelled turtles from the genera Trionyx, Chitra, Cyclanorbis, Cycloderma, Pelochelys and Carettochelys often come on land only to lay their eggs.

The other members of this group are also very large in size, for example, the Batagur turtles (Batagur), Callagur turtles (Callagur), Borneo River turtles (Orlitia), some of the South American Podocnemis and Peltocephalus turtles and Tabasco turtles (Dermatemys) while Kachuga, Hardella, Geoclemys, Erymnochelys and Emydura are normally-sized members of the group.

In some of the genera of Pond turtles already included in Group 2, there are individual representatives that could also be defined as river turtles, such as the large Central American Painted turtles of the ornata group of Chrysemys scripta.

Freshwater turtles in mountain streams

Only very few freshwater turtles have chosen rapidly-flowing mountain streams with clear water as their habitat. And indeed, in the temperate zones, the temperature of the water in such streams and rivers is too low for turtles to be able to live there. But in the mountain rivers of tropical Indochina, the water temperature ranges from 20 to 23°C. It is in just such torrents in Southern China, Vietnam, Cambodia, Burma and Thailand, which come rushing down to the valley between large boulders, interspersed with occasional deeper, calmer accumulations of water in potholes, that the curious Big-headed turtle or Casked terrapin (Platysternon megacephalum) lives. With its much flattened, longitudinally narrow shell about 20 cm in length, into which it is able to retract the disproportionally large head only minimally, and its extremely long tail, it is a grotesque phenomenon among modern turtles. Big-headed turtles conceal themselves among stones in the water during the day, and like to wedge themselves into rocky crevices much as terrestrial Pancake tortoises (Malacochersus) do in the slate rocks of East Africa. At night, they leave their refuge and go hunting. Their food consists mainly of hard-shelled molluscs and crustaceans. With their markedly hooked beak, they hold the

to c)
15 Black-Rayed Softshell (Trionyx cartilagineus)
16 Malayan Box turtle (Cuora amboinensis)
17 Temple turtle (Hieremys annandalei)
18 Black turtle (Siebenrockiella crassicollis)

to d)
19 Painted Batagur (Callagur borneoensis)
20 Batagur turtle (Batagur baska)
21 Giant Softshell (Pelochelys bibroni)
22 Leatherback (Dermochelys coriacea)

prey fast and draw it from its hiding place. Then the powerful jaws go to work. Big-headed turtles are able to crack open any mussel or crab. Even benthic fishes which, like the turtles themselves, tend to hide in rock crevices, often become their prey—snake-headed fishes, loaches and many species of barbel. With their fearsome beak, the turtles defend themselves successfully against many enemies. Many details of bodily structure indicate that the Big-headed turtle is an adept climber in its own habitat. The hooked beak, powerful claws, flat shell and, not least, the long muscular tail all help it in climbing. Swimming is less important. Short distances underwater are covered by walking and if a turtle happens to get washed away, nearby stones soon provide firm ground for the feet of this skilful climber. Many individuals—possibly even all the members of certain populations—swim so poorly that if placed in an aquarium with very deep water and nothing to climb out upon, they may drown. But it would be wrong simply to label all *Platysternon* as freshwater turtles incapable of swimming. Many learn to swim tolerably well, although without ever becoming experts.

In Southeast Asia (Southern Thailand, Malaysia, Sumatra and Kalimantan (Borneo)), *Notochelys platynota* is the second species that has elected to live in cool, clear, mountain streams. It is smaller than the Big-headed turtle and resembles the Emydid turtles (Emydidae) more closely in build, so that it can be assigned to that family, whereas the bizarre *Platysternon* is considered as the sole representative of an independent family (Platysternidae) with a single species. But in its way of life, there are many points in common. *Notochelys* also likes to be in the water between boulders, but it is predominantly diurnal. It goes on land very rarely. Its food consists of fishes, molluscs, water insects, small crustaceans and aquatic plants. As it gets older, the ratio of plant food in the diet increases. This change in feeding habit can also be observed in other turtles that are regarded as mixed feeders. In contrast to the Big-headed turtle, *Notochelys* swims well and so spends more time in the calm-water stretches of streams and rivers.

Turtles that fish in troubled waters

Numbers of freshwater turtles live in bodies of water with deep layers of mud and slime at the bottom. Hence the common name of the American family of Kinosternids or Mud turtles. All the Kinosternidae live in the murky ground layer on the bed of slowly flowing or standing bodies of water. Here they find their principal food—mud-dwelling molluscs, worms and articulates. In addition, by burrowing deeply into the mud, they are protected from danger. In spite of their predilection for this gloomy milieu, Kinosternids occasionally like to bask in the sun. The African Pelomedusid turtles (*Pelusios* and *Pelomedusa*) live a very similar life, although they are not at all closely related to the former family. Rather does the similarity represent a biological and ecological parallel. It is well known that similar life habits in animals of different origin often result in great similarities in external appearance. An outstanding example of this is provided by two groups of turtles that are not linked phylogenetically, but which both live concealed in the mud of their home waters: the Soft-shelled turtles (Trionychidae) and the Snake-necked turtles (Chelidae). In both families, there are genera with a conspicuously long neck: the Soft-shelled genus *Trionyx* and the Australian and South American Snake-necked turtles (*Chelodina* and *Hydromedusa*). Here the neck is modified into a snorkel, allowing the turtles to remain concealed in bottom mud, and yet to have a considerable radius of action for catching prey, and even for breathing in air if the water is shallow enough. In addition, the long neck permits them to "dabble" much in the manner of ducks, when they are swimming slowly in open water. But the Soft-shelled turtles are perhaps the most skilful of all in turning the mud to use. When in retreat from danger, they disappear into the mud at the bottom of the water in the way usually associated with flatfish and rays. With undulating movements of the flexible edge of the shell, they work their way down into the ground, at the same time covering their entire back with mud or sand. Similar movements allow them to "swim" along in soft mud. Finally, in addition to breathing through the lungs, they have evolved gill breathing through the mucous membranes of the mouth (see also p. 128), enabling them to remain safely submerged for a long time.

Another ecological type of freshwater turtle that lives at the bottom of gloomy waters as a lurking predator is represented by two species that have no close relational links. The Alligator Snapping turtle (Macroclemys temmincki) of southern North America, with record dimensions of up to 66 cm in carapace length and almost 100 kg in weight, is the heaviest and almost the largest of recent freshwater turtles. The great head with its hooked beak reminiscent of the Big-headed turtle is impressive, as is the long crocodile-like tail covered with lumpy scales. The carapace is relatively flat, deeply sculptured and murky blackish-brown in colour. Chin, neck and skin parts of the front limbs are covered with small warty protuberances, blurring the contours of the body, so that the huge turtle, lying immobile between tree stumps, branches or large aquatic plants, merges into its surroundings. In a very similar way, skin protuberances and the knobby, rough shell of the South American Matamata (Chelus fimbriatus) have the optical effect of breaking up the outline of the body (somatolysis). Both turtles look like gnarled branches lying motionless in the water. Covering growths of algae and moss add the final touch to make adaptation to the environment perfect. The two differ slightly only in the way they take their prey. Macroclemys is the only "angler" among the turtles (see p. 153), while Chelus captures its unsuspecting prey by suction—again a unique example within the order of turtles.

The path to the sea: turtles in brackish waters

The turtles of large, tropical rivers soon become acquainted with brackish water. As good swimmers, they also enjoy being carried along by currents and soon reach the zone in which fresh water mixes with the sea, a biotope rich in fishes and aquatic animals of many kinds, offering an abundance of food. Certain Soft-shelled turtles, particularly the giants among them, live occasionally in slightly brackish water: Trionyx cartilagineus, Trionyx sinensis, rather more rarely Chitra indica and Pelochelys bibroni. The gigantic river turtles of Southeast Asia from the family of Emydidae more often show a preference for brackish water: Orlitia borneensis, Batagur baska and Callagur borneoensis. But apart from their fondness for brack-

ish water, very little is known about the life habits of these river turtles. Clearly all these species are relatively rare in their home in Southeast Asia. They do not appear to have any communal egg-laying sites in which the females of a population can be seen in large numbers.

But the North American turtles living in brackish waters, the Diamondback terrapins (Malaclemys terrapin) are very well known. They have a distinctive colouring and inhabit the Atlantic coast of America from Massachusetts to the Yucatan Peninsula in the Gulf of Mexico. Within this extensive range, there are about seven geographical subspecies which, in some cases, differ greatly in appearance. All of them live in brackish lakes and marshes along the coastal strip or in the brackish estuaries of rivers. In southern Florida, the subspecies Malaclemys terrapin rhizophorarum inhabits the mangrove swamps. It finds its favourite foods in salt water: marine molluscs such as mussels and snails. Apart from the fact that the water is salt, the Diamondback terrapin could be classified in terms of habitat as an amphibious to aquatic water turtle of the littoral regions. Broadly webbed, powerful feet show it to be an excellent swimmer. But Diamondbacks also enjoy and need regular periods of basking in dry places. The considerable popularity achieved by Diamondback terrapins in the USA was, unfortunately, based less on their interesting biology as the only Emydid turtles of North America that are highly specialized inhabitants of brackish waters, than on their reputation as a gastronomical delicacy (see Section "Real turtle soup").

Protective legislation introduced 60 years ago averted the danger of extinction, but not of the constant reduction of habitats, which still continues today. Increasing pollution of rivers, measures of agricultural improvement in the wetlands, utilization of habitats for road construction, industrial development, tourism and other human activities have long since interrupted the continuous chain of Diamondback populations that used to extend unbroken along the entire eastern coast of the USA, leaving wide gaps in it.

Marine turtles make up the last ecological group within this order of reptiles. These turtles are also specialized for particular, different regions of the oceans. The six species of the family Cheloniidae are more or less inhabitants of the coastal (littoral) regions of the sea.

fairly estimated that 2,000 and more jars-full are consumed by the inhabitants of the villages on the river. Now, it takes at least twelve basketful of eggs, or about 6,000, by the wasteful process followed, to make one jar of oil. The total number of eggs annually destroyed amounts, therefore, to 48,000,000. As each turtle lays about 120, it follows that the yearly offspring of 400,000 turtles is thus annihilated. A vast number, nevertheless, remain undetected; and these would probably be sufficient to keep the turtle population of these rivers up to the mark, if the people did not follow the wasteful practice of lying in wait for the newly-hatched young, and collecting them by thousands for eating; their tender flesh and the remains of yolk in their entrails being considered a great delicacy. The chief natural enemies of the turtle are vultures and alligators, which devour the newly-hatched young as they descend in shoals to the water. These must have destroyed an immensely greater number before the European settlers began to appropriate the eggs than they do now. It is almost doubtful if this natural persecution did not act as effectively in checking the increase of the turtle as the artificial destruction now does. If we are to believe the tradition of the Indians, however, it had not this result; for they say that formerly the waters teemed as thickly with turtles as the air now does with mosquitoes. The universal opinion of the settlers on the Upper Amazons is, that the turtle has very greatly decreased in numbers and is still annually decreasing.

(Extract from Henry Walter Bates: The Naturalist on the Amazons. 1892)

Body form and way of life

The shell—
of skin and bone

The most striking characteristic of all turtles is the shell. Fanciful ideas about its strength abound, and from time immemorial, men have speculated upon its origins, as certain folk tales in the cultural heritage of many different peoples show. And indeed, the strength of the shell of large land tortoises is considerable. In certain zoos, one of the more questionable attractions sometimes offered is "tortoise riding". The rider, seated on a giant tortoise, can make the creature walk along by holding in front of it, and just out of reach, some favourite item of food. In its rather silly way, this experiment at least demonstrates the tortoise's ability to bear the weight of the rider not only on its shell but also on its legs. Several people must sit on a tortoise's shell before it can be hindered from walking, and the

shell can still withstand the weight. But it is essential that the pressure be evenly distributed. The animals are very sensitive to sudden pressure concentrated on a small area of the shell, and much more so to dynamic pressure. A bullet from a gun, for example, would easily penetrate the shell of a large tortoise. And if a turtle is allowed to fall, serious bone damage and injury to internal organs and particularly to blood vessels can easily result. This legendary armour, then, provides only limited protection and will not withstand all forms of attack.

The bony armour

The turtle's shell represents a barrel-vault construction on a level base. The solid fusion of the basal plate and the vault increases its strength considerably. Normally, the vault structure consists of compact bony plates which are anchored at the ridge by much smaller plates, each representing

The turtle's bony shell
This example of a compact bony shell includes various bony elements that are not invariably present in all species. Bony plates that occur only rarely are shown by dotted lines,
those normally occurring by toothed continuous lines.
Bony plates of the carapace:
1 nuchal
2 proneural
3 neural (No. 1–8)
4 metaneural I
5 metaneural II
6 pygal
7 propleural (paired)
8 pleural (No. 1–8) (paired)
9 peripheral (No. 1–11) (paired)

Bony plates of the plastron:
1 epiplastron (paired)
2 hypoplastron (paired)
3 hypoplastron (paired)
4 xiphiplastron (paired)
5 entoplastron (not paired!)
6 mesoplastron (paired), may extend as far as centre or be only marginal
7 peripheral (belongs to carapace!)

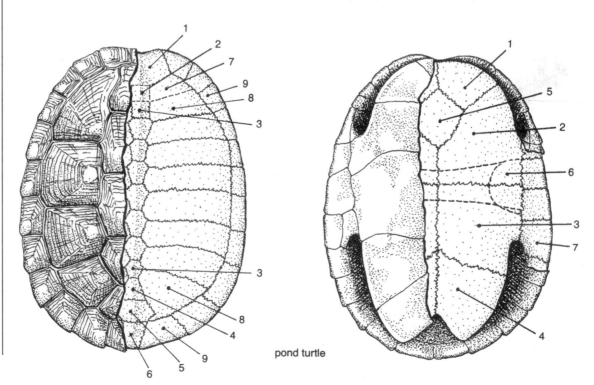

pond turtle

114

the keystone of an arch. Most land tortoises and many freshwater turtles follow this original pattern of the rigid, highly arching and massive carapace.

Various hypotheses exist to explain the origins and development of the shell. The most widely-held view links shell development with the fossorial habits of turtle ancestors. According to this view, the armour represents a special form of adaptation to life underground. A comparison is frequently made with armadillos among the mammals, that have also evolved a body covering of protective bony plates. This, of course, is only one potential means of coping with life underground. Many other vertebrates that burrow and live underground have adapted to this way of life just as successfully by means of quite different physical modifications. Because of the huge diversity in potential biological developments, it may never be possible to give an unequivocal answer to this question.

In the course of further evolution, the massive chelonian shell soon proved something of an encumberance, and numerous modifications developed in answer to the situation. In large species, the great bone mass had first to be reduced. Aquatic turtles in particular had no use for the massive shell any more. So the most radical modifications of the shell can be found both in freshwater and marine turtles. In marine turtles, the shell consists basically only of strong struts with light in-filling

surfaces between them, or with large gaps in the bone, known as fontanelles. The only land tortoise to have reduced its shell in a similar way is the rare Pancake tortoise *(Malacochersus)*. But in its case, the cause was not so much the necessity for weight reduction as the need to regain some flexibility in the body. In face of danger, Pancake tortoises inside their hiding place inflate their body and so wedge themselves firmly inside the protective rock walls.

Reduction in shell weight can also be achieved by alterations in bone structure. The bony plates in the shell of large land tortoises consist of air-filled chambers, inserted one into the other, and separated by partitions and struts of varying thicknesses (p. 134). This "air-pocketed" structure ensures lightness with strength. To a large extent, the turtle's shell reverses the most basic principle of vertebrate physiology. From the internal skeleton of the normal vertebrate, an external skeleton has developed—a remarkable exception to the general rule.

The exoskeleton provides considerable protection to the organs housed within it, but at the same time creates quite different conditions under which they must function. Respiration, digestion, locomotion, gestation and other vital processes are greatly affected by the rigidity of the shell. So turtles have either undergone specific forms of adap-

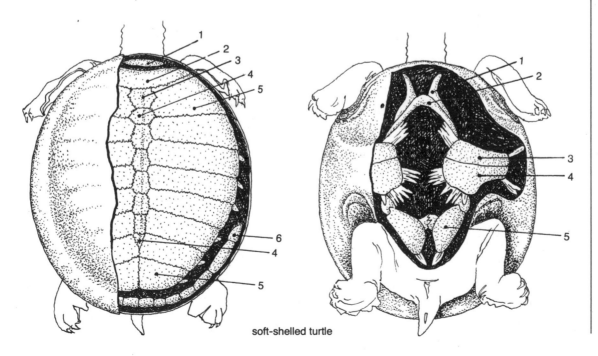

soft-shelled turtle

As an example of the shell of a Soft-shelled turtle, the carapace of a Soft Terrapin *(Lissemys)* has been chosen since its shell is less radically reduced, while a *Trionyx* Soft-shelled turtle provides the example of the plastron.
Bony plates of the carapace:
1 prenuchal
2 nuchal
3 proneural
4 neural (No. 1–7)
5 pleural (No. 1–8) (paired)
6 peripheral (paired)

Bony plates of the plastron:
1 preepiplastron (paired)
2 epiplastron (not paired)
3 hypoplastron (paired)
4 hypoplastron (paired)
5 xiphiplastron (paired)
(3, 4, 5 partially covered by callosities)
(after various authors, combined)

115

tation or else, not infrequently, have modified and even partially abandoned their most striking acquisition, the rigid shell.

In the shell's structure, it is possible to find certain indications of its origin. Not surprisingly, classical zoologists tried to explain the bony elements of the shell in terms of the metamorphosis of typical vertebrate bones. Embryological studies using the microscope, and the analysis of numerous palaeontological finds soon made it clear that the turtle shell must be a structure of varying origin. A certain part of the bony elements does indeed represent the transformation of bones in the normal skeleton of archaic saurians, but the majority of them have their origin in bony scutes in the dermal layers of the skin (osteoderms) that have fused with typical skeleton parts. The ability to form unattached bones or ossicles within the skin was characteristic of the Stegocephalians in the Carboniferous, and in the following epochs, the Saurians provided striking examples of bone structures of this kind. Among modern reptiles, crocodiles can be considered as archaic relict forms of those reptiles that also have a protective covering of membrane bones, as "armoured lizards". But even among the phylogenetically younger Squamata, the ability to develop ossifications in the dermis has not been entirely lost. The ancestors of turtles also had membrane bones of this kind in the form of free, bony plates. These plates gradually fused with the ribs, for example, and the spinal processes of the dorsal vertebrae. In this way, the upper shell or carapace developed. Examination of the cavity of the carapace clearly shows the spinal column extending underneath the covering bones. In the same way, the rudiments of the ribs reduced to bony strips can be easily recognized. The position of the rib head between two adjoining vertebrae is also noteworthy. Inside the shell of most Pond turtles and Land tortoises, the course of the ribs can scarcely be distinguished at all, but in Marine turtles and Soft-shelled turtles, it can be followed easily. In young turtles of various groups, the free ends of ribs, as the first parts of the plates, join up with the corona of the peripherals, and attach the shell in this way. There seems to be no doubt that in the course of carapace evolution, the ribs did not expand to become the plates of the carapace, but rather fused more or less completely with the broad membrane bones.

The chelonian carapace is by no means always uniform in stucture. In addition to group-specific peculiarities in large related groups of turtles, it is very often possible to observe in the carapace of individuals surprisingly wide variations from the normal skeletal structure characteristic of the species. "Surplus" bony plates occur relatively frequently. Soft-shelled turtles are particularly prone to this feature. When supernumerary elements of this kind occur asymmetrically, they can immediately be taken as an individual peculiarity; symmetrically disposed surplus bones, however, can easily lead to false conclusions. In particular, this has happened occasionally in the case of fossil finds occurring as single specimens.

The upper shell or carapace is generally composed of eight large paired pleural plates which make up the vault. The pairs of pleurals are not in direct contact, but are separated from one another by the smaller central neural plates. So, as a rule, there are also eight neurals. In certain groups such as the Side-necked turtles, there is a very strong tendency for a reduction of the neurals. In certain genera of Snake-necked turtles (Chelidae), such as *Platemys*, *Emydura* and *Chelodina*, the neurals are completely reduced, so that the pleurals abut directly above the spinal column. Other groups, such as Soft-shelled turtles and some other genera of Chelidae, have fewer than eight neurals. The row of neurals is preceded by a nuchal bone (proneural) and concludes towards the tail with one or two suprapygals or epipygals and a pygal. Proneurals and pygals always occur even when the neurals are reduced. They function as "keystones" in a girdle made up of 11 peripherals on either side which encompass the vault of the carapace. At the same time, the central peripherals form a bridge joining the carapace with the lower shell or plastron. Front and back edge of the bridge is often fortified by stable supports originating from the plastron.

The plastron is usually made up of four sets of paired bones. Set centrally between the front two pairs of bones there is an approximately circular bone, the entoplastron. In addition, the Pelomedusidae or Side-necked turtles possess a symmetrically arranged pair of small marginally situated bones, the mesoplastra. They lie between the second and third pairs of plastral bones towards the bridge. The mesoplastra are otherwise found only in archaic fossil turtles. They show the Pelomedusids to be a very primitive group. A few years ago, mesoplastra were discovered in the skeleton of a recent marine turtle, *Lepidochelys olivacea*. This finding, however, is not the norm, but an interesting individual peculiarity in certain specimens. This spontaneous occurrence of ancestral characteristics already "outgrown" is known as atavism.

In terms of their origin, the elements of the plastron derive in part from the shoulder girdle of archaic Saurians. The foremost set of paired bones, the epiplastra, represent the transformation of the clavicles, the entoplastron that of the interclavicle. The other pairs of large bones are considered to have resulted from the transformation of the ventral ribs or of fusion of the latter with dermal ossicles. Abdominal ribs are also a normal part of the skeleton of many Saurians. Among modern reptiles, only crocodilians still possess abdominal ribs or gastralia.

The principle of plastron structure is reflected in almost all modern turtles. Soft-shelled turtles (Trionychidae), however, have reduced the entoplastron completely. In its place, there is a large gap in the bone. The forward plastron bones in Soft-shelled turtles are in part reduced to rod-shaped elements.

This is true of the epiplastra, which, in addition, are solidly fused together. In front of them are frequently two additional rod-shaped praepiplastra. The remaining plastral bones in Soft-shelled turtles appear as finger-like processes.

In live specimens, extensive rough areas or callosities can be seen and felt on the plastron. Their number, site and size are an important diagnostic feature of Soft-shelled turtles. The callosities have their origin in the extraordinarily rough surface of the reduced plastron plates or in additional membrane bones that sometimes occur in the plastron of Soft-shelled turtles. In many turtles, the plastron exhibits quite large gaps in the bone (fontanelles). They are found throughout life not only in Soft-shelled but also in Marine turtles. Young turtles of other genealogical groups also show fontanelles which close up quite gradually.

One might mention again here the Pancake tortoise *(Malacochersus)* as a special case. It is the only land tortoise in which the plastral fontanelles do not close in the course of growth but become proportionally larger.

Flaps and hinges

The normal shell itself provides an effective measure of protection to chelonians. And yet certain species have improved the protective function of the shell by shell-closure mechanisms. By dividing the plastron into two movable parts, certain of the Side-necked turtles have achieved complete closure of the shell. In the vanguard of this development stand American Box turtles *(Terrapene)*, certain of the American Mud turtles *(Kinosternon)* and Asiatic Box turtles *(Cuora)*. The lobes of the plastron can be moved by means of hinges formed of cartilaginous connective tissue. Powerful muscles draw them up and hold them in place. Mud turtles *(Kinosternon)* have an immovable intermediate lobe that at the same time forms the bridge with the carapace. Thus the shell itself has remained rigid. There is a parallel example among the Pelomedusid turtles of the genus *Pelusios*. They are distinguished by the hinged front lobe of the plastron which is linked with a rigid shell.

In the other "hinged turtles", the plastron is divided directly into two sections. As a consequence, linkage by means of cartilaginous tissue has replaced fusion of the bones with the carapace. The loss of stability associated with this finds adequate compensation in the ideal dome-shaped carapace of *Cuora, Terrapene* and *Emydoidea*. The European Pond terrapin *(Emys)* still has movable plastral lobes and a cartilage link with the carapace, but is no longer able to close the shell tightly. In addition, the stability of its plastron has been much reduced because of its flat shape and the lack of strength in the pleural bones. These reduction phenomena reflect the high degree of adaptation to an aquatic way of life. Certain species of *Cuora* and *Terrapene*, on the other hand, live much as land tortoises.

Land tortoises (familiy Testudinidae) have rarely acquired the "knack" of hinging the shell to make it impregnable. Only the Spider tortoise, *Pyxis arachnoides*, has a movable lobe at the front of the plastron. Its degree of mobility varies between populations, and it is clearly rudimentary, no longer functioning as a reliable protective flap.

The slight flexibility that occasionally develops in the rear part of the plastron in elderly female tortoises of *Testudo* species is not associated with supplementary protective mechanisms. It represents rather a potential degree of compensation for

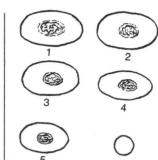

The red blood corpuscles (erythrocytes) of turtles are strikingly larger than those of other reptiles, while reptiles in general have larger erythrocytes than mammals. They differ most markedly from those of mammals in that they still have a distinct cell nucleus, as do those of fishes and amphibians. This primitive type of red blood cell does not exhibit the same efficiency in transporting oxygen and other materials as in the case of birds and mammals. The number of blood cells per millilitre of blood plasma in turtles is only 10 to 20% of that found in the human organism.

1 Mediterranean Spur-thighed tortoise *(Testudo graeca)*
2 European Pond tortoise *(Emys orbicularis)*
3 Ringed grass snake *(Natrix natrix)*
4 Blindworm *(Anguis fragilis)*
5 Sand lizard *(Lacerta agilis)*
6 Man *(Homo sapiens)* (after Reichenbach-Klinke, 1973)

Hinges for closing the shell
a) The plastron consists of two movable lobes that are linked flexibly (by means of cartilaginous tissue) to the carapace:
American Box turtles (*Terrapene*)
European Pond tortoises (*Emys*)
American Semi-box turtles (*Emydoidea*)
Malayan Box turtles (*Cuora*)
b) The plastron consists of a central part rigidly linked to the carapace and two movable lobes:
Mud turtle (*Kinosternon*)
c) Only part of the plastron functions as a movable lobe
Spider turtle (*Pyxis arach-noides*).
Pelomedusid turtle (*Pelusios*)
d) The rear part of the carapace is movable and can be drawn up:
Hinged tortoise (*Kinixys*).
e) Muscular lobes of skin are used to protect the hind limbs: Certain Flap-Soft-shelled turtles (*Cycloderma, Cyclanorbis* and *Lissemys*).

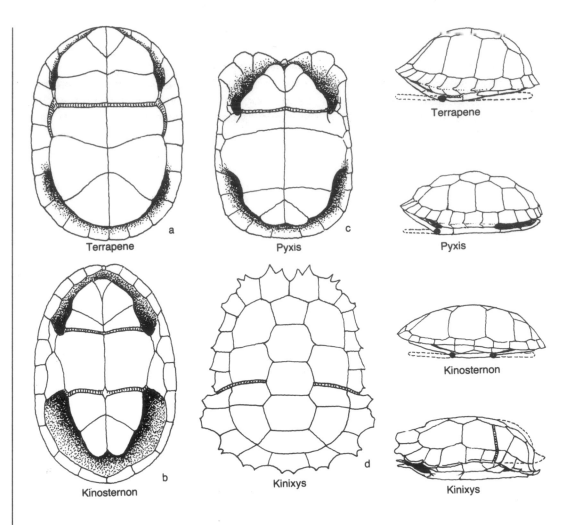

Terrapene

Pyxis

Terrapene

Pyxis

Kinosternon

Kinosternon

Kinixys

Kinixys

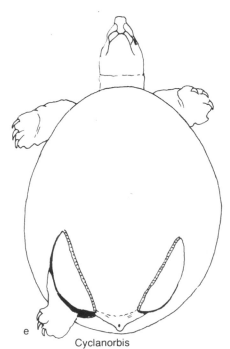

Cyclanorbis

the rigid body volume while the animals are carrying eggs.

Hinged tortoises (genus *Kinixys*) have evolved a quite different, unique mode of shell closure. The rear part of the carapace is movable and can be drawn in by powerful muscles after tail and feet have been retracted. But this remarkable hinge mechanism develops only in maturity. This again is a fundamental contrast to the plastron occlusion mechanisms that function at a very early age. But in the genus *Kinixys*, there seems to be no link between sexual function and the hinge mechanism in the carapace, and the origins of this phenomenon are still not clear.

Among Soft-shelled turtles, the subfamily Cyclanorbinae have developed a mechanism to protect their hind limbs. Flaps of cartilaginous tissue on the plastron conceal the retracted limbs. How far this represents a general protective function is uncertain. It may be that the closure mechanism serves rather as a protection against water loss by evaporation when the turtles are resting out of water. The shell closures of *Pelusios* and *Kinosternon* may also have a similar function, since they also frequently live in temporary accumulations of water and spend periods of rest in dry conditions. The "land tortoises" of the Emydidae family in the genera *Cuora* and *Terrapene* have, temporarily or permanently, an even more urgent need for protection from evaporation.

When the armour is too small

While certain turtles evolved hinge and flap mechanisms for shell closure to gain more complete protection, the evolution of other chelonian shells took the opposite direction. By modification of shell form and reduction to a minimum of entire shell parts, the shell was opened up and at the same time lost much of its protective function. Why did this happen?

Older specimens of giant tortoises from the Galapagos Archipelago and the Seychelles or from Aldabra are frequently described as Saddleback tortoises. The anterior part of the carapace is strikingly elevated and the front opening much extended. With the head drawn in, such a tortoise is unable to close the opening satisfactorily using the retracted arms. This partial surrender of the protective function of the shell could develop because the turtles, in their insular isolation, have no natural enemies that could exploit this "weakness". The raised front edge of the carapace gives the tortoise's neck a long, high reach that is very useful for grazing on shrubs and high-growing *Opuntia* cactus plants.

Water turtles of various groups have, in certain cases, also largely dispensed with the protective function of the shell. This is seen particularly in the marked reduction of the plastron. But the carapace has been retained. Snapping turtles (Chelydridae) and Central-American Musk turtles (Staurotypidae) are characterized by a very small plastron in the form of a cross of bone. This plastron now serves only to secure the dome of the carapace to its base, at least centrally. But concealment of the limbs and tail beneath the plastron has become quite impossible. And Snapping turtles can retract the large head only partially beneath the carapace. In compensation, these large turtles are very aggressive and defend themselves actively when threatened. Because of their ferocious temper and the power and sharpness of their jaws, they are feared even by man.

Members of the genera *Claudius* and *Staurotypus,* although considerably smaller, are fairly intrepid and can administer serious bites. The Bigheaded turtle *(Platysternon megacephalum)* will attack readily and bite viciously. Its plastron is of normal form, but is much too small to cover the limbs and tail. And it is quite impossible for the characteristic, large head to be retracted into the small, flat shell.

In this context, mention should be made of all the marine turtles. They too belong to the group Cryptodira that retract the neck in a vertical plane, yet they are unable to conceal either head or huge paddle-like forelimbs under their shell. The shell has retained only a limited protective function that has largely been replaced by active defense. Moreover, marine turtles are skilful swimmers and divers, so are able to evade many dangers by taking flight.

Tortoiseshell or leather

Having considered the anatomy and origin of the inner layer of bony plates in the shell, we can now turn our attention to the characteristic horny outer covering. The horny scutes or laminae of the Loggerhead and the Green turtle are greatly prized as a raw material for the craftsman, and many of the creatures have been killed to supply this demand. The horny plates of the carapace correspond exactly to normal reptilian scales.

Aware of the capacity for regeneration that is typical of the reptile skin, many native peoples in the Indo-Pacific obtain the valuable tortoiseshell by pouring boiling water over parts of the shell of a live turtle, and then removing the softened horny laminae. Usually the animals survive this cruel treatment at first, and probably in some of them, regeneration of the carapace may occur. At any rate, remarkable examples of regeneration of horny plates in wounded turtles that have been kept in captivity confirm this supposition.

Turtles possess normal horny scales on the limbs, head and neck, like other reptiles. Only the shell is covered by large shields, scutes or laminae. The arrangement of the plates, like that of the bones beneath, is based on a scheme that is characteristic of species and group. A striking feature is the considerably smaller number of horny plates compared with bony elements. Arrangement of the laminae is independent of the bony structure of the shell. Instead of coinciding, the larger laminae are clearly out of alignment with the bony plates. This construction increases the strength of the shell.

The carapace is usually covered by five centrals (or vertebrals), four pairs of laterals (or costals) and a series of marginals. At the edge of the carapace, towards the head, there is a nuchal (or precentral) and at the tail end a paired or unpaired supracaudal (or postcentral). Between them, 11 marginals on either side complete the ring. The plastron is covered by six pairs of laminae that are axially symmetrical. Side-necked turtles and the Tabasco turtle alone always have a single intergular lamina that is inserted between the two front pairs of laminae or is enclosed by them.

As with the structure of the bony layer of the shell, the arrangement of the laminae shows a large number of group-specific peculiarities. They usually reveal interesting phylogenetic and genealogical relationships, and so warrant our attention. In certain turtles, regularly arranged additional plates or pairs of plates are a striking feature. Marine turtles of the genera *Caretta* and *Lepidochelys*, for instance, have five or even as many as seven pairs of laterals. All recent marine turtles, that is, the genera *Chelonia* and *Eretmochelys*, possess, in addition, extra plastral plates. Between the carapace and the plastron, in the region of the bridge,

there is a row of four to five inframarginals on either side. This profusion of laminae is a regular feature of fossil turtle groups of the Mesozoic, while the simplified type of lamination is a characteristic of younger groups. Where additional laminae of this kind occur in recent turtles, they are usually a clear indication of the great geological age of that particular species or group.

By the possession of complete rows of three to four inframarginalia, Big-headed turtles (Platysternidae), Tabasco turtles (Dermatemydidae) and Snapping turtles (Chelydridae) reveal themselves as particularly primitive, ancient groups. Among the Chelydridae, the Alligator Snapping turtles *(Macroclemys temmincki)* have an additional, extra pair of rows of laminae on the carapace. These upper inframarginals (supermarginalia) are situated between the central laterals and the marginals. They provide an extra indication of the archaic character of these species. Only two well-developed inframarginals occur in the plastron of Mud turtles (Kinosternidae). Many chelonologists do not consider these two large plates as inframarginals, but equate them with the very small axillary or oliac (shoulder or hip) plates that frequently occur at the front and real edge of the bridge, particularly in phylogenetically "younger" turtles. But it is more correct to define these shields as inframarginals, which fits in well with the assessment of the Kinosternids as also being a relatively primitive chelonian group.

Pattern of epidermal plates
As in the review of the bony plates of the shell, all horny scutes that may occur have again been shown, although in fact, they do not all occur simultaneously in one turtle species. The pattern of the horny laminae is one of the most important aids to classification.

carapace
1 central (No. 1–5, rarely 6)
2 lateral (No. 1–4, rarely up to 9)
3 marginal (No. 1–11)
4 precentral or nuchal
5 postcentral
6 supramarginal

plastron
1 gular
2 humeral
3 pectoral
4 abdominal
5 femoral
6 anal
7 intergular
8 axillary
9 inguinal
10 inframarginal (up to 4)
(after Zangerl, 1969)

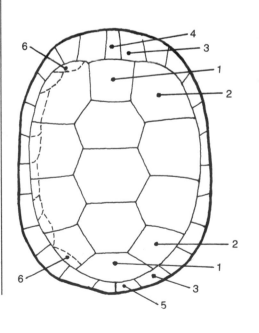

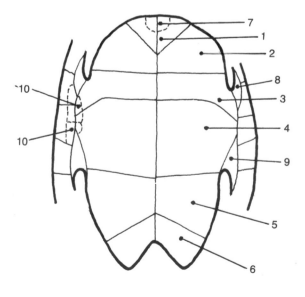

The nuchal lamina of the carapace is subject to considerable modification. There are relatively closely related species or groups in which this plate may either exist in a variety of forms or else may be completely reduced. It figures frequently in the species or group description of certain chelonians and can provide a valuable diagnostic feature in identification.

A curious example of the apparent absence of the nuchal lamina is seen in the South American Snake-necked turtles *(Hydromedusa)*. In their case, the large nuchal has been displaced from the ring of plates encircling the carapace by the front pair of marginals, and shifted to the head of the row of centrals. It gives the impression of an additional sixth central.

However, a sixth central lamina occurs constantly in the Southeast Asian species *Notochelys platynota*. This striking morphological feature clearly distinguishes *Notochelys* from related species in the family of Old World Pond turtles (Emydidae/Batagurinae). This, together with its equally atypical life habits (see p. 111), certain morphological and anatomical peculiarities and its typically relict distribution, indicate that this turtle holds a special, striking position.

It also seems curious that many turtles with reduced bony elements of the shell nevertheless have a complete set of normal horny scutes. Externally, there is no indication of the "light-weight construction" of the shell. This phenomenon is characteristic of many fossil turtles as well as of the recent marine turtles of the family Cheloniidae. Supremacy in the art of "concealing the facts" belongs once again to the frequently mentioned Pancake tortoise (also known as the Flexible-shelled or Tornier's tortoise), *Malacochersus tornieri*, which carries over its much reduced, paper-thin shell, the complete outer layer of horny scutes of the typical land tortoise.

Both in the bony plates and the horny laminae, individual variations from the group and species-characteristic norm occur frequently. Recognition of the individual character of such peculiarities is usually not difficult, because they are usually associated with destruction of the symmetry in the arrangement of the shields. But the spontaneous absence of normally present nuchals or the atavistic occurrence of this lamina in species in which it is normally reduced completely, can prove irksome in identifying individual turtles. Deviations from the norm in the occurrence of paired or unpaired post-centrals (or supracaudals) that often have taxonomic significance, can also lead to mistakes in classification.

An exception of a special kind exists in freshwater Soft-shelled turtles (Trionychidae and Carettochelydidae) and in marine Leathery turtles (Dermochelydidae). These animals have reduced the external horny plates completely and the bony shell considerably. A few horny scales can still be found on the fore and hind limbs of many Softshells, but

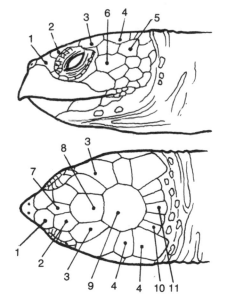

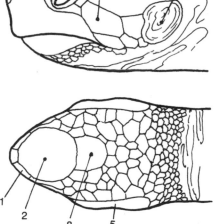

Pattern of head plates in sea turtles

Sea turtles, with the exception of the Leathery turtle, have a number of large head plates, the arrangement and the shape of which are species-characteristic. Together with other anatomical and morphological details, the existence of these plates, as a primitive feature, indicate the great phylogenetic age of sea turtles.

The specimen illustrated is a Loggerhead turtle *(Caretta caretta)*. The plates, equally discernible in both sketches, bear the same numbers. The other marine turtles have, in general, fewer large head plates.

 1 nasal
 2 prefrontal
 3 supraocular
 4 parietal
 5 tympanal
 6 massetericum
 7 internasal
 8 frontal
 9 syncipital
10 occipital
11 interoccipital
12 tympan

The shields of the upper surface of the head together make up the pileus, with an arrangement of plates that is species-characteristic.

The head plates of a land tortoise

In land tortoises, most of the large head plates have been reduced to small scales. Any larger plates that still remain are given the same names (and numbers) as in the case of sea turtles.
(after Schreiber, 1912)

Turtles in which the pattern of the laminae shows striking peculiarities (not to be confused with deviations from the species-characteristic pattern of plates frequently occurring in individual turtles).
a) Tabasco turtle *(Dermatemys mawi)* with a complete row of inframarginals.
b) Giant Mud turtle *(Staurotypus)* with large axillaries and inguinals that are recognizable as rudiments of the row of inframarginals.
c) Purple-bellied terrapin *(Notochelys platynota)* with a normal 6th central lamina.
d) South American Snake-necked turtle *(Hydromedusa)* with a nuchal lamina that has been displaced by the joining pairs of marginals into the row of centrals, where it could easily be mistaken for a 6th central lamina.

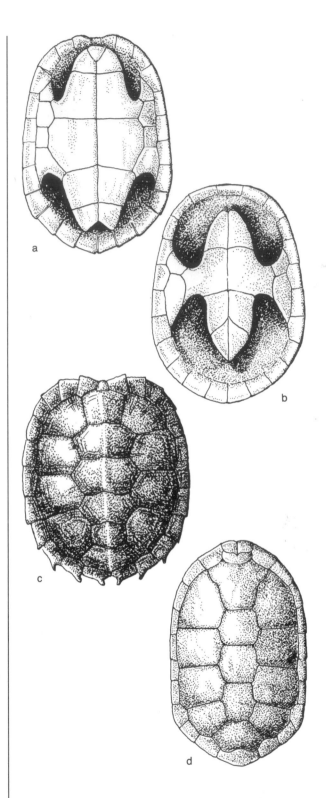

otherwise the body is completely covered by a thick, leathery skin. On the carapace, the rudimentary bony shell reveals itself as a fairly large, oval disc with a very rough surface, covered by thin skin, through which the grainy structure of the bone surface can be detected. There are rough patches of this kind on the plastron as well, in the centre of the leathery skin. Mention has already been made of these callosities.

In comparison with the skin surface of other chelonians with a complete covering of horny scutes, the leathery skin of Soft-shelled turtles is, of course, physiologically more efficient. Like many other animals, Softshells are able, for example, to carry out part of the process of gaseous exchange through the skin. Linking this fact to the highly aquatic way of life of the Trionychids, one can interpret the leathery skin as the optimal adaptation to life in the water. The same is true of marine Leathery turtles. Undoubtedly the high degree of specialization in both groups of turtles is the result of a long, independent evolutionary process. The origin of these turtles has to be put at a time considerably earlier than that suggested by the earliest fossil finds of clearly identifiable Soft-shelled and Leathery turtles.

The shell in its entirety is not only the most fundamental and remarkable structure in turtle physiology, but also a reflection of their phylogenetic and genealogical relationships, mirroring the interrelationship between their way of life and the modifications in form that resulted from it. In his assessment of turtles, a chelonologist could well make use of the saying: Show me your shell and I shall tell you who you are.

Chewing without teeth— special features of the testudinid skull

The turtle skull shows many features that characterize the entire order of Testudinids. Probably the best known is the absence of teeth. Why turtles should have lost their teeth completely is difficult to explain satisfactorily. The Triassic turtles still had remains of a dentition that was already highly regressed. Toothless jaws are perfectly able to function as a fruit press or as nutcrackers when they are moved by powerful muscles. It may be that the ancestors of turtles fed in this way, and they may also have crushed the solid shells of primitive molluscs to get at the soft flesh—we do not know.

But the absence of teeth was another result of evolution for which widely varying groups of turtles soon compensated. The upper jawbones and the two rami of the lower jaw, which except in a few Snake-necked turtles (Chelidae) are fused into a solid uniform rod in which no suture is visible between the bones, were covered by a horny sheath. The function of teeth is taken over by the horny covering of the jaws. Predaceous water turtles have extremely sharp, completely level jaw coverings. They work together on the scissors principle. In many species, such as Snapping and Big-headed turtles, as well as in a few sea turtles, the tip of the covering of the upper jawbone is bent downwards in a hook. The underlying bones of the skull, the maxillae and the premaxilla lying at the tip, determine the hooked beak shape. The grab-hook of the Alligator Snapping turtle *(Macroclemys temmincki)* and of the common Snapping turtle *(Chelydra serpentina)* make it possible for quite strong prey to be held fast, while the Big-headed turtle *(Platysternon megacephalum)* is the only turtle that occasionally makes use of its hooked beak to climb, much as a parrot does. The beak of the Leatherback *(Dermochelys coriacea)* is unique in form. The rim of the upper jaw forms two cusps that are isolated by a deep notch at the tip of the snout and by notches on the sides of the upper jaw covering. This double hook structure allows the turtle to take a particularly firm hold on the slippery jellyfishes that make up a large part of its diet.

Some substitute for teeth is just as important to herbivorous turtles as it is to their carnivorous cousins. But serrated jaw coverings are more suitable for biting off plant parts than are smoothly sharp edges. Many land tortoises and pond turtles that are predominantly vegetarian have regularly serrated, horny jaw coverings. Once again, the bones of the upper jaw often determine the contour of the substitute teeth. Particularly interesting are the horny jaw sheaths of large land and freshwater turtles *(Megalochelys, Chelonoidis, Batagur, Callagur, Hardella, Kachuga,* etc.), that extend far into the inner mouth, covering almost the entire length of the maxillae and which have several rows of protuberances lying one behind the other that function as regular grinding teeth to break down vegetable

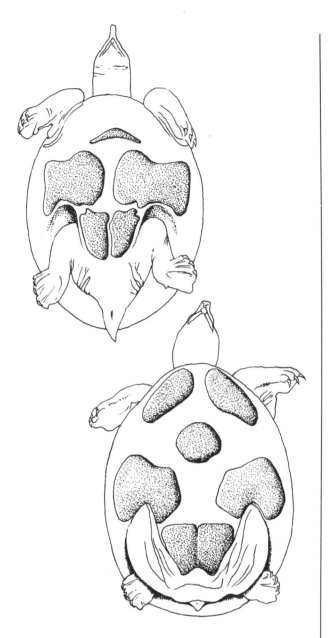

food. Because of the knobby prominences of the maxilla, the "horny denture" fits snugly onto the underlying bones. In most turtles, the skull curves outwards at the temporal region. In this way, space is provided for the powerful jaw muscles *(musculi adductores mandibulae)*.

In land tortoises and Soft-shelled turtles, only a narrow bony bar has remained behind the eye sockets as a pseudotemporal arch (formed by the *quadrato jugale)*, whereas Snapping turtles and some others have broader areas of bone made up of several cranial bones (jugale, postorbitale, quadrato jugale). Without closer examination, the skull opening could be confused with the skull ap-

Form, number and position of the callosities in the leathery skin of the plastron of Soft-shelled turtles are characteristic of genus or species. The callosities are rough, gristly and bony areas that can be seen and felt on the surface of the skin. Above a Three-clawed turtle *(Trionyx)*, below an Indian Soft Terrapin *(Lissemys)*.

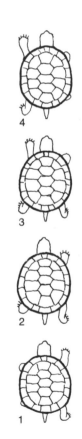

4

3

2

1

Synchronous movement of diagonally opposed limbs—normal quadrupedal locomotion in turtles (with exception of sea turtles) (see pp. 125–126).

123

erture in other reptiles. Of course, it fulfils the same function, allowing muscles to pass through it to the lower jaw, but it is a secondary development. Originally, the turtle skull was a compact structure lacking temporal fossae or openings (anapsid type of skull), as the Triassic turtles clearly show. Modern marine turtles approximate very closely to this primitive closed structure. But many specialists believe that this closed skull form could also be a secondary acquisition, like the opening-up of the skull in "pseudo temporal fossae" in other turtles.

But the interpretation of the marine turtle skull as primitive seems to fit in better with the repertoire of other primitive features in these animals that undoubtedly represent a very ancient group of the Cryptodira, whose separate development certainly began very near to the original roots of the chelonian tribe. The question of whether the anapsid skull structure of turtles is indeed comparable with that of the Cotylosaurians and therefore primitive, can nevertheless not be regarded as finally decided. From time to time, new research findings bring it to the fore again. For example, Rainer Zangerl, an American herpetologist, discovered a rudimentary skull vacuity *(Foramen parietale)* in a number of recent turtles, presenting new puzzles in the interpretation of their origin.

Snake-necked turtles of the genus *Chelodina* have the most widely opened skull among the Side-necked turtles. In general, they show an incurving (emarginated) temporal region without any remnants of a bony bar. But the curious shallow skull of the Matamata *(Chelus fimbriatus)*, that still has a temporal bridge, is also impressive. Another peculiarity of the chelonian skull is the complete reduction of the nasal bone (nasale). The external nostrils join to form a single wide opening. The position of the internal nostrils (the choanae) may be near the front of the mouth or quite far back. T. S. Parsons, an American zoologist, studying the structure and path of the choanae, was led to some interesting comparisons. He found considerable deviations from the nasal structure of other reptiles, but instead, morphological links with amphibians. The structure of the ear region of the turtle skull is very characteristic. In the hypertrophy of the middle ear region, which takes the form of lateral occlusion by a bony wall, the American chelonologist Eugene Gaffney recognized an important characteristic of all "modern" turtles coming after the Triassic turtles, which he called Casichelydia. He considered the meeting of the pterygoids at the base of the cranium with the effect of closing the gap that existed at that point in Triassic turtles, to be another important feature common to all modern turtles. As a consequence, the cranium of the turtle is a very compact structure, in the consolidation of which an important part is played by the quadrate bone (quadratum). But the lumen of the brain case appears quite modest in scale.

An important factor in determining relationships between turtles is the route taken by major blood vessels. The path of the internal carotid artery is, according to Gaffney, of particular significance.

Jaw shape in various turtles
a) Big-headed turtle *(Platysternon megacephalum)*
"Parrot beak" for eating snails and for climbing.
b) Softshell *(Trionyx)*
Fleshy upper lips protect and cover the extremely sharp-edged horny sheaths of the jaw.
c) Alligator Snapper *(Macroclemys temmincki)*
A "raptor's beak" for taking prey.
d) Leatherback *(Dermochelys coriacea)*
Double-hooked raptor's beak for catching jellyfish and fishes.
e) Aldabra Giant tortoise *(Megalochelys gigantea)*
Short beak with broad masticatory ridges for chewing hard parts of plants.
f) Indian Roofed or Dura turtle *(Kachuga tecta)*
Serrated edge of the horny sheaths for biting off tough water plants.

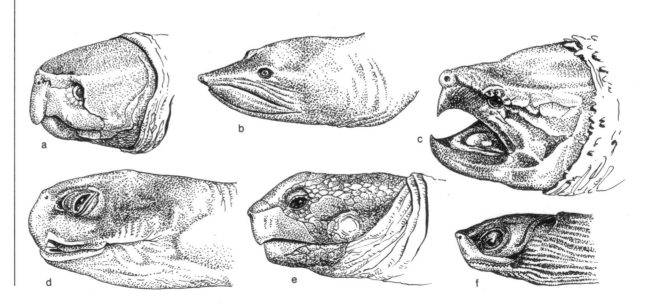

Cryptodira or Pleurodira—neck retraction in horizontal or vertical plane

The neck of chelonians is worthy of special consideration since its structure and the manner in which it moves constitute the basic distinction between the two major groups of modern turtles, Cryptodira and Pleurodira. The method of head retraction is the result of the varying mobility of the neck vertebrae. The number of cervical vertebrae in all turtles is eight. But they differ greatly in length and form (the snake-like necks of Chelidae and Trionychidae). Mobility is determined by the form and arrangement of the lateral vertebral articulations, the zygapophyses. In the cryptodires, the zygapophyses are widely separated from one another, so that the cervical vertebrae can be bent in an S-shape in a vertical plane and the neck retracted into the shell.

Because in the pleurodires (the Side-necked turtles) on the other hand, the zygapophyses are set close together, they can retract the neck only sideways in the horizontal plane. Another remarkable feature is the flexibility of the neck vertebrae and the enormous diversity in the individual centra. For example, in the European Pond terrapin (*Emys orbicularis*), the cervical spine is made up of seven different types of vertebra. The centra differ in the shape of the front and end surfaces that in either case can be flat, concave or convex in any combination. The shape of certain neck vertebrae can sometimes even vary between individuals of the same species, as has been found particularly in land tortoises (*Kinixys* and others). Some mention has already been made of the lower parts of the spinal column. The ten dorsal vertebrae are fused to the carapace bones, while the two sacral vertebrae lie freely beneath the epipygals of the carapace. The tail consists of the 18 to 32 free caudal vertebrae. The number is very variable so tail length can vary greatly. All chelonians can draw in the tail sideways under the shell, much in the way in which a Side-necked turtle retracts its head. This is mainly because of similarity in the form of the vertebrae. Finally, mention should be made of the remarkable structure of the tail of the Matamata (*Chelus fimbriatus*). It ends in a rod-like bony sheath that is made up of dermal bones, and to some extent represents "tail armour". No similar structure occurs in any other recent chelonian. Among fossil turtles, only the remarkable "bull-horned" turtles (family Meiolanidae) from the Eocene and Pleistocene in Australia and South America had similar armoured tails.

Are turtles good walkers?

Many jokes have been made about the leisurely gait of the tortoise, and its slow pace has become proverbial. But in reality, most chelonians are decidedly nimble, and even land tortoises are good walkers. Certainly their speed is modest, but they have great staying power. On their daily walk in

The chelonian skull and its typical components
The side view of the upper skull shows the following bones:
1 prefrontal
2 frontal
3 parietal
4 postfrontal
5 supraoccipital (developed as a ridge at the back of the head)
6 squamosal
7 premaxillary
8 maxillary (edentulous)
9 jugal
10 quadratojugal
11 quadrate (with condyle)
Usually a nasal bone is absent; only the majority of Sidenecked turtles and a number of fossil groups of turtles have retained the nasal.
The lower jaw is composed of:
12 dental (edentulous)
13 coronoid
14 angular
15 supraangular
16 articular (with articular surface)

View of roof of mouth
Bones that already feature in the side view are numbered as above. Other bones visible are:
17 vomer
18 palatinum (with internal nasal opening)
19 pterygoid
20 basisphenoid
21 basioccipital (with condyle)
(modified after Steiner, 1977)

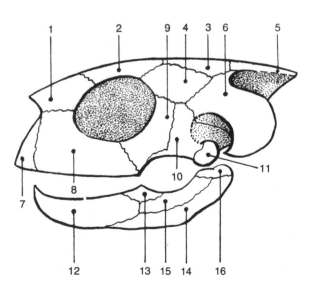

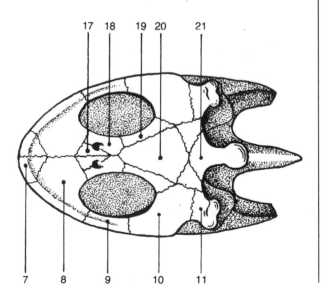

Limbs and forms of locomotion in turtles
Modification of limbs in relation to way of life
1 Pond turtle:
scaled feet armed with claws have a wide range of potential uses, webbing of feet is moderately developed, that of the hind limbs more highly developed.
2 River turtle:
claws and scales reduced, webbing of feet very highly developed. Hind and fore limbs fully palmated.
3 Sea turtle:
claws greatly reduced, front extremities modified into paddles or flippers have taken over swimming function.
4 Soft-shelled turtle:
claws and scales reduced (the "Three-clawed turtle"), webbing on feet very highly developed.
5 Land tortoise:
claws and scales highly developed, fore limbs flattened into shovel-like digging implements, hind limbs modified into pillar-shaped "elephant's feet".

Reduction of bones of hand and fingers in a land tortoise (left) compared with a pond turtle (right). The bony elements of the foot are modified from a general-purpose to a fossorial foot.

search of food and back again, many species cover several hundred metres. Mention has already been made of the well-defined "roads" made by the giant tortoises of the Galapagos Islands, leading from the coast into the mountain plateaus. They are particularly impressive since, as they walk, land tortoises do not "crawl" but carry their heavy body raised up off the ground.

With few exceptions, water turtles are excellent swimmers, showing great endurance and achieving considerable speeds. Marine turtles are masters of long-distance and high-speed swimming (with a top speed of about 74 km/h). But adult animals are no longer able to walk normally on land. Because of the weight of the massive body and the lateral arrangement of the limbs, they are only able to haul themselves forward in a series of lurches by the simultaneous use of all four limbs, scraping along the ground as they do so. Young marine turtles, on the other hand, walk quite normally with alternate leg movements.

Freshwater turtles can usually walk very well on land, even when they are fully grown. They too carry the weight of the shell as they progress. A few terrestrial Emydid turtles have even become good walkers, and many freshwater turtles are able to climb well (Kinosternids, Platysternids, many Emydids). The method of swimming employed by freshwater turtles differs fundamentally from that of sea turtles. Whereas all marine turtles have developed powerful, paddle-shaped forelimbs as the major propulsive organs, freshwater turtles have webbing over a large area of the hind limbs that provides the principal driving force. Only the common Batagur turtle (Batagur baska) deviates sharply from this general rule, with forelimbs that resemble somewhat the paddle-shaped limbs of sea turtles. To a varying extent, the same is true of Soft-shelled turtles (Trionychidae and Carettochelydidae) and other predominantly aquatic turtles such as the Painted Batagur (Callagur borneoensis) and the Tabasco turtle (Dermatemys mawi).

Basically, the pectoral girdle is fused into the structure of the shell, so that it consists of only two unattached bones, the scapula with an elongated process, the acromium, and the coracoid bone. The position of the pectoral girdle in the shell and inside the ribs is a typical chelonian feature which makes turtles unique among reptiles. However, the

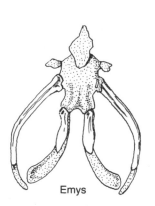

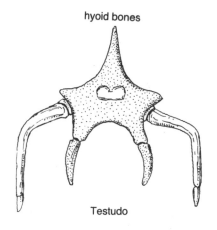

hyoid bones

Emys

Testudo

Trionyx

The hyoids consist of bony and cartilaginous substance (dotted or white). In Soft-shelled turtles, the hyoid apparatus becomes considerably ossified during the turtle's lifetime, in tortoises and pond turtles, it remains cartilaginous.
Ventilation of the nose brought about by movement of the hyoid bone serves the vital sensory function of olfactory perception as well as assisting respiration.
(after various authors)

pelvic girdle corresponds substantially with that of other reptiles. It is composed of the three normal bones, the pubis, ischium and ilium. To a large extent, the form of the pelvis determines the way in which the particular turtle walks or swims. It is at the same time a characteristic feature of specific relational groups. The condition of attachment of the pelvis also differs fundamentally. In cryptodires it lies freely within the shell, while in pleurodires, it is fused to the plastron.

Inevitably, the shell restricts the mobility of the limbs. The arms are characterized by the forward rotation of the elbow joint; the shell itself prevents the normal drawing-back action. The knee joint is also shifted to a somewhat sideways position. In large land tortoises, these bones, and in particular the joints, have to support enormous loads. The limbs of land tortoises have the columnar, club-footed shape of an elephant's leg. Only the claws extend from it, whereas in the forelimbs of fossorial species of land tortoises (*Gopherus*, *Geochelone*, *Agrionemys*, *Testudo*, etc.), the last phalanges extend into the claw-sheaths. In this connection, there is a tendency in land tortoises to a shortening of the bony elements of carpus, tarsus and the digits, and a reduction in the number of phalanges (*Agrionemys* is the "four-toed tortoise"). However, Emydids, Snappers and Big-headed turtles, Mud turtles and Side-necked turtles have well-developed fingers and toes that are joined together only by webbing. In soft-shelled and marine turtles, the extremities, particularly the fore limbs, are again more integrated, with only a few of the free claws visible (*Trionyx* is known as the "three-clawed turtle").

How turtles breathe

The normal method by which terrestrial vertebrates ventilate their lungs by movements of the thorax is not available to turtles since they are enclosed in a rigid shell. The existence of the exoskeleton made it necessary for them to develop means of respiration that are used only partially by other vertebrates. In addition to pulmonary breathing, many animals also use abdominal breathing. Its basis is an additional action of suction and compression involving body cavity and lungs.

The turtle's lungs lie at the zenith of the shell. A skin of connective tissue, the diaphragma, separates them from the underlying organs (heart, liver, stomach, intestinal tract). The viscera are also enclosed within a membrane which is attached to the diaphragma. Two paired groups of muscles, working with antagonistic action, act alternately upon this membrane and so alter the volume of the abdominal cavity. The transversus abdominis muscle originates from the inner surface of the carapace; as it contracts, the volume of the abdominal cavity is reduced and part of the air is expelled from the lungs. As this muscle relaxes, its opposite number, the obliquus abdominus muscle which originates from the skin of the hind extremities, is able to contract and pull back the membrane, and air is drawn into the lungs. This process is supported by the rhythmic drawing-up and opening out of the arms. In this way, the shoulder girdle supplements the suction-and-compression action of lung ventilation. A third mechanism that assists in respiration is movement of the hyoid bone at the base of the tongue. The hyoid apparatus, a system of bony and cartilaginous rods, causes the constant rise

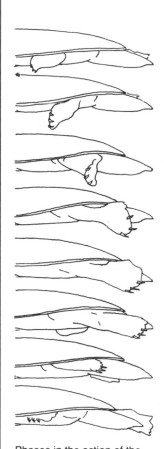

Phases in the action of the hind limbs of a Soft-shelled turtle while swimming ("frog-like" action, powerful thrust then drawing up of legs). A notable feature is the alteration of the area of the foot in the individual phases.
(after various authors, combined)

and fall of the throat. This permits pressure-change respiration on land. At rest, and in conjunction with the respiratory muscles of the body cavity, it provides adequate ventilation, and the muscles of the shoulder girdle can rest. Air exchange by movement of the hyoid bone also has an olfactory function. This can easily be observed in the way turtles recognize one another by sniffing, or inhale to inspect food. Water turtles are able to smell actively in water by movements of the floor of the mouth arising from the hyoid bone that draw a stream of water in and out through the nose. This is the preliminary stage of a specialized form of respiration occurring in Soft-shelled turtles. The throat of Trionychids is lined with short finger-like projections or villi of skin which have a plentiful blood supply and like gills, are capable of gaseous exchange in water. Softshells, buried in bottom mud, extend only the head or the snorkel-like, thin snout and rhythmically fill and empty the throat by pumping, in what has been accurately described as pharyngeal "gill" respiration.

As already mentioned, respiration through the skin also plays an important role for Soft-shelled turtles. At rest, a Softshell can obtain all the oxygen it requires by a combination of cutaneous and pharyngeal "gill" respiration. But in some Soft-shelled turtles, another form of lung ventilation has been observed. In these animals, the lungs are enclosed in a thin muscular sheath that corresponds to the intercostal muscles of other reptiles. These muscles compress the lungs and then release them, producing a respiratory mechanism that is largely independent of the diaphragma and the membrane of the body cavity. This technique might be called bellows respiration. Water turtles of various groups hibernating in water seem also to be capable to some extent of achieving a modest gaseous exchange through the lining of the pharynx. With metabolism reduced to the minimum necessary for survival, oxygen requirement is very slight and this form of respiration can be adequate for a stationary turtle. It is possible that anal sacs filled with water also serve as supplementary "substitute gills."

In diving, the lungs of water turtles also function as air bladders. Since it is possible for air to be exchanged from one lung to the other, changes of direction can be brought about when a turtle is diving or surfacing. Disturbances in this specialized function of the lungs can best be observed in turtles in captivity that have caught a cold. The affected animal can no longer dive and swims on the surface.

Some river turtles have adapted well to diving to considerable depths. So that their lungs can withstand the extreme pressure, they have bony lung chambers. The lung chambers are formed by the lateral bony walls of the carapace. The genera of Asiatic Emydid turtles that are highly specialized as divers (*Batagur*, *Callagur*, *Hardella*, *Kachuga* and *Orlitia*) possess lung chambers of this kind.

The long necks of Snake-necked turtles and Softshells enable them to take in air snorkel-fashion while remaining submerged. Similarly, the snout of Soft-shelled turtles (Trionychidae), Papuan Softshells (Carettochelydidae) and Matamatas *(Chelus fimbriatus)* functions as a snorkel to inhale at the surface of the water. The animals either take a rapid gulp of air and immediately dive down again or else make use of natural cover under water and draw in air slowly with only the tip of the snout projecting cautiously from the cover.

As an aid to diving, marine turtles have a special closure mechanism for the nostrils. It does not function on the basis of muscular action but is effected by swelling of the connective tissue lining the nostrils. Increased blood supply and congestion in the vessels distends the nasal mucous membranes that are underlaid with connective tissue, preventing the passage of water.

Pharyngeal "gill" respiration
Buried in mud, the Soft-shelled turtle rhythmically fills its throat with water and empties it again. Folds in the skin of the pharynx, rich in blood vessels, are capable of gaseous exchange, so that Soft-shelled turtles can remain on the ground underwater lying in wait for prey for a long time without coming up for air.

The respiratory muscular system
Groups of muscles working with antagonistic action rhythmically alter lung volume. At rest, turtles sometimes support ventilation of the lungs by action of the forelimbs and by moving the base of the throat by means of the hyoid bone.
(modified from McCutcheon, 1943)

exhalation

inhalation   action of forelimbs

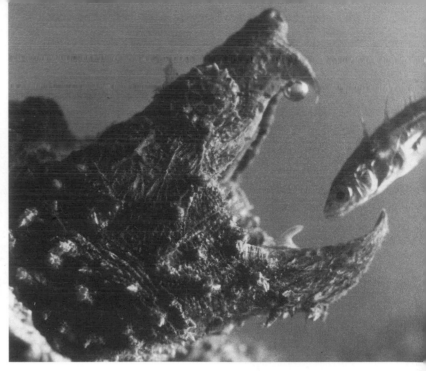

previous page:

Reeve's Chinese terrapin *(Chinemys reevesi)* eating a water snail.

Alligator Snapper *(Macroclemys temmincki)* catching prey by "angling".

Common Red-eared turtle, the "Elegant turtle" *(Chrysemys scripta elegans)* eating a fish. The fish is held by the fore limbs, and fragments are torn from it.

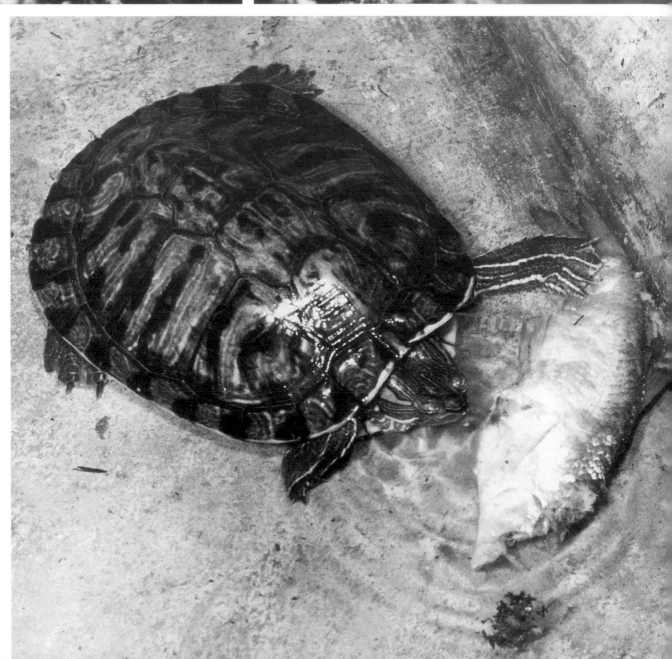

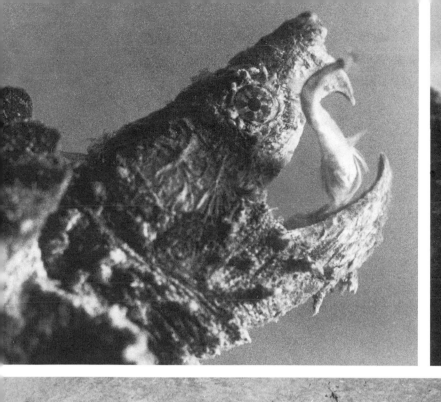

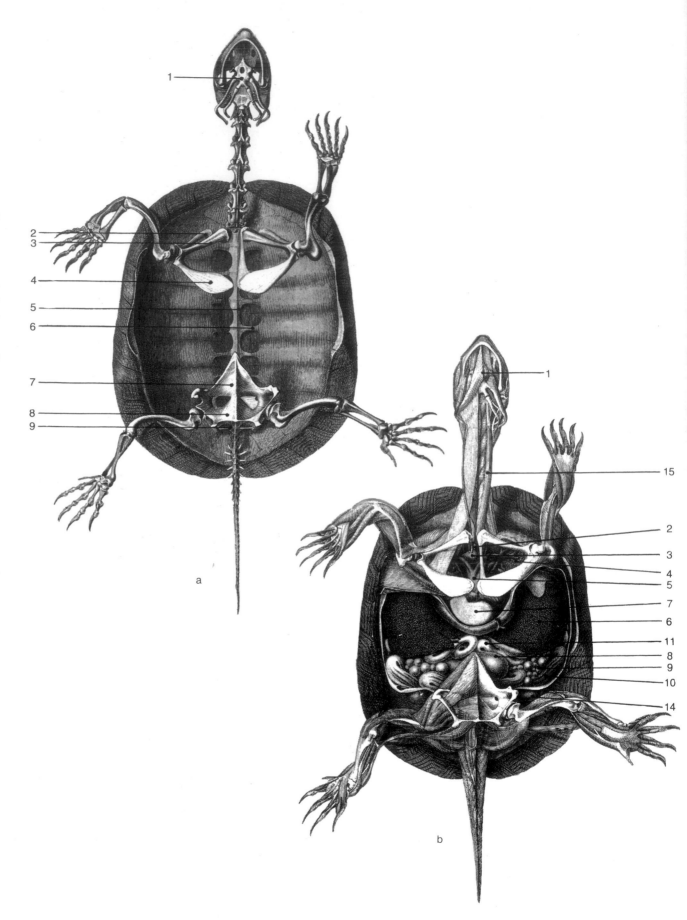

Skeleton and internal organs of the European Pond turtle *(Emys orbicularis)*. Reproduced here are three original plates (copperplate engravings) from Bojanus' famous work *Anatome testudinis europaeae* (1819−1821). In spite of its age, this book has remained a standard work on testudinate anatomy up to the present day.

a) skeleton from below, plastron removed:

1 hyoid bone
2 postscapula or preco-
 racoid
3 scapula
4 coracoid
5 dorsal vertebra
6 rib attachment
7 pubis
8 ischium
9 ilium

b) and c) different views of internal organs and muscles. Numbers denote the same organ or muscle in both illustrations

1 salivary gland of the
 tongue
2 trachea
3 thymus gland
4 lung
5 heart
6 liver
7 stomach
8 bladder
9 ovaries
10 oviduct
11 intestinal loops
12 kidney
13 oesophagus
14 anal sacs
15 muscles allowing head
 retraction
16 respiratory muscles

132

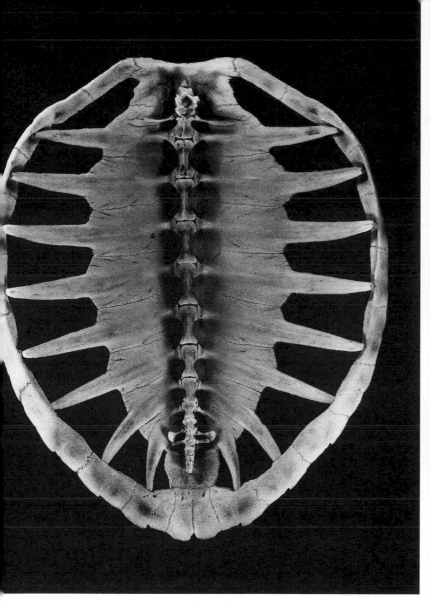

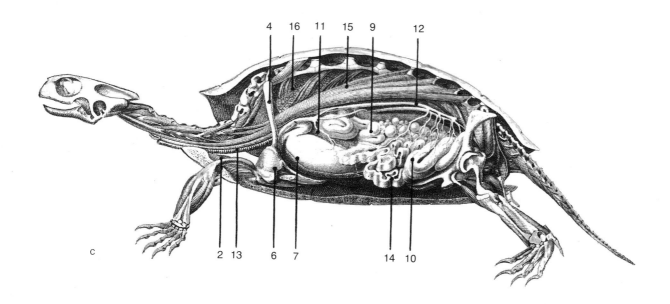

c

4 16 11 15 9 12

2 13 6 7 14 10

Skeleton of a young Hawksbill turtle *(Eretmochelys imbricata)*, interior of carapace. Note the very large gaps in the bone (fontanelles) and the skeletal structure of the supportive elements of the shell.

Skeleton of a young Hawksbill turtle *(Eretmochelys imbricata)*, interior of plastron. Here again, the very large fontanelles and the skeletal structure of the supportive elements of the shell are conspicuous.

133

Skeleton of an Indian Soft terrapin *(Lissemys punctata)*. Plastron with cartilage linking the bony plates and cartilaginous thigh flaps.

Section through bone of the carapace of a Seychelles Giant tortoise *(Megalochelys gigantea)*. The spongy structure of the thick bone ensures stability with lightness.

Skeleton of a land tortoise. Leopard tortoise *(Geochelone pardalis)*. Near side of shell removed. (Staatliches Museum für Tierkunde, Dresden)

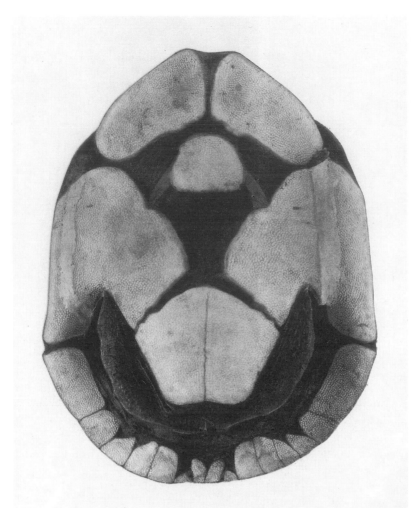

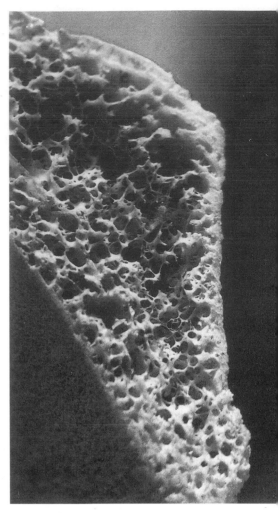

Skeleton of a soft-shelled turtle, the Ganges Softshell (*Trionyx gangeticus*) (Staatliches Museum für Tierkunde, Dresden)

135

Skulls of turtles
above left:
Alligator Snapper *(Macro-clemys temmincki)*
length of skull: 165 mm
above right:
Green turtle *(Chelonia mydas)*
length of skull: 180 mm
below left:
Matamata *(Chelus fimbriatus)*
length of skull: 98 mm
below right:
Snapping turtle or Logger-head Snapper *(Chelydra serpentina)* length of skull: 90 mm

Skulls of turtles
above left:
Seychelles Giant tortoise *(Megalochelys gigantea)*
length of skull: 150 mm
above right:
Krefft's turtle *(Emydura kreffti)*
length of skull: 35 mm
centre left:
Indian Soft terrapin *(Lissemys punctata)*
length of skull: 106 mm
centre right:
European Pond turtle *(Emys orbicularis)*
length of skull: 39 mm

below left:
West African Hinge-backed tortoise *(Kinixys erosa)*
length of skull: 56 mm
below right: Ornate slider *(Chrysemys scripta)*
length of skull: 42 mm
(Staatliches Museum für Tierkunde, Dresden)

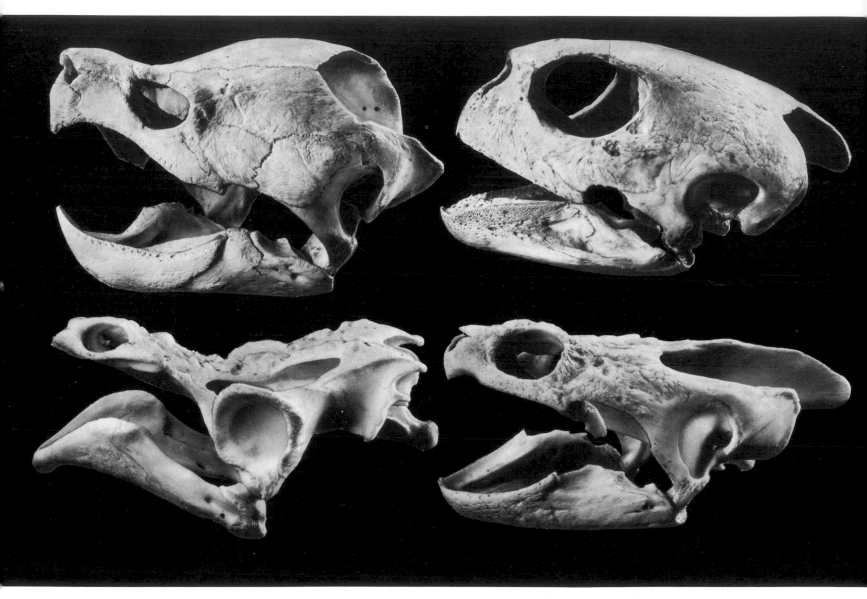

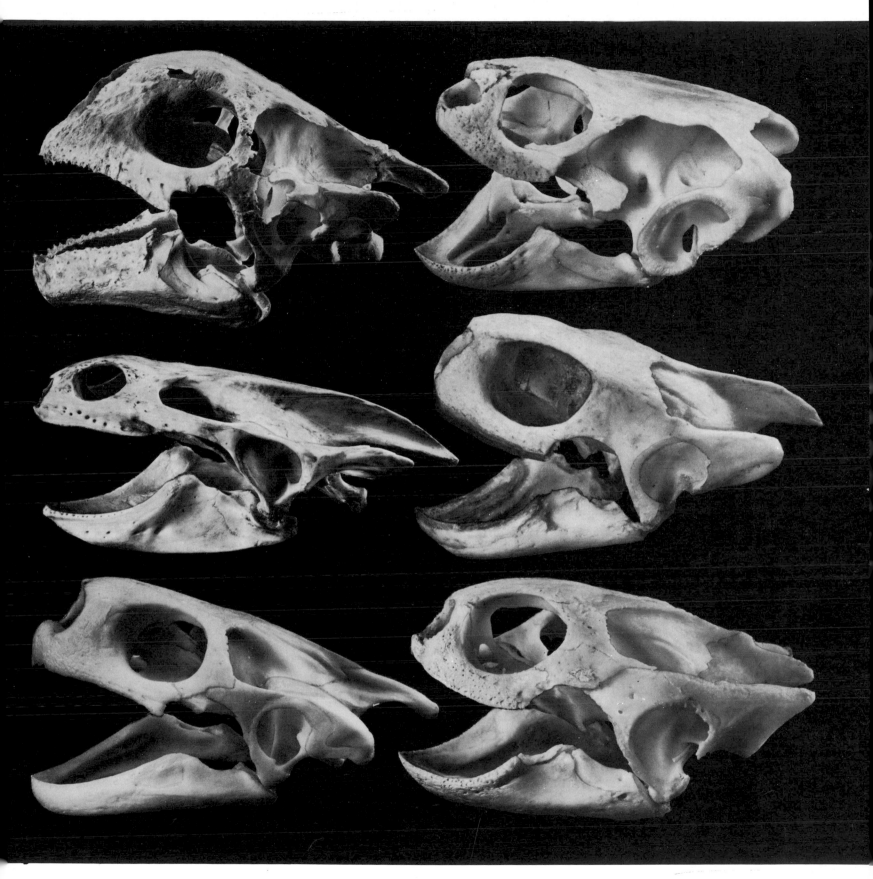

Horny sheaths from the jaw of a Seychelles Giant tortoise *(Megalochelys gigantea)*
left: lower jaw
right: upper jaw
The broad masticatory surface and the tooth-like serrations are characteristic.

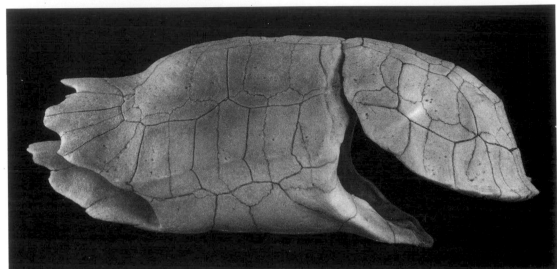

Closure of the plastron by means of movable lobes in the American Box turtle *(Terrapene carolina)*.

Shell of the Forest or Schweigger's Hinged tortoise *(Kinixys erosa)* with movable posterior flap on the carapace as an occlusion mechanism.

Bell's Eastern Hinged tortoise *(Kinixys belliana)* Note the articulation of the carapace just in front of the hind legs.

Eastern Spiny Softshell *(Trionyx spiniferus)* The coloration of all Soft-shelled turtles darkens at an advanced age, the patterning disappears almost completely.

Different stages in the life of the Madagascan Radiated tortoise *(Asterochelys radiata)*. There are striking changes in shape of shell and in markings. Very often, elderly individuals are almost entirely black instead of yellow.
Above: very old turtle, unusual coloration.
Below: adult turtle.
Right: young turtle.

A very old specimen of Seychelles Giant tortoise on the Island of Anse Malabar.

Plastron of an American Box turtle *(Terrapene carolina)* from Rhode Island engraved with the dates 1844 and 1860. This individual was caught in 1953.

142

Spined turtle *(Heosemys spinosa)*. Pond turtle from Indochina that lives terrestrially. Juveniles with characteristic markings on carapace and plastron.

Chinese Soft-shelled turtles
(*Trionyx sinensis*) mating.
The male bites into the
front edge of the female's
carapace.

Hatchling of African Spurred
tortoise *(Geochelone
sulcata)*.

Half-grown Leopard tortoise
(Geochelone pardalis) from
East Africa.

following page:

Basking under a lamp in a
terrarium, Pond turtles like to
clamber over one another,
just as they can be seen to do
in the wild.

Highly albinistic Florida Soft-shelled turtle *(Trionyx ferox)*. Albinos occur rarely among turtles.

Siamese twin Horsfield's tortoise *(Agrionemys horsfieldi)* found in 1978 in Soviet Tadzhikistan. It lived only a few months.

A Soft-shelled turtle *(Trionyx steindachneri)* being held correctly by the feet. It was caught for a check-up in an open air terrarium. Serious bites can be avoided by quick action and a firm grasp. (Note the long neck!)

146

Diving for Snakenecks (*Chelodina*) and Shortneck turtles (*Emydura*) in Australia.

John Cann, one of Australia's leading experts on turtles, catching an Emydura turtle in mud.

The Giant tortoise enclosure
at the Zurich Zoo
If the tortoises are properly
fed, tough grasses and
shrubs can survive, provided
there is adequate space
available for the animals.

Covered area with tropical
plants, plenty of space for
movement, deep soil floor,
partially heated, and large
pond. In the foreground,
stone seats for visitors.

Glass case housing
freshwater turtles belonging
to Marcel Peltier, Olten,
Switzerland. On the left,
more vivaria and a basking
place for little African foxes or
fennecs that have the free
run of the room.

The author's outdoor terrarium. The photographer is
standing in the land tortoises
section that is separated from
the terrapin enclosure by a
simple wooden palisade. The
surrounding wall is of sandstone blocks with overhanging coping stones. The pool
and bed for marshland plants
are cemented.

two pages later:

Amboina Box turtle (Cuora
amboinensis), the most widely distributed representative
of the genus in Southeast
Asia.

Turtles in search of food

The diet of most chelonians is mixed and depends upon seasonal availability. Land tortoises are predominantly herbivorous, water turtles predominantly carnivorous. Only a few highly specialized species or groups deviate from this basic rule. Snappers (Chelydridae), Big-headed turtles (Platysternidae), many Mud turtles (Kinosternidae) and Softshells (Trionychidae), for instance, are pure carnivores, whereas exclusively vegetarian feeders obviously do not occur. There is an interesting variation in the principal components of the diet depending upon age. The young of many water turtles that as adults are herbivorous (*Dermatemys*, some *Kachuga* species, *Hardella*, *Notochelys*, some *Chrysemys* and others) eat largely or almost exclusively animal food. A similar development is seen in certain marine turtles. In Softshelled turtles, on the other hand, a shift probably takes place within a basically animal diet. Features of the jaw suggest that certain species may eat fish as juveniles, but molluscs and crustaceans as adults.

Turtles adapt extremely well to the sudden availability of seasonal food in large quantities. For example, water turtles exploit the mass occurrence of lower crustaceans, the annual surfeit of tadpoles, the spawning season of fishes, and during this time, these animals constitute their main food. Land tortoises and terrestrial pond turtles make full use of the growth period and fruiting times of particular food plants. Curious examples of this are provided by the Painted turtles of the Antilles (*Chrysemys terrapen felis*) on Cat Island in the Bahamas, which have a great fondness for delicious "custard apples", the fruit of the West Indian tree *Anona reticulata*, or the Papuan Soft-shelled turtles (*Carettochelys insculpta*), that lie in wait for Pandanus fruits to fall into the water. In this vegetable element in their diet, they differ radically from most of the True Soft-shelled turtles (Trionychidae).

Food is located both by eye and by nose. Turtles have relatively good vision, particularly in the red range. They have no difficulty in the visual recognition of food. The nose functions even better. Turtles perceive strong-smelling food such as carrion very well, and home in on it accurately, even in cloudy water or among dense plant growth where they cannot see the target.

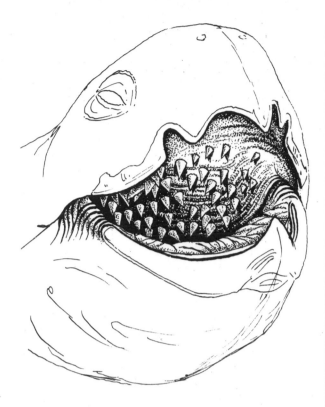

The jaw of the Leatherback (*Dermochelys coriacea*) is edged with numerous small cornified processes that are slightly movable and are directed backwards. They serve as "substitute teeth" in maintaining a hold on slippery food such as jellyfishes. (after Schumacher, 1973)

Their keen sense of smell is particularly useful to those chelonians that are coprophagous. Land tortoises readily eat the dung of herbivorous mammals since nutrients contained in it can be useful to them. Water turtles such as *Podocnemys* remain underneath the overhanging branches of trees near the bank where birds are nesting and where droppings fall regularly into the water.

Various water turtles have highly specialized methods of taking prey. Soft-shelled turtles often excel at catching fish, lunging with lightning speed using the full reach of the neck, with an accuracy that defeats even nimble fishes. Species that specialize in eating molluscs, such as *Platysternum*, *Malayemys* and others, patiently—and very successfully—seek out the hiding places of snails and mussels. Even very ponderous turtles are often clever hunters. The Matamata (*Chelus fimbriatus*) is expert at lying in ambush. Its body, and particularly the head and neck with their fringe of ragged skin, are not recognized as dangerous by fishes. They often swim near the Matamata's snout, and suddenly the turtle opens its mouth widely. The suction produced carries water and the fish along with it into its jaws. The Alligator Snapping turtle (*Macroclemys temmincki*) catches its prey in a unique and elegant way. It "angles" with a bait or lure in the form of a reddish bifurcate worm-like projection on its tongue, that it moves in irregular jerks inside the dark cavern of its open mouth. When a fish takes this apparent bait, the hooked beak closes in a flash (see p. 130). The Alligator Snapping turtle might be described as a living baited trap.

Digestion, excretion and water balance

The length of the turtle's digestive tract varies depending upon its feeding habits. That of herbivores is considerably longer than that of carnivores. Food reaches the distensible stomach after being broken up and mixed well with saliva. Turtles hold larger pieces of food with their forelimbs and bite or tear fragments from it. The morsels are further crushed in the mouth before they are swallowed. Many turtles ingest ballast materials to stimulate intestinal action or perhaps as "grindstones" for the stomach. Such material may be indigestible

parts of the food but, in particular, includes sand and small stones. Freshwater and marine turtles sometimes also ingest algae as "roughage". For the development of the large bony skeleton, turtles require a good deal of calcium which they obtain in the form of chalky soil or sand.

Among the turtle's organs of digestion, the bulky liver is particularly striking. It is of special importance in its metabolic function and for the purpose of storage. The turtle's ability to digest animal fat is notably slight. Most animal fat is secreted undigested. However, turtles are well able to produce their own bodily fats which are particularly important to the seasonally active species. Chelonians are well adapted to long periods of fasting. Land tortoises in arid regions can go without food for weeks without suffering any harm. The large species can, of course, hold out longest. Giant tortoises taken on board sailing ships as live food stores often survived for a year without food.

Food waste is generally excreted in the typical reptilian manner. An interesting feature is the excretion of the nitrogenous products of decomposi-

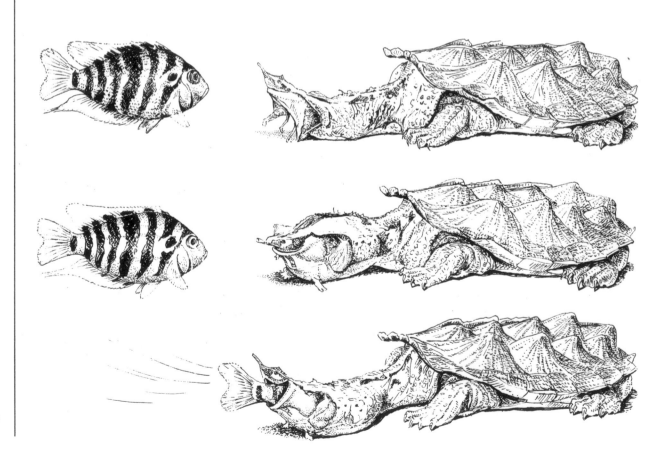

A Matamata takes its prey by suction.

tion such as result from the digestion of protein. In order to maintain the greatest economy in their water balance, land tortoises do not excrete nitrogenous waste dissolved in the urine, but re-absorb the water and excrete ammonium salt of uric acid which contains little water and is almost insoluble. This crumbly white mass is usually passed together with the faeces. Water turtles do not need to go through this physiologically demanding process and excrete urine containing soluble urea and ammonia. A particular problem closely linked with water balance arises from the loading of the organism with salt. It affects marine turtles and turtles in brackish waters. They must continually eliminate from the body excess salt that is taken in, in particular, with their food. But the kidneys of turtles, unlike those of marine mammals, are incapable of removing excess salt that is dissolved in the blood. Curiously enough, in turtles, the function has been taken over by the lachrymal glands. They have enlarged, and secrete salt in a gel-like liquid. This is why marine turtles and Diamondback terrapins *(Malaclemys terrapin)* "weep salt tears".

Heat balance

Compared with mammals and birds, the body temperature of reptiles is much more dependent upon ambient temperature. Chelonians draw a large amount of the heat they need in order to function adequately from the sun. Characteristically they do this by basking. It was thought at one time that many crepuscular and nocturnal water turtles did not bask. Now the opposite is known to be true of almost all species. Even Mud turtles *(Kinosternon)* climb up on to overhanging trees and shrubs to sunbathe. If danger threatens, they drop like stones into the water.

Sometimes the sun is sought even under extreme conditions. Painted turtles *(Chrysemys picta)* have been observed underwater enjoying the first rays of spring sunshine while ice still covered the water in which they lived. Such behaviour is undoubtedly characteristic of all water turtles of the temperate zone. To remain healthy, turtles require particular temperatures that vary from species to species. Variations of this kind can be observed in

The effect of various climatic factors on a pond turtle. Sunlight either has a direct effect or is reflected from clouds, water or large surfaces in the environment such as trees, rock walls etc. The reflection of thermal radiation is particularly effective, while the ultraviolet component of light is more often absorbed. Air or the movement of air and water—its depth and movement—are further important factors affecting the temperature balance of turtles. In basking, the turtle makes full use of the available heat by extending its limbs, by selecting the optimal angle of incidence for direct solar radiation and by giving preference to absorbent surfaces with low conductivity (dark-coloured tree trunks). Diving to a great depth causes considerable cooling. Basking by floating on the surface of slowly flowing water provides the best possible means of temperature regulation, particularly for pond turtles in tropical waters. While basking, the eyes are often kept shut to protect them from excessive ultra-violet radiation.
Since turtles have no sweat glands, they can lower the body temperature only by breathing in air or by contact with their surroundings (air, water, the ground).
(modified after Hutchison, 1979)

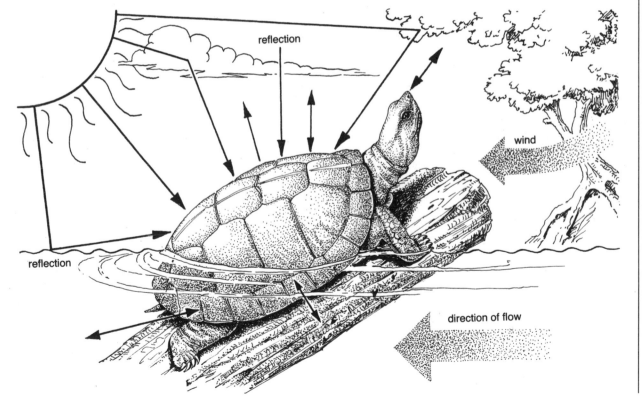

reflection

reflection

wind

direction of flow

the different degree of activity in species living in associations. There are certain temperatures peculiar to species at which a wide variety of biological processes are initiated. With an air temperature of 12 to 15°C, for instance, when other land tortoises will not even leave their sleeping quarters, the Pancake tortoise *(Malacochersus tornieri)* is already feeding. The activities of reproduction, egg and sperm formation and much more depend strictly upon temperatures that are species-characteristic. Few statistics are available in this sphere which for most species of turtle has been poorly researched.

Decline in the ambient temperature in autumn and reduction in the duration and intensity of light trigger off the physiological preparation for winter in chelonians of temperate latitudes. Food intake ceases, winter quarters are sought out. For many species, hibernation is an obligatory resting period essential for the initiation of the reproductive rhythm.

Much the same is true of turtles in tropical regions that are attuned to a strict alternation of dry and wet seasons. In contrast, the inhabitants of tropical forest regions are somewhat more independent, since their seasons are associated with only minimal changes in temperature and humidity. The considerable dependence of turtles upon the ambient temperature is further increased by their slight body mass and the poor insulation provided by the horny scutes that cover them. In this context, it might be recalled that the largest modern turtle, the Leatherback *(Dermochelys coriacea)*, is the only marine turtle that manages to penetrate relatively far into northern waters in its migrations. Its volume and metabolism make it better able to stand up to unfavourable ambient temperatures for some time. The muscles in the limbs of this "long-distance swimmer" are served by a particularly well-developed vascular system. A good deal of heat is generated during swimming and so body temperature remains high. When the turtle rests, it immediately reduces the cardiac rate in order to retard circulation and restrict heat loss. In addition, the leathery skin over an insulating layer of fatty tissue reduces considerably the amount of heat lost to the surroundings. Therefore, the American turtle expert Wayne Frair named the Leatherback with good reason a "warm-blooded turtle in cold northern waters".

Dull-witted or clever?

Highly contradictory views are held on the capacity for sensory perception and the intellectual capacities of turtles, as our chapter heading suggests.

Of the senses, smell and sight are the most important in the life of turtles. Other senses are much less well developed, particularly hearing. The most efficient sensory organ in chelonians is the olfactory apparatus consisting of the nose itself and the associated organ of Jacobson. In other reptiles, such as lizards and snakes, this hollow organ is completely separated from the nasopharyngeal cavity, and in their case, has achieved its highest degree of perfection. Both nasal cavity and the organ of Jacobson are lined with sensory epithelia which allow the perception of smell. Mucous glands keep the epithelium constantly moist. In some aquatic turtles, the external nasal openings are situated well forward at the end of a flexible snout, so the animal is able to breathe air without raising its head out of water. Soft-shelled turtles, Papuan Softshells and the curious Matamata have a snout of this kind. Aquatic turtles can also smell very well under water; they open the mouth slightly, draw in water through the nose and then immediately empty it out again through the mouth.

A sense of smell is vitally important in finding food. Particularly in cloudy water, turtles find their food almost exclusively by olfactory perception. Odorous substances contained in mucous secretions from snails, worms and other prey as well as chemical stimulants occurring in the juice of plants are perceived even in very low concentrations. Turtles respond even more readily to the olfactory stimulus coming from animals on which they prey, the smell of carrion, of fish and of the blood of creatures that have perhaps been attacked in the water by larger predators. Terrestrial tortoises also recognize many food plants and fruits by smell and are irresistably attracted by particular "delicacies"— aromatic fungi, overripe fermenting fruit, carrion and dung.

Smell is also the most important means of recognizing members of the same species and potential mates. Distinctions of this kind are facilitated by the secretion of aromatic substances that are species-characteristic and sex-specific, from glands situated particularly in the anal region. When wandering tortoises meet, the standard form of greeting is an intensive mutual sniffing with nodding head movements. Sea turtles also sniff at one another in this way, and water is clearly a much more favourable medium for the transmission of odorous substances than air.

Together with the sense of smell, vision plays an important part in the turtle's life. The eye is of typical reptilian structure, comparable with that of crocodiles and lizards, though differing from that of snakes. Externally, a pair of well-developed lids provides good protection. The chelonian upper lid is particularly large. The eye is served by two glands, the true lachrymal gland and the Harderian gland, a characteristic feature of reptiles. In marine turtles, the lachrymal gland is enormously enlarged. In addition to discharging secretions that care for the eyes, it has the function of ridding the body of excess salt taken in with food. A lachrymal duct to carry away some of the secretions into the nose and mouth cavity is absent in chelonians. Consequently the secretion of liquid from the eyes is particularly copious. This explains the origin of the legend that as they are nesting, turtles "weep with pain, or for their eggs".

The visual efficiency of chelonians is considerable in every respect. Many species are able to perceive moving objects from a great distance and all have good form perception. Turtles living amphibiously probably have the best eyesight, judging by the great distance at which they take flight from an approaching danger. But land tortoises can also see a very long way. In addition to long distance vision and a sense of form, the chelonian eye is remarkable for its degree of colour discrimination. In the red range, turtles are able to distinguish quite slight differences, and their colour sensitivity even includes part of the infra-red range. Together with the sense of smell, this well-developed colour perception is very important for finding food. Undoubtedly the overall visual efficiency of the chelonian eye is also closely associated with the turtle's remarkable sense of direction and home-finding ability.

It is often difficult to discern the turtle's ear externally. Sometimes the ear drum or tympanic membrane lies freely on the surface without any protection, although usually it is covered by an inconspicuous skin or by several small or one large scale. In its anatomical structure, it rather resembles the lizard's ear. A striking feature is the division of the middle ear (the tympanic cavity) into two compartments. The funnel-shaped outer chamber contains a cartilaginous bony rod that links the tympanic membrane directly to the small auditory ossicle,

Sensory capacity in turtles
The turtle's optical sense of orientation is based on the position of the sun and on information obtained from the surrounding terrain; the perception of food, of animals of the same species and of enemies is also visual.
The olfactory organ is used to find food that cannot be detected visually and to distinguish members of the same species and potential mates.
The seismic sense enables the turtle to perceive approaching danger, but hearing certainly has scarcely any practical importance.

157

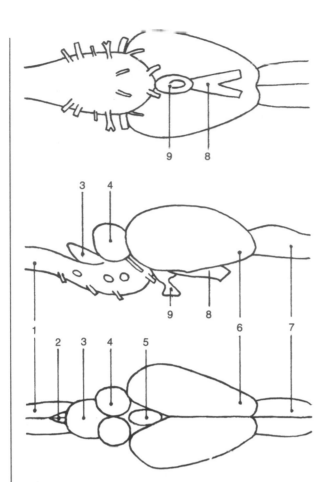

Brain of a turtle
from top to bottom, ventral view, side view and dorsal view.

Those processes not named represent the starting points of cerebral nerves.
1 medulla oblongata –
  after-brain or extension of the spinal cord
2 tela choroidea
3 cerebellum –
  hinder or lower part of brain
4 tectum opticum –
  parts of the mid-brain or mesencephalon
5 pineal organ –
  "pineal eye"
6 telencephalon –
  anterior brain
7 bulbus olfactorius –
  olfactory processes of the anterior brain
8 chiasma optica –
  intersection of the optic nerves
9 hypophysis –
  pituitary body of the brain
(after Powers and Reiner, 1979)

the columella, that leads to the inner ear. In the inner ear, the large labyrinth is a striking feature. In spite of its complicated structure, the acoustic perception of the ear is obviously very limited. Although at one time, chelonians were generally believed to be completely deaf, it has since been shown that they are well able to hear low frequencies of up to 1000 c.p.s. Their optimal range of hearing lies in the low tones between 200 and 500 c.p.s.

In this context, it might well be mentioned that turtles themselves are by no means mute. During mating, the mounted males produce calls ranging from squeaks to grunts. The females are also capable of making noises of this kind, as can be observed in the "pseudomating" of unpartnered females. Very rarely, land tortoises produce vocal sounds when they are suffering great pain. But in general, the turtle's sensitivity to pain is slight, at least on large areas of the shell. The relevant receptors occur only sparsely and are widely spaced, so that even serious injuries to the shell appear to be borne "stoically". Heat sensitivity in the skin, in-

cluding the shell area is much more highly developed. Temperature perception is, of course, vitally necessary for reptiles in which the capacity for physiological compensation is so restricted. The turtle's acute sense of temperature stands it in good stead when it is selecting a basking place or looking for a suitable egg-laying site. The combination of changes in light and heat gives the animals a certain sense of time, so the turtles that are not active at twilight sense when the time is approaching for them to withdraw to their night quarters.

Finally, one might mention the ability of chelonians to perceive ground vibrations transmitted through the ear. What role the inner ear plays in the animal's seismic sense is not clear, since so far, the function of the inner ear has been only inadequately studied.

From what has been said, it seems that tortoises and turtles do not deserve their reputation for stupidity. They are at least equal to other reptiles in intelligence. Although their sense of direction and navigational capacity represent an outstanding achievement among reptiles, it would be just as wrong to attribute to them a special "cleverness", setting them above other related groups. In addition to instinctive patterns that are inherited, the ability to learn undoubtedly also plays a part in the behaviour of chelonians. How rapidly and reliably turtles are able to learn has been shown in comparative ethology by a wide range of training experiments. People who keep tortoises as pets can often give remarkable reports of achievements of this kind. But to find out about territorial behaviour, hierarchical organization, loyalty to habitat, the use of fixed trails, individual feeding preferences or even variations in temperament in tortoises of the same species requires the patient observation of often very subtle "signs" made by these animals at all hours of the day and over a long period of time. Anyone who takes the trouble to do so will learn much of interest. And anyone who tries to observe turtles living amphibiously in the wild, will be surprised by the tremendous wariness and the rapid reactions of these animals. Just as astonishing is the speed with which tortoises and turtles that have lived only a short time in captivity become accustomed to being fed and will even pester their keepers for food. This demonstrates their ability to learn, but to call it particularly "clever" would be an exaggeration.

Finally, an examination of the chelonian brain responsible for all intellectual capacities, shows it to be very similar to the brains of other reptilian groups. Because of the importance of the sense of smell, it is not surprising that the *bulbi olfactorii* that are associated with the sense of smell are strikingly large and thick compared with those of other reptiles. In terms of relative and absolute brain size, chelonians hold a position among reptiles that shows them to be typical but respectable representatives of their class.

Sexual behaviour in turtles

The amatory passion of turtles is legendary. In Japan, turtles are considered as the symbol of the sexual drive, and the Ancient Roman authority Claudius Aelianus is able to report some remarkable facts on that subject . . .

Like most manifestations of life, sexual activity is also strongly linked to the annual rhythm in the life of chelonians. In a temperate climate, it is the arrival of spring that directly initiates the period of reproduction, in the tropics it is the rainy season.

Only a few marine turtles that spend the whole year at certain nesting beaches seem to be independent of season in this respect. But it is probably true that these animals also show distinct annual peaks in the number of individuals arriving to mate and lay eggs. Probably the "late arrivals" are only members of particular populations that have their true habitat in a different climatic zone. The process of sperm production is already completed during the preceding summer while the turtles are living under optimal conditions of feeding and temperature.

Spermatozoa are stored in an organ close to the testis, the epididymis, and the males are ready to mate immediately after hibernation when they set out to seek a partner. The sexual products in the female are also produced in the previous year. At the end of the summer, when the animals are in peak condition, growth of the follicles begins. The winter state of torpor stops the process. This interruption in growth appears to have a beneficial effect on the later maturing of the follicle.

In spring, before fertilization, the eggs have already achieved 70 to 90 % of their full size. Many females produce eggs several times over. In Painted turtles (*Chrysemys*), five to six clutches within a few weeks have been observed. Small, tropical land tortoises that lay only one or two eggs, compensate by having several (six to ten) ovulations within a year.

The search for a partner is carried out by the males. To this end, they undertake quite extensive wanderings that may lead them several kilometres from their winter quarters. Marine turtles cover the greatest distances. The females usually remain in their normal habitat. Partners are recognized initially by sight. Experiments using decoys have shown that a male ready to mate will run at any moving object of approximately the right size. But recognition of its own species and of the opposite sex follows by olfactory means, as the turtles sniff at one another. Since the nose is the most acute of the sense organs in chelonians, errors in distinguishing between species living in the same habitat are virtually excluded. Even aquatic turtles recognize one another by smell. Indeed, water is an excellent vehicle for carrying dissolved odorous substances, so that even water turtles living in mud and soil find their sexual partners without difficulty. The production of these odiferous secretions, which in the males have a strongly musky scent, takes place in the anal glands. It is to these glands that Musk turtles (*Sternotherus*) owe their common name. The scent barrier that divides species is sometimes supplemented by species-characteristic behaviour patterns. Movements typical of species or group, which are particularly distinctive in sea turtles, are a useful aid to recognition.

Jousting and courtship display

The males of many species vie with each other for the favour of the females. This is very widespread among land tortoises, but many water turtles behave in the same way. Fights between males, which are part of normal reproductive procedure, are strongly ritualized. No serious injuries are inflicted upon an opponent in these combats. Perhaps best known are the "jousting displays" between Gopher tortoises (*Gopherus*), but almost all other land tortoises also "fight" each other if they meet during the rutting season. The object is always to throw the opponent onto its back, thus eliminating it as a competitor for a fairly long time. The attacker runs at its rival, using its own body as

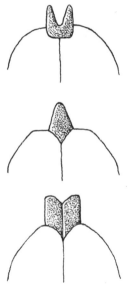

Gular spurs in some land tortoises
from top to bottom:
African Spurred tortoise
(*Geochelone sulcata*)
Madagascan tortoise
(*Asterochelys yniphora*)
Gopher tortoises (*Gopherus*)

Courtship behaviour among chelonians
In each case, the ♂ is drawn in realistic detail, the ♀ only in outline.

normal courtship in land tortoises
1 The male "greets" the ♀ with ritualized head nodding. This phase also allows for olfactory recognition of the mate.
2 The ♀ is invited to copulate by repeated ramming of her flanks. The tail of the male swells and curves, sometimes the penis is already extruded.
3 Mounting is followed by copulation. At this time, the ♂ produces squeaking noises. (after various authors, combined)

Courtship and jousting tournaments in Gopher tortoises on left: normal procedure when ♂ and ♀ meet:
1 "Greeting" by head nodding
2 Actual and feigned biting causes the ♀ to stand still, draw in the head and extend the anal region.
3 Copulation is similar to that of other land tortoises

On right: Procedure when ♂♂ meet:
4 Recognition of a rival is followed by ramming at the opponent's flanks and attempts to overturn him by leverage (a "jousting tournament").
5 As soon as one of the males is on his back, the victor makes off rapidly and attempts to mate with a ♀. (after Auffenberg and others, combined)

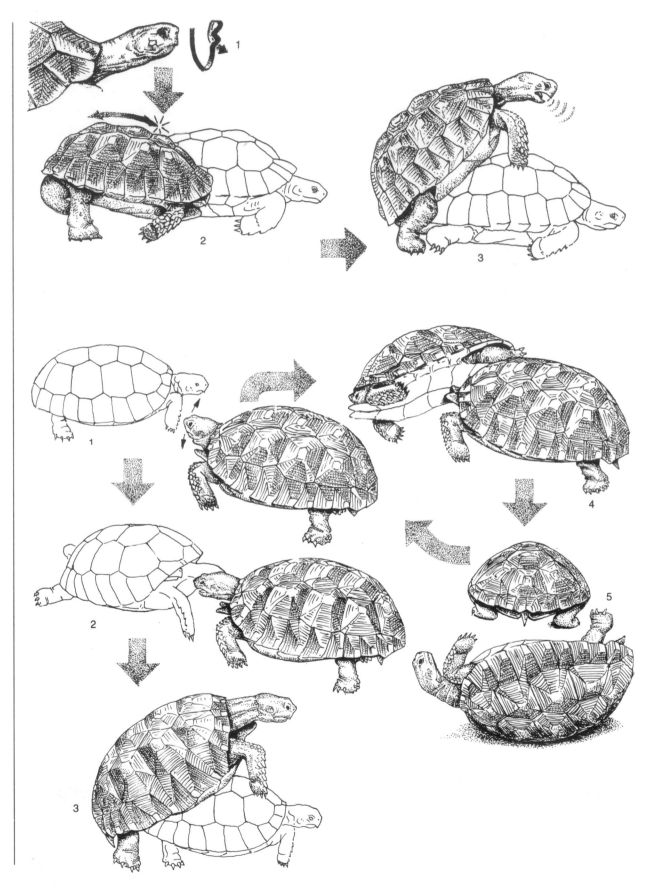

a ram to overthrow the opponent. This is most likely to succeed if the attack is launched against the opponent's flanks. But since both combattants try to use the same line of attack, the pair may circle one another several times, or when patience runs out, one may launch a frontal attack. In doing battle, Gopher tortoises make full use of the spur-like extension of the gular laminae which they use like a crowbar. The Madagascan tortoise *Asterochelys yniphora* and the South African *Chersina angulata* (the Bowsprit tortoise), the extinct Mascarene Giant tortoise, *Cylindraspis*, and to a lesser extent the Spurred tortoise *(Geochelone sulcata)* and Schweigger's Hinged tortoise *(Kinixys erosa)* have similar projecting spurs. To use them for ramming, the tortoises retract the head and approach the opponent as closely as possible. Then the body is moved slightly back and suddenly jerked forward in a powerful thrust. When the ploy succeeds, the loser has considerable difficulty getting back onto its feet.

The courtship displays of land tortoises resemble in many ways the fights between rival males. The male circles the female, bringing her to a standstill so that olfactory contact can be made. A resting female is stimulated by weaker rammings against her flanks. Finally the male bites at the fe-

male's arms, causing her to retract head and forelimbs. With the head drawn in, it is more difficult for the female to close off the cloacal region. The biting attack is the direct preliminary to copulation that follows immediately.

Rivalry and courtship can also be observed in water turtles. Rivalry between males is usually expressed by threat displays with widely gaping jaws. If this does not suffice, the rival may be bitten seriously. Sometimes fighting and injuries will follow if the defeated opponent is unable to escape. Courtship ritual is dispensed with entirely in many freshwater turtles. After olfactory recognition, the females of Mud turtles (Kinosternidae), Soft-shelled turtles (Trionychidae) and others, are often mated immediately in what seems a rapine attack.

Terrestrial and semi-aquatic Pond turtles (Emydidae) perform simple courtship rituals on land *(Pyxidea, Heosemys, Terrapene)*. Their behaviour is rather similar to the mating actions of land tortoises.

Other species mate in water after making circling movements, olfactory contact and courtship bites. American Painted turtles *(Chrysemys)* have an elaborate courtship pattern. The males swim in circles round the chosen female in open water. They try to stimulate the female to mate, using one of two

Courtship ritual in Painted turtles
The ♂ "strokes" or "taps" the head of its partner with its elongated claws to stimulate a readiness for mating.
left: In *Chrysemys concinna* and *Ch. floridana*, the "stroking" ♂ swims above its mate.
right: In *Chrysemys scripta* and *Ch. terrapen*, the "stroking" ♂ approaches its mate frontally.
(after Cagle, 1944)

Final phase of copulation in an American Box turtle *(Terrapene carolina)*.
After mounting and copulation, the ♂ frequently falls back and remains in this position for some minutes. Sometimes it is dragged along backwards by the female. Usually the ♂, still attached by the penis, remounts the ♀ after some time and concludes copulation in this position.
(after photographs by P.H. Stettler, 1982)

161

Common form of underwater courtship among pond turtles

1 The ♀ makes olfactory contact with the ♂.

2 "Greeting" in the form of ritualized head-nodding by the ♂.

3 When prepared to mate, the ♀ bites at the head of the ♂.
At this, the ♂ draws in its head, its tail swells. Spontaneous erection of the penis is possible.

4 The ♂ mounts and by biting the back of the female's neck, forces her to retract the head and extend the anal region.

5 Copulation takes place. (after Hidalgo, 1982)

Sexual behaviour in turtles

"The land-Tortoise is a most lustful creature, at least the male is; the female however mates unwillingly. And Demostratus, a member, I may add, of the Roman Senate—not that this makes him a sufficient voucher, though in my opinion he attained the summit of knowledge in matters of fishing and was an admirable expounder of his knowledge; nor should I be surprised if he had made a study of some weightier subject and had dealt with the science of the soul. — This Demostratus admits that he does not know precisely whether there is any other reason for the female declining to copulate, but he claims to vouch for the following fact.

group-specific modes of behaviour. The males of the first group of Painted turtles (Chrysemys concinna, Ch. floridana and Ch. rubriventris) swim close above their mate, tapping or "stroking" the female's head with the conspicuously long claws of the front limbs. The males of the other group (Ch. scripta, Ch. terrapen) swim frontally towards the female, stretch the forelimbs well out forwards and once again, touch either side of the female's head with rapid, vibrating movements of their elongated claws. These different patterns of approach and touching act as a barrier to misalliances between members of the two groups of species.

Sexual characteristics

Quite elementary biology lessons include the well-known and simple rule for ascertaining the sex of a turtle. The female has a level plastron while that of the male is slightly concave, enabling him the more easily to remain mounted on the female during coitus. And this basic rule does indeed make it possible to determine the sex of very many turtles, but it fails in the case of certain large groups (and curiously enough, sometimes even for apparently closely related genera).

The range of universally valid, sexually-determined differences in form can be extended somewhat. Females are usually larger and heavier than males. Disparity in size in favour of the female is particularly marked in certain Emydid turtles, for example, in Painted turtles (Chrysemys), Map turtles (Graptemys), Roofed turtles (Kachuga), while in other representatives of the same family, the difference is detectable but slight. This is true of the European Pond tortoise (Emys), the American and Old World Pond turtles (Clemmys and Mauremys), and many other genera. And in Soft-shelled turtles (fam. Trionychidae), South American Podocnemids (Podocnemis), large River turtles (Callagur, Batagur and Orlitia) and finally in Marine turtles (Cheloniidae), the females are also decidedly larger than the males. But there is often little difference in size between male and female Land tortoises (Testudinidae) and Mud turtles (Kinosternidae). For example, in Giant Land tortoises (Megalochelys and Chelonoidis), African and Asiatic Land tortoises (Geochelone), Indochinese Land tortoises (Manouria) and in dwarf genera like Homopus, Pyxis and Malacochersus, both sexes are of about equal size. Exceptions include Mediterra-

nean Spur-thighed tortoises (Testudo graeca) and Horsfield's tortoises (Agrionemys horsfieldi) in which very old females grow much larger than males. Both sexes of Snappers (Chelydridae) and Big-headed turtles (Platysternidae) also achieve the same maximum size.

Reversal of the sex-specific sizes is a rare exception. In the Hardshelled terrapin (Melanochelys trijuga), for instance, the males are conspicuously larger.

As for the shape of the shell, it has been found that in many Freshwater turtles (Emydidae) as well as others, individuals with the same length of carapace can have striking differences in carapace height. Males are often substantially flatter than females.

An important morphological character that distinguishes the sexes is the length of tail. The male usually has a longer tail than the female. An even more important feature is the distance between the hind rim of the plastron and the cloacal opening, which is considerably greater in males and shows a thickening caused there by the presence of the penis.

The males of many land tortoises have a large nail on the end of the tail, the function of which will be discussed later. In most chelonians, both sexes are similar in marking and colour. Bright colouring in the male that is characteristic of the squamata, rarely occurs. Curiously enough, modest rudiments of it can be detected in the eye colour of Box turtles (Terrapene) and European Pond tortoises (Emys orbicularis). In the males of these species, the iris is orange to reddish-brown, while that of females is yellow to yellowish-white. Brighter male colouring is shown to a discreet degree in male Spotted turtles (Clemmys guttata) whose head spots are orange in contrast to the yellowish spots of females. Slight differences in colour exist in various other Emydids (Chrysemys, Graptemys, Cuora, Kachuga) and even in Land tortoises (Manouria impressa). In a number of Snake-necked turtles of the genera Elseya and Emydura, as well as the recently discovered Fitzroy River turtle (Rheodytes leucops), the males have more intense colouration on the head, with yellow or reddish tones. Also worth noting are discrepancies in the colouration of skin-covered soft parts. The males of Sacalia bealei and Cyclemys dentata, for instance, unlike the females, have conspicuous light colouring

The female couples only when looking towards the male, and when he has satisfied his desire he goes away, while the female is quite unable to turn over again owing to the bulk of her shell and because she has been pressed into the ground. And so she is abandoned by her mate to provide a meal for other animals and especially for eagles. This then, according to Demostratus, is what the females dread, and since their desires are moderate, and they prefer life to pleasurable indulgence, the males are unable to coax them to the act. And so by some mysterious instinct the males cast an amorous spell "that brings forgetfulness of all fear".

It seems that the spells of a Tortoise in loving mood are by no means songs, like the trifles which Theocritus, the composer of sportive pastoral poems, wrote, but a mysterious herb of which Demostratus admits that neither he nor anyone else knows the name . . . . If the males hold this herb in their mouth there ensues the exact opposite to what I have described: the male becomes coy, but the female hitherto reluctant is now full of ardour and pursues him in a frenzied desire to mate; fear is banished and the females are not in the least afraid for their own safety."

(Claudius Aelianus: *On the Characteristics of Animals*. XV, 19)

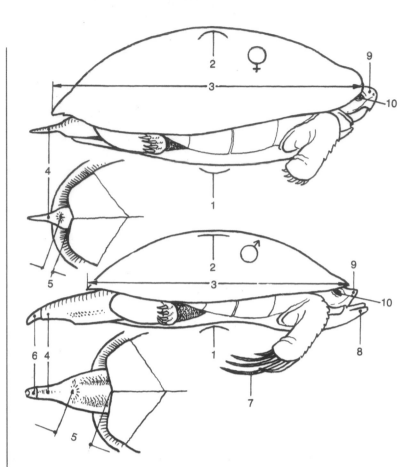
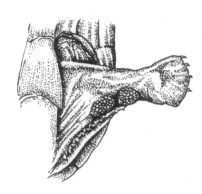

Sexual dimorphism in turtles
The diagram shows all the most important secondary sexual characteristics, although in fact, they do not all occur together in a single species.

1 Curvature of the plastron: convex in ♀, concave in ♂.

2 Curvature of the carapace: in ♀ more steeply curved and greater absolute height of shell, in ♂ flatter and absolute height of shell is less.

3 Difference in total length mostly in favour of ♀.

4 Form and length of tail: greater absolute length and thickness of tail in ♂.

5 Distance between cloaca and back edge of plastron: significantly greater in ♂ than in ♀.

6 Nail at end of tail barely suggested in ♀, large and curved in shape of a shoehorn in ♂.

7 Elongated claws on fore limbs in the ♂ of many pond turtles.

8 Gulars prolonged into ramming spurs in the ♂ of certain land tortoises.

9 Extension of the nasal region in the ♂ of certain pond turtles.

10 More intense eye colouration (colour of iris) in the ♂ of certain pond turtles.

Rough warty areas on the hind limbs of the ♂ Musk turtle (Sternotherus). The animal is shown lying on its back. The ♂ is enabled to maintain a firmer hold on the edge of the shell of the ♀ during copulation.
(after a photograph by H. W. Rudloff, 1981)

where the forelimbs join the body. The significance of this distinction is not clear.

The most striking example of the male assuming brilliant "nuptial dress" is found in the Callagur turtle (Callagur borneoensis) in Southeast Asia. The skin of the upper surface of the head turns red, the sides of the head white, the extremities bluish-grey. Even the longitudinal stripes of the carapace that are normally blackish-blue stand out with added intensity, while the ground colour of the carapace becomes much lighter.

Morphological peculiarities in males of certain species of chelonians have already been mentioned as adaptations to mating: the spurred gular laminae of Gopher tortoises and the extremely long claws of Painted turtles.

An extremely "practical" sexual characteristic is found in male Musk turtles (Sternotherus odoratus). At mating time, they develop two rough warty areas of scales on the thighs that help them to maintain a grip on the female's carapace during copulation.

The external sexual organs of male and female turtles are very similar in basic structure. The penis of chelonians, unlike that of snakes and lizards, is an unpaired organ. It arises from the ventral cloacal wall and when erect, projects backwards; in many turtles, the tail is used as a guiding organ for the penis during copulation. In certain Land tortoises (Testudo, Pyxis), this function is taken over by the nail at the end of the tail, which in the male is very large and curves in a sickel-shape. The chelonian penis is relatively large and in the case of certain freshwater turtles (Kachuga, Graptemys, Chrysemys as well as Trionyx and others), in which the male is much smaller than the female, it can be almost as long as the plastron. This is necessary for copulation to be possible at all, in view of the extremely great discrepancy in the size of the partners.

The smaller clitoris of the female differs only in size from the male penis, so that in spite of numerous general and specific sex characteristics, it is sometimes difficult even for the specialist to ascertain the sex of some species. Examples of this include the Spurred tortoise (Geochelone sulcata) and the Argentinian land tortoise (Chelonoidis chilensis).

Table 6   Number of eggs per clutch

1 egg:	*Malacochersus, Chersina, Psammobates,* (particularly *P. geometrica*), *Kinosternon angustipons*
2–4 eggs:	*Clemmys guttata, Clemmys muhlenbergi, Cuora amboinensis, Homopus* species, many species of *Kinosternon,* all species of *Sternotherus, Platysternon, Indotestudo,* other species of *Psammobates*
up to 10 eggs:	many species of *Pelusios,* all *Gopherus,* many *Graptemys, Terrapene* species, numerous small and middle-sized Emydidae
10–30 eggs:	most medium-sized and large land tortoises *Testudo, Geochelone, Chelonoidis, Asterochelys, Chelydra, Macroclemys,* larger *Chrysemys* species, species of *Chelodina* and *Emydura*
more than 50 eggs:	large *Podocnemis* and *Peltocephalus, Chelonia depressa,* large species of *Trionyx, Chitra, Pelochelys*
more than 100 eggs:	*Caretta, Chelonia, Eretmochelys, Lepidochelys*
records of 150 eggs or more:	*Dermochelys* and *Chitra*

Union of the sexes always occurs with the male mounted on the female. Freshwater and marine turtles also mate in water. The males endeavour to maintain a grip on the rim of the female's carapace with their claws, which they are better able to do when the size of the two partners is evenly balanced. Male freshwater turtles, approximately equal in size to the female, bite at their partner's neck, forcing her to retract her head and thereby open up the cloacal region. Many species of Emydids also occasionally bite at the female's neck *(Mauremys).* Soft-shelled turtles using their extremely long necks are able to bite into the front rim of the female's carapace (p. 144). If the difference in size between the partners is too great, the male may be unable to gain a hold on the female's body, and tips off backwards. Then the pair are linked together only by the very long penis, and the male is towed along behind the swimming female.

Turtles have no pair bond, and mating is entirely random. There is no social intercourse beyond the sexual act, such as can frequently be observed in the squamata (lizards, snakes). The females usually mate with several males so that fertilization of the eggs is ensured. Moreover, female turtles are capable of storing sperm and fertilizing eggs that ripen later on *(amphigonia retardata).* So far, the "record" is held by a Diamondback terrapin *(Malaclemys terrapin)* living in captivity, that laid fertile eggs four years after the last mating.

The number of eggs and the number of clutches in the course of a year fluctuates greatly. The lowest reproduction quota is shown by small species of land tortoises that produce only one or at most two mature eggs per clutch, although they lay three to six times in a year. The most prolific are marine turtles that have clutches of up to 150 eggs and which, moreover, are capable of producing 2 or 3 such clutches in a year. Further data are given in Tables 6 and 7.

Table 7   Number of clutches per year (according to information from various sources)

1 clutch:	*Clemmys* species, *Chelydra,* many *Kinosternon* species
2 clutches:	*Homopus* species, *Kinosternon* species, *Sternotherus* species, *Emys, Emydoidea*
3 clutches:	*Homopus* species, *Malacochersus,* some *Kinosternon, Batagur, Chinemys reevesi, Deirochelys, Graptemys,* many *Chrysemys, Geochelone elegans*
4 clutches:	*Chrysemys picta, Terrapene carolina, Chelonia depressa, Rhinoclemmys funerea*
5 clutches:	*Malaclemys, Chrysemys scripta, Caretta, Trionyx spiniferus Graptemys pulchra*
7 clutches:	*Geochelone pardalis*
10 clutches:	*Chelonia mydas*

Incubation temperature can affect the sex of baby turtles

In recent years, a number of herpetologists have observed distinct links between the eventual sex of the reptile embryo and the temperature at which the egg has developed. Animals in which such a link has been observed include many Pond turtles (Emydids), Marine turtles and certain representatives of the Mud and Musk turtles (Kinosternids) and Gopher turtles. If the eggs are incubated at a temperature close to either limit of the range of temperatures suitable for egg development, the resulting young will be predominantly or exclusively of the same sex. Observations have shown that eggs incubated at 25°C (that is, the lower limit of the viability range) produced a preponderance of males, while the young from eggs incubated at 31°C were mostly female. In strictly controlled experiments, it was found that only the middle third of the total incubation period is decisive for the determination of the sex of the embryos. After that time, temperature has no effect upon the animal's sex which is already fixed irreversibly. Among turtles, the effectiveness of temperature as a factor determining sex seems to vary from family to family. For example, the low incubation temperature was more reliable in its effect upon the eggs of various Emydids; it was easier to induce males than females. With Snapping turtles, the situation was reversed. The discovery of the phenomenon of temperature-controlled determination of sex is one of biology's most recent findings, whereas the genetic determination of the sex of an embryo by means of various sex chromosomes has been known about for a long time. In this context, it is interesting that in a number of *Trionyx* species and in the genus *Staurotypus*, determination of the sex of the progeny is genetically controlled and independent of temperature.

There can be no doubt that the manner of sex determination has played an important part in the evolution of turtles and in the history of their distribution. It is also an important factor in the competition between species of turtles with different reproductive patterns living in similar ecological conditions. Where sex determination is dependent upon temperature, long-term climatic changes can affect the population structures of turtle societies and even destroy reproductive potential. Extinction of the species in this part of its range is the result. To a limited extent, the turtles can themselves counter these effects of temperature by their selection of nesting sites. This may also explain their ability to live in areas where conditions represent the extreme limits of feasible existence.

Table 8 Observed incubation periods under natural conditions

(the occurrence of the same species in different categories illustrates the dependence of incubation upon geographical situation)

Minimum time recorded:	
30 days:	*Trionyx sinensis*
average times:	
50 days:	*Chelonia mydas, Caretta, Podocnemis expansa*
60 days:	*Emydura macquarrii, Clemmys insculpta, Malaclemys, Terrapene carolina, Chrysemys scripta, Melanochelys trijuga*
90 days:	*Podocnemis unifilis, Chelydra serpentina, Emys orbicularis, Graptemys, Chrysemys picta, Chrysemys scripta, Terrapene carolina*
150 days:	*Chelodina longicollis, Kinosternon leucostomum, Terrapene carolina, Gopherus, Chelonoidis elephantopus, Pseudemydura*
250 days:	*Chelodina expansa, Chersina, Homopus, Geochelone pardalis*
360 – 420 days:	*Chersina, Geochelone pardalis, Chelodina expansa*
maximum time recorded:	
540 days:	*Geochelone pardalis*

The eggs are spherical (in marine turtles) to cylindrical (in certain emydid turtles), with a parchment-like shell (still flexible) or hard-shelled. The soft-shelled eggs are predominantly laid by marine turtles and some river turtles, that is, by animals that produce immense numbers of eggs, while the smaller clutches of the other species have hard shells. Land tortoises in arid regions with very long incubation periods for the eggs (see Table 8), lay those eggs with the hardest shells. While the number of eggs clearly depends upon the size of the particular species of turtle and fluctuates greatly, egg size is relatively constant. Dimensions of the individual egg are determined by a minimum requirement of food and liquid reserves and space for the embryo. So the only alternative for the smaller species is to reduce the number of eggs to a single one, while the giant forms make use of their advantage in size by producing large numbers of eggs. Thus reproductive evolution in the various turtles is uniformly set at a relatively low level. Absolute egg dimensions stand at a minimum of 20 mm in length, a maximum of 76 mm in length. The absolutely largest eggs have been found to belong to *Rhinoclemmys funerea*, a medium-sized species (carapace length about 250 mm). Giant forms such as Galapagos tortoises *(Chelonoidis elephantopus)* and Batagur turtles *(Batagur baska)* have eggs "only" 70 mm in length. The relatively smallest eggs (round eggs 20 mm in diameter) are those of the medium-sized Soft-shelled turtles *(Trionyx)*, that have a carapace length of 250 to 400 mm. On the other hand, the diminutive Boulenger's tortoise *(Homopus boulengeri)*, with a carapace length of 110 mm, lays a cylindrical egg 39 mm in length. In relative terms, it must be the largest chelonian egg.

Egg laying in all chelonians follows the pattern already familiar from the biology of marine turtles. Excavation of the egg chamber is very difficult for tortoises in dry regions. Very many tortoises possess their own bodily reserves of water in the anal sacs. These are paired, bladder-like membranous pouches opening into the cloaca. In the West African Hinged tortoise *(Kinixys belliana)*, the anal sacs are so large that they can fill half the body cavity. Those of *Emys, Mauremys* and some other Emydids are also quite large. As they are constructing the egg chamber, they empty out the water in small quantities or all at once, to soften the ground for digging. Once the eggs are laid, interest in the offspring is completely lost by all turtles. As far as brood care goes, chelonians once more reveal themselves as very primitive reptiles.

The ages of a turtle

From embryo to hatchling

The life of every turtle starts in the egg. The embryo's chance of development and the length of the incubation period depend upon the microclimatic conditions at the egg-laying site. One vital factor is temperature. In addition, air humidity and the dampness of the substratum also play an important part. Nevertheless, turtle eggs belonging to one and the same species have been found to develop successfully within a relatively broad range of conditions and durations. A remarkable feature in certain species is the often extraordinarily long time the eggs take to develop. Long incubation periods of this kind have been observed particularly in land tortoises of arid regions. The dry periods of several months in the tropical "winter" probably also represent resting phases in embryonic development. Table 8 shows the incubation periods for various species of turtles.

The first active event in the life of a turtle is its emergence from the egg. Once it is sufficiently mature to hatch, it attempts to break the shell of the egg. At the tip of the snout, on the premaxillary bone of the upper jaw, is a horny epidermal thickening known as the egg caruncle. Other reptiles such as snakes and lizards have a sharp-edged egg-tooth in this position that they use to slit open the parchment-like shell of the egg. But here the main work of breaking through the shell is probably carried out by the fore limbs in conjunction with stretching movements made by the baby turtle in the egg. Hatching may take several hours or even days. The young turtle interpolates frequent and quite long intervals for rest. After emerging from the egg, it stretches out its body. Now no longer in the curved embryonic position, it is 10 to 25 per cent longer than the egg from which it hatched. The shape of the carapace is linked with this irreversible stretching of the spine. An umbilical scar is distinctly visible on the plastron. If the process of hatching was a rapid one, the umbilical cord and even a pea- or bean-sized remnant of yoke from the yoke sac may still be attached. The umbilical cord dries off within a few hours. All young turtles are fairly similar in form. But the hatchlings of land tortoises are already higher-backed than baby water turtles. In outline, they can be longish-oval or almost circular. The carapace of all hatchlings is still

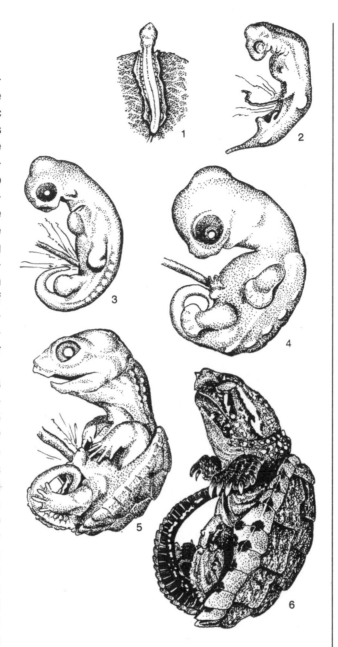

Embryonic development of the Snapping turtle *(Chelydra serpentina)*.

1 Back view of embryo after 20 days
2 Side view after 30 days
3 Side view after 6 weeks
4 Side view after 8 weeks
The shell is already recognizable, no fingers or toes have yet developed on the limbs.
5 Side view after 12 weeks
The shell already shows division into shields; fingers and toes have formed. Pigmentation is beginning to develop.
6 Side view after 19 weeks
Fully pigmented baby turtle ready to hatch. The egg caruncle clearly visible on upper jaw.
(after Yntema, 1968)

very elastic and provides little protection. Nevertheless fundamental features typical of group and species can already be detected in it.

The arrangement of the horny plates is already determined unalterably in the individual. Right from the start, hatchlings always retract their head either in a vertical or a horizontal plane. And even as babies, the Cryptodires with "heads that are too large", such as Big-headed turtles, Snappers or Marine turtles are unable to draw the head into the shell. Thus the hatchlings are in essence miniature versions of their own species. In a few species,

A European pond turtle *(Emys orbicularis)* hatching. (after photographs by W. Leuck, 1982)

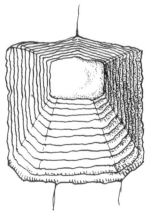

Horny scutes in the carapace of a turtle with concentric "growth rings" round the central area, the areola. The development of growth rings and grooves corresponds exactly to the process described for the plastron.

however, the young differ in appearance from the adults rather more sharply. Young Pancake tortoises *(Malacochersus tornieri)*, for example, are not flat, but have a normally curved, typical land tortoise's carapace. The flattening and reduction in the bony mass of the shell only happens later on. But it is the young Leathery turtles *(Dermochelys coriacea)* that differ most strikingly from their parents. Their shell has a distinct mosaic-like structure, a remnant of the secondary osteodermal shell that we are already familiar with from the evolution of these animals. Also noteworthy are the remains of individual plates at the front of the carapace that can be distinguished clearly in the young of the New Guinea Plateless turtle *(Carettochelys insculpta)*. They are also evidence of the evolutionary history of Soft-shelled turtles. Very rarely, twins are produced from a turtle's egg. Usually they are too small to be able to survive. Siamese twins, very extensively linked together have been found repeatedly. An abnormality of this kind, with two heads, four fore limbs and only one tail and two hind limbs was found in Tadzhikistan in October 1975. It was a Horsfield's tortoise *(Agrionemys horsfieldi)*. The creature lived for a few months, but like all animals with such extensive malformation, died while still a juvenile. It is now in the Zoological Museum in Kiev as a prepared specimen.

Colour anomalies are also observed occasionally in various species. Animals with partial or complete absence of pigmentation are particularly conspicuous. Partial or total albinism is found most frequently in Soft-shelled turtles (genus *Trionyx*), but has also been observed in Painted turtles (genus *Chrysemys*). The laboratory breeding programme for Galapagos Giant tortoises in the Darwin Station has also produced some albinos. In the wild, these individuals are unlikely to survive, but in a terrarium they often live for a long time.

The second major achievement in the life of a turtle is its independent action of digging its way out of the egg chamber. Since hatching and emergence from the nest require so much energy, the exertion frequently proves too much for the weakest animals. Either they die while still in the egg or never get out of the egg chamber. The successful hatchlings dig their way out of the ground and follow the paths laid down by their genetically fixed programme. Water and marine turtles make for water as fast as they can, while land tortoises seek out a habitat in terrain with good cover.

Growth

During the life of many turtles, body shape changes in the course of growth. Species that are naturally small are less affected than giant forms. An important factor in the normal growth of the bony shell is calcium metabolism. To develop such large quantities of bone, sufficient calcium must be present in the diet, or the turtles compensate by ingesting decayed animal bones, snail shells, egg shells or disintegrating limestone rock. Vitamin D is necessary for the conversion of the calcium, and it, in its turn, has to be activated to D3 by ultraviolet light. Disturbance of this complicated interaction can be brought about even by an excess of the vitamin. But in all cases, whether as a result of lack or excess of Vitamin D, or else of calcium deficiency, the result is rachitic shell deformities and softening of the shell. If the weakness is overcome and the bone hardens, the animal may remain grotesquely crippled. Tortoise and turtle owners are only too familiar with this difficult aspect of caring for young

Changes of form and marking during a turtle's lifetime

a) Bell's Eastern Hinged tortoise *(Kinixys belliana)*
The young have not yet developed the transverse hinge on the dorsal carapace. The shell is still smoothly curved, the carapacial shields have circular markings, which in old age, break up into a radiating pattern or give way to a complete absence of markings.

b) Spined terrapin *(Heosemys spinosa)*
The hatchlings are almost perfectly circular with curiously extended marginals and a clearly defined dorsal keel. The adult gradually assumes an elongated form. The protuberant spines on the marginals remain distinct only in the posterior part of the carapace. The dorsal keel is also reduced. Associated with this development is a marked loss of intensity in the juvenile coloration which fades to a brownish monotone.

c) Margined tortoise *(Testudo marginata)*
The young animal has an evenly curved carapace. The carapacial shields have dark marking towards the edges. Only the adult animals develop the species-characteristic spreading of the posterior rim of the marginals and the contraction of the shell at the middle of the body. In very elderly animals there is a distinct tendency to darkening (melanism).

169

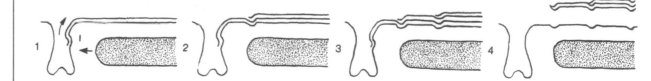

Growth of epidermal laminae and ecdysis in turtles
Phases of growth in the plastron of a Painted turtle *(Chrysemys)*. The turtle is lying on its back.
1 The bone is shaded dark, the horny layer indicated as a line. Arrows show the direction of growth. To the left of the bone there is a furrow between the horny scutes. The first groove in the horny scute lies in the furrow. It is pushed to the right.
2 The groove has moved its position, a second horny layer raises the first ones.
3 A second groove has become visible, at the same time, a third horny layer has formed beneath it and thickened the two older ones.
4 By a process of skin-casting, which occurs on the shell of only a few species of emydid turtles, the fused horny layers are cast together as a single plate. Underneath, a new horny layer forms, taking the shape of the grooves. In most turtles, instead of the skin being cast, new horny layers are continually formed, but they are thicker only at the outer edges (the growth rings). They are retained throughout life. The grooves, on the other hand, may become appreciably flatter and less conspicuous with growth.
(after Moll and Legler, 1971)

animals. But deformed turtles found in the wild show that trouble of this kind can also arise under natural conditions. Growth of the bony shell means that the covering horny plates must also grow. The laminae grow outwards from an originally central field, the areola. The surface of the areola is grainy in juveniles, but becomes smooth with increasing age. At every phase of growth, bulging growth bands are added round the areola. Their width varies, so that the rings always lie concentrically round the areola. In the early years of life, provided they are still distinct, the "growth rings" make it possible to count the phases of growth. If they are used as a guide to the animal's age, it must be remembered that two or three phases of growth may occur in a single year. So assessment of age is always approximate. As the animal gets older, the concentric rings often disappear completely and the shell becomes quite smooth or takes on new structures. When Painted turtles *(Chrysemys)* get old, they often develop longitudinal furrows that extend across the boundaries of the carapacial laminae, giving the shell surface the appearance of a washboard. Skin casting in chelonians can be observed only on neck and limbs. Regular sloughing of skin from individual horny scutes is normal only in a few Pond terrapins such as *Chrysemys* and *Cuora* and in certain Side-necked turtles such as *Emydura*, *Chelodina* and *Elseya*. In many turtles, the attainment of adulthood is associated with remarkable changes in form. The development of secondary sexual characteristics accounts for a certain number of these changes, but others are not specifically sex-linked. As the animals get older, they often lose keels and ridges on the shell. Serrations on the carapace typical of young turtles are frequently progressively smoothed out as they get older (e.g. *Heosemys*, *Rhinoclemmys*, *Melanochelys* and others). In the same way, the streamlined, boat-shaped shell of large River turtles *(Batagur*, *Callagur*, *Orlitia*, *Dermatemys*, *Podocnemis* and others) is also the result of a long period of growth

during which the form changes. Striking alterations occur in the shells of many land tortoises. Hinged tortoises (genus *Kinixys*) do not develop the hinge on the carapace until late in life. And the movable plastral lobes in many *Pyxis* species and in females of *Testudo graeca* become clearly apparent only in old age. In many land tortoises, the splaying of the rear marginals into a shape like the brim of a hat also develops very late. A well-known example is provided by the Margined tortoise *(Testudo marginata)* that gets its name from this rim on the carapace. The young have completely smooth edges. Very elderly specimens of Hermann's tortoise and the Iberian tortoise *(Testudo hermanni* and *Testudo graeca)* also develop these wavy carapace rims. In old Spurred tortoises *(Geochelone sulcata)* and a number of species of *Psammobates*, the marginals even curl upwards. Phenomena of this kind are typical of changes linked with ageing in chelonians. They take the place of a growth in length, which slows down progressively after maturity is reached and finally stops completely. But since the turtle grows throughout its life, misshaping of this kind is caused. The saddle-back shell of elderly Giant tortoises in which the anterior part of the carapace grows upwards, is a further example of this phenomenon. Closely linked with the change in form is a change in colour and marking. Juveniles are usually much more clearly marked and have more vivid colour contrasts. In old turtles, the markings often disappear, the colours fade or darken. Certain Emydid turtles in particular tend to darken, indeed, in many species of Painted turtles the process is described as senile melanism. But other Emydids such as Temple turtles *(Hieremys annandalei)* also turn almost black in old age. Other striking changes in colouration occur in the course of the life of, for instance, the Malayan Pond turtle, *Notochelys platynota*, and other species. Sexual maturity, or at least the minimum size necessary for it, is achieved slowly and quite late by turtles. The smallest species reach the age of fertility most rapidly. They may become sexually active at five years of age. Giant forms such as marine turtles and large land tortoises take some 15 to 25 years to reach sexual maturity. In many species or perhaps only particular populations, the turtles are believed to be as old as 50 years of age before they are capable of reproduction. But these wide divergences in the duration of maturation have little effect on reproductive rates. The "precocious" dwarf species produce very few eggs, often only one, whereas the "late-maturing" giants produce correspondingly large numbers of eggs per clutch. The proverbially great longevity of chelonians is linked to their slow individual development. Here again, there is a correlation between absolute size of a species and the length of time it lives. Small species have a life span of about 40 to 60 years only.

But even medium-sized species such as European Land tortoises of the genus *Testudo* can live to be 120 years of age. There are well-known examples of even smaller Box turtles *(Terrapene carolina)* reaching "Biblical" age. The maximum recorded age of over 150 years for Giant tortoises may not represent the maximum age potential of these animals. Various workers have suggested that they are certainly capable of living for 200 years. The high life expectancy of single individuals can make it possible for particular species to be saved from extinction by a programme of controlled breeding in captivity, such as has been carried out successfully on the Galapagos Islands with individuals that were the last remaining specimens of many populations.

Diseases and parasites

In spite of their proverbial longevity and tenacity of life, turtles can fall ill. They are badly affected by viruses, bacteria, protozoa, skin fungi, a wide variety of worms and insects, they can suffer intestinal upsets and catch colds. Their remarkable capacity for healing when wounded is well-known. If the shell is damaged following an attack by an enemy, a forest fire or any other accident, the bone and skin tissue show considerable capacity for regeneration. The process of regeneration can take place successfully even with up to 50 per cent of the carapace destroyed. The fact that the bony shell is originally derived from the skin helps to explain this phenomenon.

Chelonians suffer badly from parasites. Land tortoises are usually host to large numbers of ticks. When these blood-feeding arachnids have sucked their fill, their abdomen can swell to the size of a bean. Only then do they relinquish their hold on the host. If they are torn off before that, the mouth parts may remain in the skin causing protracted suppuration. Hermatozoa, very small, blood-feeding parasites that are also arachnids, are very mobile and usually attack their host only at night. Not only do blood-feeders damage the host by drawing off blood, but they also transmit pathogenic micro-organisms. Familiar among them are the unicellular haemogregarine and haemoproteus that destroy the red corpuscles of the host. In addition to blood parasites (haematozoa), large numbers of intestinal parasites live inside chelonians. This is really not surprising in view of the chelonian habit of feed-

External parasites (ectoparasites) and organic growths on chelonians
The diagram illustrates the great variety of ectoparasites and organic growths commonly found in turtles, although all are unlikely to occur simultaneously in a single species.
1 Algae and mosses, harmless organic growths found on various freshwater and marine turtles.
2 Fungoid and bacterial cultures between the scutes, in the junctures or under damaged plates.
3 Flatworms (Turbellariae), represented by the genus *Temnocephala*, reside harmlessly in the skin folds of various water turtles.
4 Cloacarides are host-specific, highly specialized mites living in the cloaca of water turtles.
5 Leeches frequently live parasitically on water turtles, and in the tropics, also on land tortoises.
6 Ticks (Ixodidae) are very common on the soft parts of tortoises. Blood suckers.
7 Mosquitoes sometimes occur on tortoises as highly specialized blood-sucking organisms; in North America, for example, mosquitoes of the genus *Aedes*. All blood-suckers transfer virus infections, parasites, unicellularia.
8 Mites (Acari)
9 Balanids (Chelonibia)

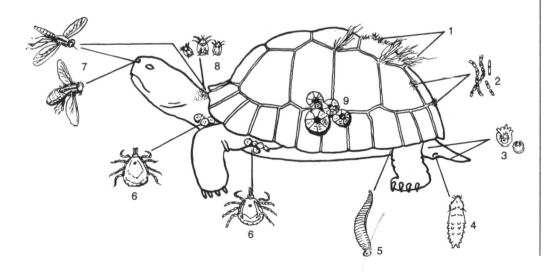

Internal parasites (endoparasites) in turtles.

Again, a wide variety of potential parasites is shown, but they are unlikely to occur all together. A characteristic of many endoparasites is their complicated development through various larval forms and intermediate hosts. Turtles serve such parasites both as ultimate and intermediate hosts.

Organs most likely to be affected by parasites:

A mouth and nasal cavities
B blood
C oesophagus
D stomach
E lung
F blood vessels
G kidney
H liver
I urinary bladder
J intestines, particularly rectum

Principal endoparasites:

1 Single-celled blood parasites (Haemogregarinae) in the erythrocytes.
2 Flatworms (Trematoda) live in a wide variety of organs.
3 Hookworms (Monogenea) live in the bladder, in the rectum and the buccal and nasal cavities.
4 Amoebae are unicellular intestinal parasites, frequently pathogenic (causative agents of amoebic dysentry and other diseases).
5 Tapeworms (Cestode)
6 Thorn-headed worms (Acanthocephala)
7 Roundworms or threadworms (Nematoda)
8 Liver fluke, belonging to the order Trematodes.

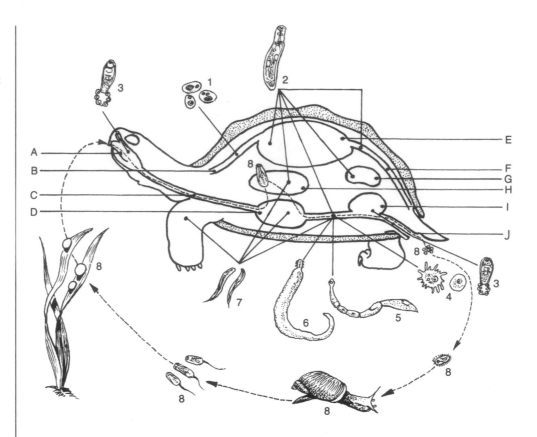

ing on carrion and dung as well as consuming ground-dwelling and germ-infested arthropods, molluscs and worms. Land tortoises and freshwater turtles are usually all carriers of large numbers of dangerous intestinal bacilli such as salmonella and arizona bacteria and amoebae. But in most cases, they are probably strains of these agents that are highly specialized to live inside the body of poikilothermic animals. There is therefore little likelihood that the diseases can be transmitted to mammals or from animal to man. The subject of the parasitic fauna of wormlike intestinal parasites that are found in chelonians is a complicated one. As many as 14 different species of parasitic flatworms (Trematoda) and threadworms (Nematoda) have been found in a single population of Painted turtles (Chrysemys picta) in the USA. In addition, tapeworms and hookworms live in the turtle's intestines. Among the trematode worms, the various species of liver fluke are particularly dangerous for their hosts. They penetrate the liver, lung and spleen, causing serious damage to these organs. But in the course of their development, liver flukes go through a complicated change of host and alternation of generations, so that direct transmission is ruled out. Snails serve as intermediate host. These, of course, are a favourite item of food for all chelonians, so that under natural conditions, infestation with liver fluke is almost the norm. Apart from their occurrence as parasites in the digestive tract, nematodes also penetrate the brain, liver and heart of turtles. They function without intermediate hosts and because of their immense excretion of eggs, can be transmitted from turtle to turtle.

There are certain other noteworthy peculiarities among parasites that affect chelonians. In North America, for example, there is a species of mosquito that prefers to draw blood from various genera of Emydid turtles (Emydidae). As it sucks, it transmits certain viruses which in their turn are specialized to live in turtle blood. But the most remarkable parasites on turtles are probably the cloacal mites that have been found in Snapping turtles (Chelydra serpentina) and Painted turtles (genus Chrysemys). They are highly host-specific, living in the folds of the mucous-membrane lining of the cloacal region that is rich in blood vessels, and from which they obtain blood. They are undoubtedly transmitted only by sexual intercourse, so that chelonians have their own "venereal disease".

To sum up, it must be emphasized that in spite of the fact that the turtle's body houses a large number of parasites, there is virtually no danger of the transmission of disease to humans and animal pets. Nevertheless, due consideration should be given to hygienic measures, both in the interest of the creatures themselves as well as of those handling them in captivity. For reasons of hygiene alone, if not from much more serious considerations, turtles and tortoises should not become playthings for children. The conscientious turtle keeper can do much to prevent disease and infestation in the animals in his care, making use of the wide range of preparations that are available for this purpose.

Turtles as pets and as "guinea pigs"

Although an encouraging number of terrarium enthusiasts are nowadays devoting themselves to discovering more about living conditions in the terrarium and constantly achieving breeding successes with new species, while at the same time a number of major zoos are working with equal commitment on programmes of turtle breeding, much still remains to be done. Experimental biologists carrying out research into a wide range of biological processes in recent years have found turtles to be suitably robust animals to work with, and have also played a considerable part in the planned breeding of turtles. In addition to their use in the testing of pharmacological products, turtles frequently serve as "model" animals in research into processes of circulation and metabolism, immune reactions, neurological and psychological manifestations. They have been employed successfully in space research. In the Soviet interplanetary probe No. 5 in October 1968, a number of Horsfield's tortoises *(Agrionemys horsfieldi)*, as the most highly developed organisms in a "mixed"

crew of astronauts that otherwise consisted of insects and micro-organisms, flew for the first time with cosmic speed beyond the orbit of this planet, and were the first vertebrates to circle the moon.

The ingenuous animal lover often sees only those animals that are sacrificed to science. And certainly, the number of animals "expended" in laboratory tests is often unjustifiably high, and the aims of the research could sometimes be achieved just as well with fewer victims. But even here, the high cost of animals has already set a reasonable limit to their use. In addition, it should be borne in mind that the scientists themselves did much to promote the breeding of laboratory animals. In the USA, for example, physiologists and anatomical scientists studying the embryogenesis of turtles were the first to achieve success in the continuous breeding of Snapping turtles and Soft-shelled turtles in the laboratory. The Painted turtle farms that today supply almost all those animals bought as pets, were originally set up in response to the demand for Painted turtles as laboratory animals. In future, only efficiently run, large-scale breeding establishments will be able to produce at an acceptable cost the numbers of animals that are required to reinforce endangered populations in the wild. Undoubtedly it will again be the initial breeding successes achieved by enthusiastic individual turtle keepers that provide the groundwork of experience on which farm breeding will be based. But an exact formulation of the conditions under which it will be possible to implement measures of support for threatened species can be provided only by ecologists and scientists working in the field. Only the cooperation of all, from scientist through turtle keeper and enthusiast to the last man acting with an awareness of nature, can ensure that turtles, as the most ancient of recent land vertebrates will, after millions of years of existence, be enabled to go forward unimpaired into the third millennium of an urbanized world . . .

Every day, the motif of the turtle is to be found in a wide variety of places, as the trademark of various firms, on revenue stamps and labels, in catalogues, on posters, coats of arms and even on coins. But nowhere do turtles occur in such large numbers as on postage stamps.

They first appeared in 1932 on stamps issued by the Cayman Islands Post Office: the Green turtle (Chelonia mydas) and the Hawksbill turtle (Eretmochelys imbricata). From that time on, turtles were a popular motif repeatedly used on the stamps of various countries. And which turtles were primarily depicted on postage stamps? Marine turtles (Cheloniidae) with about 45 issues hold the lead, and their only possible rival would be Seychelles Giant tortoises (Megalochelys gigantea). These endemic tortoises have appeared on 18 stamps issued by the Seychelles Post Office since 1938, some of which consisted of sets of different values. Many countries in the tropics, on whose shores there are well-known nesting grounds for marine turtles, vie with one another in the quantity and quality of such stamps. There is a noticeable predominance of those sea turtles that are commercially useful. Green turtles with more than 25 issues and Hawksbills with 15 far outnumber any others. The Loggerhead (Caretta caretta), that provides no marketable tortoiseshell or meat, has drawn the attention only of Ascension and Jugoslavia, while the Ridleys (Lepidochelys) have been ignored completely. The Italian Post Office takes credit for the first appearance of the giant Leatherback (Dermochelys coriacea) on a postage stamp. Under the slogan "il mare deve vivere", this issue called for conservation of the ocean—still a matter of urgent topical concern, with a particularly successful graphic design. In 1966, the Leathery turtle also provided the motif for a special date stamp for the Berlin Post Office. This was on the occasion of

Turtles for philatelists and numismatists

リュウキュウヤマガメ

自然保護シリーズ 第9集

Nature Preservation Series 9

First Day of Issue   March 25, 1976

First-day cover of a Japanese nature conservation series, the 9th issue of which is dedicated to the Spengler's turtle (Geoemyda spengleri) (Collection of Losansky, Frankfurt/Oder)

a touring exhibition mounted by the *Meereskundliches Museum Stralsund* (Stralsund Museum of Oceanography) that presented to an astonished Berlin public a museum specimen of a Leatherback colossus. The animal had strayed into the Baltic and finally died in the Rostock Zoo.

Remaining with marine turtle stamps, there is an interesting souvenir sheet that was issued by the Maldive Islands. The background shows the entire coastal landscape with a broad sandy beach crossed by the unmistakeable track of a Green turtle. Some Cayman Island stamps, first issued in 1950 and again in revised form in 1971, are also very informative. They show farms where baby marine turtles are reared. From 1932 onwards, the Cayman Islands Postal authorities issued some twenty stamps featuring marine turtles.

But in other tropical coastal countries, the issue of a sea turtle stamp was something of a rarity, although those that appeared introduced original touches. The Tonga Islands tried their hand, with a Nature Conservation issue that was produced as a foil stamp, and in 1966, the Democratic Republic of Vietnam made an unintentionally noteable contribution in the form of a stamp depicting a Loggerhead that was described as a Leatherback. Cuba's postal contribution must appear regrettable to anyone supporting nature conservation. In 1967, the "World Championship in Underwater Hunting" took place there—in itself a questionable undertaking. To celebrate the occasion, a special stamp was issued which depicts the harpooning of turtles as a sport of the upper classes.

Returning to a much more admirable cause, there are many creditable and attractive issues devoted to animal and nature conservation. Outstanding is the Japanese stamp issued in 1976, depicting the biologically interesting *Geoemyda spengleri*. A matching special date stamp and first day cover make up the set, which effectively promotes the cause of nature conservation. Other countries also devote special issues to endangered species of turtles with an appeal for their conservation: Kenya for its Pancake tortoise *(Malacochersus tornieri)*, Brazil for the critically endangered Arrau turtle *(Podocnemis expansa)*, Papua New Guinea for its curious endemic Plateless River turtle *(Carettochelys insculpta)*, and finally the German Democratic Republic, Albania, Jugoslavia and Poland for the conservation of the European Pond turtle *(Emys orbicularis)*, in their own territory. Stamps from Albania, Romania and Spain featuring European Land tortoises *(Testudo)*, and those issued by Fernando Po and Mali with the impressive Spurred tortoise *(Geochelone sulcata)* and by Togo with a Schweigger's Hinged tortoise *(Kinixys erosa)* also serve this purpose. The most recent link in this chain is a stamp issued by Madagascar on which two highly endangered species of valuable and beautiful Land tortoises are depicted: the large Radiated tortoise *(Asterochelys radiata)*, generally considered the most splendid of all tortoises, and beside it, the diminutive Spider tortoise *(Pyxis arachnoides)*. Only the first species is named. It is impossible to say whether the artist mistakenly took the small tortoise for the "baby" beside its "mother", or whether part of the wording was simply omitted. And the Afghan Post Office was rather unfortunate when its endemic four-toed Horsfield's tortoise *(Agrionemys horsfieldi)* was drawn with five claws on its right front foot.

A selection of postage stamps with turtle motifs (Collection of Losansky, Frankfurt/Oder).

The rich cultural history of turtles is also reflected in stamps. A classic example is the Australian 20 cent stamp showing a drawing carved on the back of a turtle. Drawings cut into the bark of trees are traditional examples of the culture of Australian aborigines. A Korean stamp depicts a turtle carrying a stone tablet or stele as part of Buddhist cultic ritual, once again as a typical illustration of that country's deep-rooted ancient culture. Togo presents a wooden toy tortoise, while New Caledonia makes its contribution to the campaign "Philately and School" with its own original and humorous version of La Fontaine's fable of the race between the Hare and the Tortoise. It would be possible to extend considerably the list of such examples showing the use of the turtle motif and the interaction of cultural relationships. One final glance at postage stamps shows the Christmas stamp issued by the Seychelles in 1971, reproducing a child's drawing of the arrival of Santa Claus riding on a Giant tortoise.

Turtles on coins are found more rarely. But the oldest turtle coins are so famous that every numismatist who has had anything to do with Graeco-Roman coinage is familiar with them. They are silver pieces from the Greek island state of Aegina from the 6th to 4th century B.C. At that time, Aegina was an important commercial power. The struggle for economic and political leadership was concluded in 457 with the conquest of Aegina by the Athenians. The coins from Aegina may be seen as reflecting the historical events in the form of a cleverly worked out code. A marine turtle is depicted on the obverse of the small irregularly-shaped coins. At the front, the powerful paddle-

Ancient silver coins from
Aegina, Greece
above left:
drachma with a land tortoise
(∅ 17–19 mm)
about 350–320 B.C.
above centre:
triobol (three obol piece) with
a land tortoise
(∅ 12 mm)
about 350–338 B.C.
above right: stater with a land
tortoise
(∅ 18–20 mm)
about 350–338 B.C.
below left:
stater with a sea turtle
(∅ 19.5 mm)
about 470 B.C.
below centre:
same stater, reverse showing
quadratum incusum
below right:
obol with sea turtle
(∅ 9 mm)
about 470 B.C.
Aegina's coins were struck
from a spherical blank of defined weight. The lower die
stamped the pictorial motif on
the obverse, the upper die the
mint mark (quadratum incusum) on the reverse side of
the coin.
Aegina's currency consisted
of the following coins:
one stater or didrachma =
two drachmas
one drachma = two triobols
or six obols
one obol = two hemi-obols
(Staatliche Kunstsammlun-
gen Dresden, Münzkabinett)

like flippers and the large head can be distinguished clearly. The heart-shaped carapace is highly stylized. Of the carapacial shields, all the central laminae and sometimes also the front marginals are picked out as dotted lines in certain of the mintings. But often the shell lacks all structural details. It is therefore no longer possible to determine which species of marine turtle served as the model. But the artistic generalization is strikingly well done, and the creatures are unmistakably marine turtles. In the 5th century B.C. the picture on the coin changes suddenly. It is now land tortoises that feature on the obverse. This change coincides with the occupation of the city by Attic troops and the end of Aegina's hegemony of the sea. The silver coins showing tortoises, struck in different sizes and denominations, were in no day inferior to earlier mintings. The tortoise's carapace is so accurately stylized that there is no difficulty in recognizing the Margined tortoise *(Testudo marginata)* as the model.

The turtle and tortoise coins were extraordinarily widespread in Ancient Greece. Their popular name was simply "chelonai"—turtles.

This heyday of the turtle coins was followed by an interval of more than two thousand years before the creatures again appeared on coins. The setting is once again maritime, but far removed from Europe. In 1934, the Fiji Islands put sixpenny pieces into circulation that bore a highly stylized but unmistakable representation of a Loggerhead turtle *(Caretta caretta)*. The small silver coin was minted until 1943, with a fluctuating or rather diminishing silver content. This coin was to introduce a new era of turtle motifs on coins. Although the years of the Second World War and the period of austerity immediately after it caused something of a hiatus, the new "boom" in turtle coins really got underway at the end of the sixties. In 1967, the small Pacific kingdom of Tonga struck a bronze or brass coin as a 1 or 2 seniti piece that was reissued several times in the same form up to 1974. One side is adorned with the portrait of the monarch Taufaahau Tupou IV, while the other bears a lifelike depiction of one of the best known of chelonian personalities, the famous "Tui Malila". Land tortoises are quite unknown on the islands of the South Seas, and so this large tortoise that lived for a long time in the King of Tonga's park, was one of the marvels of the region to the islanders. But Tui Malila was also a puzzle to the scientist. The first question was how the creature could have come to the island. Tradition had it that it had been presented by Captain Cook to the Queen of Tonga on his third visit in 1777. The tortoise lived freely in the garden of the royal palace. One day it almost fell victim to a forest fire. It survived, but severe scars were left on the carapace. They can be distinguished clearly on the coin. In old age, Tui Malila became blind and was able to eat only what was laid immediately in front of it. It died on May 19th 1966. When Tui Malila was being examined by scientists during its preparation as a taxidermic specimen in Auckland Museum in New Zealand, it was found that exceptional old age had caused it to become unrecognizably dark and discoloured, but that in fact, it was a Radiated tortoise *(Asterochelys radiata)* from Madagascar. The New Zealand zoologists Robb and Turbott, who had revealed the true identity of Tui Malila, thought it very unlikely that this could be the selfsame tortoise that Captain Cook had brought to Tonga as a Giant tortoise. If it were, it must have been over 200 years old, since it was already adult on arrival at the island. But up to now, 152 years is the maximum authenticated life span for a land tortoise, and many experts would set the normal life expectancy lower than this. So somehow, the Tonga Islanders must have introduced an "illegal successor" to the presumed dead James Cook tortoise during those 189 years. This also seems unlikely. Perhaps one day, using microscopic examination of bone growth or other processes, it will be possible to determine the approximate age of the animal, and in this way, solve the problem of its identity. But Tui Malila can easily wait for this final mystery to be cleared up. Meanwhile, in the foyer of the International Dateline Hotel in Nuku'alofa, the capital of Tonga, tourists and local people can admire Tui Malila mounted as a museum specimen. They will certainly take home with them as a souvenir one of the small coins bearing the portrait of this enigmatic tortoise.

In the years that followed, coins showing turtles turned up in many places. Marine turtles, in particular Green turtles (Chelonia mydas), were popular motifs. They occurred in 1972 on the 10 cent piece of the Cayman Islands, 1974 on a silver coin worth 50 colones in Costa Rica, 1976 on 10 rupee coins in the Seychelles and in the same year as a nine-sided 1 dollar piece on the island state of Tuvalu, and on a postage stamp.

In 1978, Ascension Island and the Isle of Man each followed with a 1 crown piece struck in silver and cupro-nickel respectively, both of which show a slightly stylized but quite recognizable Green turtle beneath the British lion. In 1975, Papua New Guinea, one of the many young nation-states that came into being after the Second World War, chose one of the most interesting of its turtles, the Plateless River turtle (Carettochelys insculpta), as the motif for its small token coin, the 5 toea piece. Justly proud of the success of this coin, the young state also used the design on a postage stamp which was then carried throughout the world.

In this same year, land tortoises twice made an appearance on coins. From 1972 to 1974, a seven-sided 5 rupee piece in silver or cupro-nickel was in circulation in the Seychelles, carrying a stylized drawing of a very old, typically-shaped specimen of Seychelles Giant tortoise (Megalochelys gigantea) against the contour of a small island.

An event in 1977 proved something of a sensation for numismatists and for turtle enthusiasts interested in cultural history. On the occasion of the 25th anniversary of the accession to the throne of Queen Elizabeth II, a large 25 pence coin in silver or alternatively in cupro-nickel was struck for the Island of St Helena in the Atlantic that is administered by Britain. The obverse shows a Seychelles Giant tortoise that lived in the grounds of Government House. This animal, known as Jonathan, was taken to St Helena in 1882. It is popularly said to have belonged to Napoleon, but unfortunately this cannot be true. The Corsican Emperor of France had already been dead for some time when Jonathan followed him into exile. But it is true that during Napoleon's time, two other Giant tortoises lived on the island, and undoubtedly the ex-emperor, who was fond of animals, must have known of them. They had been taken there in the 18th century, but their remains are lost.

Last but not least! The most recent turtle to appear on a coin is minted in solid gold. In 1980, Panama struck a 100 balboa coin containing 8.16 g of gold. The design shows a highly stylized turtle which it is impossible to identify in detail. Known as the "golden turtle", it is a rare and valuable coin.

Modern coins with turtle motifs

top row:
Tuvalu, 1976
one dollar, with Green turtle *(Chelonia mydas)*, cupro-nickel, ⌀ 33 mm
Fiji Islands, 1953
sixpence, with Loggerhead turtle *(Caretta caretta)*, silver, ⌀ 19 mm
Costa Rica, 1974
50 colones, with Green turtle *(Chelonia mydas)*, silver, ⌀ 38 mm
second row:
Tonga Islands, 1967
two seniti, with Radiated tortoise *(Asterochelys radiata)*, bronze, ⌀ 29.5 mm
Seychelles, 1976
10 rupees, with Green turtle *(Chelonia mydas)*, silver or cupro-nickel, ⌀ 35 mm
Cayman Islands, 1972
10 cents, with Green turtle *(Chelonia mydas)*, cupro-nickel, ⌀ 20 mm
third row:
Tonga Islands, 1974
onc seniti, with Radiated tortoise *(Asterochelys radiata)*, brass, ⌀ 27.5 mm
Papua New Guinea, 1975
five toea, with New Guinea River turtle *(Carettochelys insculpta)*, cupro-nickel, ⌀ 19.5 mm
bottom row:
Ascension Island, 1978
one crown, with Green turtle *(Chelonia mydas)*, silver or cupro-nickel, ⌀ 38.6 mm
Seychelles, 1972
5 rupees, with Seychelles Giant tortoise *(Megalochelys gigantea)*, silver or cupro-nickel, ⌀ 30 mm
St. Helena, 1977
25 pence, with Seychelles Giant tortoise *(Megalochelys gigantea)*, silver or cupro-nickel, ⌀ 38.7 mm
(Collections of Heinemann, Helbra and Drescher, Eberswalde)

Proverbially, the way to a man's heart is through his stomach, and there are many "turtle lovers" who are familiar with the animal solely in the form of turtle soup. The representative of the chelonian order chosen by gourmets as their favourite is the Green turtle *(Chelonia mydas)*. Green turtles and other marine turtles are a traditional food for many people living on tropical coasts. They have been hunted and eaten for thousands of years without any serious threat to the stocks of these species.

The absence of suitable methods of preserving the meal prevented more turtles from being killed than could be consumed right away. The only way supplies could be stored was as live animals kept in bamboo cages in the tidal zone of a beach. Turtles sometimes lived there for weeks before they were slaughtered. The South Sea Islanders rarely use turtle flesh for soups, preferring to cook it as pieces of meat wrapped in the leaves of various green vegetables. It was only when sailing ships from Europe regularly plied the tropical seas in the 16th century that the fate of the marine turtles changed. As a cheap living food supply, they were often taken on board in large numbers, where they existed miserably for weeks before being killed. The only attention they received during this time was to have a few bucketfuls of sea water flung over them each day. It was in this way that the first sea turtles came to Europe, where, in the 19th century, they ranked alongside caviar, oysters, crayfish, lobsters and other seafoods as an exotic delicacy of marine origin. In the cuisine of fashionable society in western Europe, sea turtles were usually prepared as a soup, and rather more rarely as a ragout. The principal characteristic of turtle meat is that the broth in which it is cooked becomes extremely gelatinous on cooling. It has no characteristic taste of its own like the other delicacies mentioned. So it is not surprising that the impact of the dish lies entirely in the seasoning. Everything that the spice rack can offer, from cayenne pepper, curry and ginger to every possible strongly-flavoured native pot herb is used in the recipes. Finally, madeira or some other wine is added, and Lady Curzon's famous recipe swears by a generous dash of sherry. Looking at these recipes, it is clear that the least indispensable ingredient is the turtle meat. It is the cartilaginous substance close to the shell, particularly that in juvenile individuals, rather than the meat, that produces the abundant gelatine. Known as "calipee", this material is dried and exported, unfortunately still in alarming quantities, from the tropical countries of its origin, to be used in the conserved food industry. As a cheaper substitute for the gelatine-producing calipee, calf's head and calf's feet were already being used in the 18th century, and so "mock turtle soup" came into being. It can scarcely be distinguished from the real thing. "Ragout à la tortue" became "Mock turtle ragout", and some cookery books simply call it calf's head "en tortue", which means just the same thing. It is to be hoped that today, the marketing of turtles by the tinned food industry to the supermarkets of the consumer society is at last coming to an end. In Europe in the Middle Ages, it was primarily the European Pond tortoise *(Emys orbicularis)* that was regularly eaten during Lent, since it was considered as permitted fish and not as proscribed meat. This was perhaps a more appropriate classification in respect of its taste than from a zoological point of view. After the Reformation, periods of fasting were abolished across large areas of Central Europe. But this did not prevent the Lutherans, with a sharp eye for business, from exporting whole wagonloads of freshwater turtles from Brandenburg, for instance, to the Catholic areas of southern Germany, where they sold them at a good profit. This practice contributed in no small measure to the serious decline in the stocks of European Pond tortoises, particularly in central and east Prussia.

What the Pond turtle was for Europe, the Diamondback terrapin *(Malaclemys terrapin)* was to become for America. In the 19th century, this terrapin living in brackish waters on the western and southern coast of the USA became accepted as a delicacy throughout the land. The flesh of *Malaclemys* is rather more tender than that of other emydids, and its taste is said to lie somewhere between chicken meat and fish. As a result of its dubious career on the dinner tables of fashionable society, the Diamondback terrapin was exterminated in extensive parts of its range. The decrease in numbers in the wild, together with the growing demand, awakened interest in the farm-breeding of Diamondbacks, and so the first commercial turtle farms were established, which still today supply the luxury gourmet trade with all it requires of what has since become a very expensive delicacy. But before this, the Diamondback had been a cheap item of food for the common people. In the southern states, the frequency with which turtle dishes were served to the negro slaves working on the plantations, in combination with other unacceptable living conditions, even led to rebellions—probably the only time turtles have played a role in politics.

Among the rich turtle fauna of North America, there is a second species that, like the Diamondback, achieved some importance as an edible turtle. This is the Chicken turtle *(Deirochelys reticularia)*. Its vernacular name indicates that its flesh has a taste closer to that of poultry. This species was not bred on special farms, and in many places, as a result of the widespread interest in the sport of fishing in the USA, its numbers were greatly reduced. Today, like the Diamondback terrapin, the species is widely protected. Many American Indians, the original inhabitants of North America, also consider various species of Painted turtles *(Chrysemys)* and Map turtles *(Graptemys)* to be edible, whereas those species of Mud and Musk turtles (Kinosternidae) that smell strongly of musk, and Snapping turtles (Chelydridae) are not consumed, even though they are relatively common. In other parts of the world, the situation is fairly similar. Various species of land tortoises in particular are eaten readily by many African races, whereas the commonly occurring, musky-smelling Pelomedusid turtles *(Pelusios* and *Pelomedusa)* are usually rejected.

On the islands of the Indian Ocean, Giant tortoises have been a long-standing item of food. Seychelles Giant tortoises *(Megalochelys gigantea)* were also imported on to other islands where they were not already indigenous, to be looked after or even bred as a source of meat. The island of Zanzibar is a familiar example, where the quite considerable numbers of Giant tortoises owe their existence to these very profane motives. Certain rare species of turtles that are highly prized by the pet trade are, unfortunately, equally highly appreciated in their native home as meat. On Madagascar, for instance, the beautiful Radiated tortoise *(Asterochelys radiata)* is a highly esteemed delicacy. Strict legislation makes it virtually impossible to export these beautiful animals for study purposes or for breeding, but for the tourist, however, there is no difficulty in

A recipe from Vienna in 1777 provides an example of just such a Lenten meal of *Emys orbicularis*:

"Tortues servies en Caille
Turtles served in their shells

Cut the head and legs from the turtles, blanche them in a pot of boiling water, then clean the outside of the shells and put them in a pot again with root vegetables and herbs and a little salt, fill up with clear pea bouillon, place on the fire and cook gently until tender; take them out and remove the shells; cut the turtles neatly into quarters and put those parts that are removed, such as the liver and eggs, into a casserole with fresh butter, a few mushrooms and a whole onion, put over the fire, sprinkle a little fine flour over the whole and add some of the same liquor in which the turtles stewed, cook the sauce well, then add the turtle meat, cook with salt, and leave the whole to stand until required. Clean the shells, dry them well and when it is time to serve the meal, bring the turtles to the boil, add a little finely chopped parsely, mix in a few egg yolks, add the juice squeezed from one or more lemons, set the shells on dishes, put the turtle meat into them and serve at table."

having a meal of Radiated tortoise, or even of buying one at a market for butchering. During a study tour in New Guinea, Thomas Schultze-Westrum, who carried out valuable research into the Papuan Plateless River turtle *(Carettochelys insculpta)*, was able to find out a great deal about the biology of this curious turtle that was reputed to be very rare, but he also learned that *Carettochelys* was considered a great delicacy by the native Papuans. The turtles were by no means as rare as had originally been assumed. But to the foreigners who wanted to buy freshwater turtles from them, (not to eat, but to prepare as specimens or to take with them live—behaviour quite incomprehensible to the natives—), the local fishermen had usually offered only the less desirable species and had witheld the delicious *Carettochelys* for themselves. Such was the simple explanation of the supposed rarity of this species.

But the consumption of turtle meat, and particularly of land tortoises, is still widespread in many Balkan countries today. Even quite recently, it was possible to see herdsmen in Bulgaria preparing an occasional meal of the Greek or Iberian tortoise *(Testudo hermanni* and *Testudo graeca)* that they roasted over a campfire. The wretched creatures were simply skewered on a stick and cooked over the flames, then broken open and the meat eaten. Crude though this method may be, it should be noted that far fewer tortoises have been destroyed in this way than by being carried off by tourists.

There is a novel custom practised on the Seychelles Archipelago. The Aldabra Giant tortoises *(Megalochelys gigantea)* living there are popular as food, and so are kept and fattened in simple open-air pens. An adult giant tortoise yields between 50 and 150 kg

Marine turtle eggs for sale at the Sunday street market in Bangkok.

of meat. A traditionally-minded Seychellois will give a present of a young Giant tortoise to a newborn child; the animal is looked after in the family until the child marries. Then the tortoise is killed and prepared for the wedding feast. Since the Seychelles Giant tortoises are anyway semi-domesticated, this custom scarcely affects the natural stocks of the species at all. In the rookeries of marine turtles, the eggs are looked upon as an inexpensive food supply. They are equally acceptable whether they come from species held to be inedible or from Green turtles. Marine turtle's eggs are a popular item of food particularly on the Greater Sunda Islands and in Central and South America. Eggs are collected in millions causing drastic depletion of the turtle population. Marine turtle's eggs are eaten boiled like hen's eggs or fried, or are used in the preparation of other dishes; Indians and South Sea Islanders in particular simply eat them raw. A final example of the exploitation of turtles as a source of food is the use of the eggs of various species of *Podocnemis* terrapins that live in the north of South America, mainly in the Amazon and Orinoco river systems. For centuries, the creatures had been hunted by Indians at egg-laying time, and their eggs collected for the extraction of oil; as a result of commercial influences introduced by European settlers, these activities increased to such an extent that many species, in particular the Arrau turtle *(Podocnemis expansa)*, are now critically endangered. The turtles lay their eggs along the sandy banks of the great rivers which are then visited by crowds of egg collectors. Only a few of the eggs are used in the same way as hen's eggs; the majority are processed for oil. The eggs are crushed in tubs and a little water is added. After fairly lengthy stirring, the fat from the yokes rises to the surface and is skimmed off as oil. The oil is preserved by boiling. Today, artificial preservatives are also added. Turtle oil is amber to chestnut brown in colour and completely clear. It is popular as cooking oil while batches of poorer quality are used as fuel oil. An account written at the middle of the last century gives a vivid picture of the enormously wasteful exploitation of the Podocnemid turtles. With the depletion of their stocks, an important source of food was lost to the Indians, on which they could have lived for countless generations, as their forefathers had done, without seriously damaging the impressively large turtle population. As in the practice of harvesting tortoiseshell, it is not the utilization of the creatures by primitive races that leads to their extinction, but the immoderate intervention of profit-seeking "civilized" nations into the life and nature of tropical countries and their peoples.

In the religions of various peoples, the turtle is venerated as a sacred animal. So representations of turtles in paintings, as small sculptures or even as impressive, monumental sculptures are one of the characteristic elements in the art of, for example, the Asiatic civilizations. Interpretation of their symbolic content opens up a vast chapter in the history of the civilization of ancient China, Japan, India and of many other peoples. The turtle motif also provides cultural links with the Indian civilizations of historical and present day America.

In Bangkok, the capital of Thailand, there is a Buddhist Temple complex known as "Wat Po". Its centrepiece is a pond that is interspersed with artificial rocky islands with delicately wrought bridges and miniature pagodas. Large numbers of turtles live in the

The compassionate man

A compassionate man once caught a turtle. He wanted to make it into soup, but without burdening his conscience with the sin of killing it. He boiled some water in a large pan, and lay across it a stick upon which he placed the turtle, saying to it "If you can cross to the other side of the pan, I will grant you your freedom". The turtle was perfectly well aware of the man's intentions, but did not want to die. It summoned up all its will-power and accomplished the impossible.
"Well done," cried the man, "but please, do try it once again."

(Ting Shi)
A fable from ancient China
Altchinesische Fabeln.
Leipzig, 1976.

Turtle temples and sacred turtles

The constellations of the Chinese

The spring symbol of the Blue Dragon is in opposition to the winter constellation of the Turtle or the Black Warrior, which corresponds approximately to our constellations of the Archer (Sagittarius), the Water Bearer (Aquarius) and the Winged Horse (Pegasus). In the South Pacific and Japan, the turtle is a popular image for the process by which islands and continents come into being; it rises up out of the sea and becomes land. Its beautifully marked shell is divided up like tracts of land. Schlegel recounts the following fable: In the west of the mountain range of Youen Kiao is the Star Pond. The divine turtle with eight feet and six eyes lives in the pond. On its carapace it carries the northern constellation of the Great Bear, the Sun, the Moon and the eight celestial regions. On its plastron, the five mountains and the four canals, that is, the geographical region inhabited by the Chinese of that time. Beyond the Dragon's tail, the head of the Turtle appeared in the heavens . . .

From: Friedrich Normann: *Mythen der Sterne* (Myths of the Stars), "The Constellations of the Chinese". Gotha, 1925.

water, among which black Temple turtles *(Hieremys annandalei)* are predominant. As an adult, this placid freshwater turtle is almost entirely vegetarian. Visitors to the temple feed the animals with bananas and other fruit or with vegetables. The growth of algae on the temple turtle's shell is taken as a sign of its longevity. In Buddhism, the turtle is the symbol of immortality. This concept is closely linked to the Buddhist views on reincarnation and transmigration of souls. For example, the faithful see the sacred temple turtles as the temporary dwelling place of the souls of men as they make their arduous way through a variety of earthly existences to attain eternal Nirvána. Consequently it is taboo to disturb or kill these animals. There are other famous sites at which sacred turtles are cared for in Bangladesh, India and Burma. Probably the best known is the turtle shrine of Chittagong in eastern Bangladesh. Here the sacred turtles are representatives of a species of soft-shelled turtle that lives only in this great "tank" or reservoir with an area of some 5,000 m and a depth of up to 5 m. So far, they have not been found in any natural body of water. In 1875, the zoologist Anderson described these animals as an independent species. He gave them the name *Trionyx nigricans*. From the few specimens of this species that have so far been available for scientific examination in Museums of Zoology, it appears that this remarkable and rare animal can be assigned to a taxonomic position between the Indian Ganges Soft-shelled turtle *(Trionyx gangeticus)* and the Indochinese Soft-shelled turtle *(Trionyx cartilagineus)*. Recent estimates put the total population of the species at less than 150–200, including all age groups. Adult temple turtles attain a carapace length of up to 70 cm. As omnivores, the animals live almost exclusively on the food (fruit, pieces of meat and fish) given to them by the visitors of the Holy Shrine. While feeding them, devout Moslems try to touch the leathery backs of the turtles and then moisten their brow with the water. The significance of this custom is unclear. According to Mohammedan legend, the shrine of Chittagong dates back to the Moslem Saint Bayazid Bostami. On a missionary journey in about the year 830 A.D., he is said to have founded the turtle shrine by turning the evil spirits of the place into turtles. According to another version, the turtles are the metamorphosed forms of sinners who offended against Allah and his holy missionary. As a punishment and warning, they now live on as turtles until their redemption. A third version tells how Saint Bayazid brought the turtles with him from his home in Iran. It is much more probable that the turtle temple already existed in the earlier pre-Buddhist history of Chittagong and because of its popularity, was simply taken over by Islamism, a religion otherwise hostile to reptiles. The turtle cult is not a feature exclusive to Buddhism, but had already been taken over from earlier Chinese and Indian religions. Probably the Indian veneration of the sacred soft-shelled turtles is based on the Brahmanic-Hindu idea that these animals are an embodiment of the ancient river goddess Jumna.

Probably the most important role assigned to the turtle is that contained in ancient Chinese and Hindu myths concerning the origin of the world. In Hinduism, the turtle is considered to be the second incarnation of the immensely powerful god Vishnu. After a great flood, Vishnu transformed himself into a great turtle on whose back the world was able to arise anew. Meanwhile, the other gods had tried in vain to raise up the earth again from out of the vast ocean. The Indian subcontinent is said to be the remains of

Turtle temple of Wat-Po in Bangkok. Besides the Temple turtles *(Hieremys annandalei)*, *Siebenrockiella crassicolis*, the Amboina Box turtle *(Cuora amboinensis)* and at times other representatives of the rich turtle fauna of South-east Asia are kept here.

this vast carapace. Similar ideas exist in ancient China. There, Kwei, the dragon turtle, was the first creature to emerge from chaos and help to bring order to the world. The regular arrangement of the plates of the turtle's shell is associated in these myths with the concept of an ordered system. To the Chinese, the rune-like furrows on the turtle shell were enigmatically encoded "plans" for the organization of the world. In addition, the arrangement of the plates was construed as a mystical system in which individual laminae embody particular characteristics such as longevity, constancy, endurance, as well as health and happiness. The ornamental arrangement of the turtle shell was incorporated into the astronomical and astrological beliefs of various peoples who defined groups of stars as the constellations of turtles. Finally, the patterns on the turtles' shells also assumed numerical symbolism. In China, the "magic squares" formed by the concentric furrows on the carapace are said to be the origin of the games board and of card games.

Interestingly enough, the turtle plays a very similar role in the mythology of certain Amerindian peoples, such as the Algonquian Indians and the Iroquois. They also see "mother turtle" as a creature supporting a world that is entirely surrounded by water. No doubt the forefathers of the Indians brought these myths with them from their ancient Asiatic home. Probably all later Asiatic religions and philosophies borrowed the idea of the turtle as supporter of the world from the same ancient sources of natural religions.

The enormous esteem in which the turtle is held in ancient Eastern Asia as the creator of order in the world and the symbol of immortality also finds expression in monumental figures of turtles sculpted in stone or bronze that are part of the historical tradition of China, Korea, Mongolia and other countries. Representations of turtles often adorn the graves of important figures in ancient China. It is not unusual for the glorious deeds of the dead man to be inscribed on the carapace that is in the form of a flat plate. The most splendid of the turtle monuments, however, are those in which a stele bearing a detailed inscription stands upright on the back of the animal. Tablet-bearing turtle monoliths of this kind were erected on Chinese territory wherever they could give visual expression to the significance of particular public places—temple buildings, intersections of important routes, bridges or the sites of historical events. The most famous example of a stone turtle monument is the granite monolith some two metres long that is found on the site of the ruined city of Karakorum in the Mongolian steppes. It marks the place where the palace of Ogotai, son of the world conqueror Genghis Khan, stood in the 13th century. In 1380, Chinese troops conquered the Mongolian Empire and razed the capital to the ground. It is not known whether they spared the stone turtle, or whether it was set up by the Chinese after their victory. The large stone tablet bearing the inscription that would provide this information is missing. It may have been used in the building of the monastery town of Erdeni-dsu, the imposing ruins of which tower up only a few hundred metres beyond the enigmatic turtle. Erdeni-dsu, the oldest and largest Lamaist monastery in Mongolia, was built in 1586 under Abatai Khan, not far from the ruined city of Karakorum. (The endpaper shows the Karakorum turtle.)

The temple turtle (Hieremys annandalei), a "sacred turtle" from Indochina.

Innumerable small statues with turtle motifs can be found in the countries of Eastern Asia. Among the small bronzes, those showing a turtle with a white crane are particularly striking. This popular motif illustrates the Buddhist legend of the turtle carrying the crane across a raging torrent. The crane bears in its beak a Lotus blossom as a candle-stick to bring a light to the Holy Buddha. Another turtle sculpture that is frequently found in Japan shows two turtles, one mounted on the other. It represents the turtle's great diligence in mating and its gregarious nature. Here, one might also mention the Chinese legend in which the turtle maintains a forbidden relationship with a snake. It is from this sphere—perhaps the only negative aspect of the turtle's nature—that the Chinese draw the term of abuse "turtle-ness" with which they revile an ill-bred person of dubious origin.

In classical Graeco-Roman antiquity, the turtle plays a certain part as the revered attendant of many a deity, for example, of the goddess Urania, patroness of marriage, and of Pallas Athene, goddess of wisdom. In pre-classical civilizations, turtles were already considered the symbol of prudence and intelligence. In many fables, the tortoise shows itself a match for its rivals by virtue of its superior wisdom. For example, the tortoise wins a race against the hare, or in the versions of other countries, against the ostrich, the antelope, the deer. It even triumphs over the hero Achilles in a competition that the Greek mathematician and philosopher Zenon organized as an intellectual-cum-sporting event. ·

From the medicine of classical antiquity, in which the turtle plays a varied role, there is a direct line to the superstitious belief in the miraculous powers of turtles held by various peoples. Many Africans and Indians wear turtle shells or even small live turtles as amulets against misfortune and disease. Scutes from the shell are often an ingredient of secret remedies or simply a talisman against harm of various kinds. Papuan soothsayers, many American Indians and even ancient Greek oracles frequently made use of the shell of turtles as a mystery-shrouded tool of prophecy. Even up to the last century, Italian peasants used live tortoises as a miraculous means of averting an impending hailstorm. To this end, the animals were buried in the ground, lying on their back, along with a few lumps of earth, in the threatened field or vineyard. African tribes in southwest Africa used tortoises or their shells in a very similar way as a mystical protection against lightning. The creatures were simply tied to the roof of the house when there was a storm, or else "prophylactic" turtle shells, filled with magic charms, were incorporated into the roof of a house when it was built.

Finally, the turtle plays a considerable part in fairy tales, myth and legend. The folklore of South American and Pacific peoples is particularly rich in turtle stories. In them, the turtle is almost invariably presented as a genial, intelligent, helpful and lovable creature. It is to be hoped that in the future, this friendly attitude of people towards the turtle will contribute to the conservation of the chelonian fauna of the world.

The constellations of the Taulipang Indians (-Venezuela-)

". . . Before the Great Flood, the stars were people. They said: "What shall we be (after the Flood)?
Agouti, paca, tapir, stag? All these get eaten.
So it is better for us to become stars, so that men may see us from down below".
They sang, as they ascended, a beautiful song.
First the chameleon went up.
After him came the dolphin.
He said: "As a dolphin, I am going into the heavens."
Then the Tartaruga turtle rose up.
It can still be seen, together with its eggs, in the heavens.
Then came the crab . . ."

Robert Henseling:
Sternbilder primitiver Völker (Constellations of primitive peoples) Potsdam, 1925.
(The constellation referred to is Orion; one of the nebulae is the eggs.)

Valuable tortoiseshell

The most valuable material obtained from turtles is tortoiseshell. This beautiful raw material that is easily worked into a wide variety of products has proved as costly to the Hawksbill turtle *(Eretmochelys imbricata)* and to the Green turtle *(Chelonia mydas)* as have the valuable pelts of certain fur-bearing animals or the decorative plumage of many birds. Tortoiseshell (or "carey") is the name given to the horny plates of the carapace of these two species of marine turtles. They are very similar in appearance. A harmonious range of yellow, brown to reddish tones, sometimes with a touch of dark brown or even olive green, alternate in an irregular undulating pattern, comparable perhaps to the appearance of the veneer of certain root woods or the stratification in polished stones. While the tortoiseshell of the Hawksbill is several millimetres thick, and at the base can even reach almost a centimetre in thickness, that of the Green turtle is uniformly thin. The scutes on the carapace of the Hawksbill overlap considerably like the tiles of a roof, which causes thickening and irregular growth. In contrast, the carapacial laminae of the Green turtle are smoothly juxtaposed and are at no time imbricate. The tortoiseshell from both species is exactly the same in its technical quality. It is easily cut, engraved, moulded or drilled, it can be polished to a permanent brilliant lustre and can be bonded to wood and other surfaces with various adhesives. In earlier days isinglass was used for this purpose. But the feature that greatly extends its potential range of use is its high plasticity when heated in water or oil. The soft material can readily be shaped to the required form in a mould. Moreover, separate pieces of tortoiseshell can easily be welded together to make an extended surface. Native peoples for whom turtle flesh is a popular item of

"Kap-kaps", breast ornaments made from a polished disc of mussel shell (*Tridacna* spec.) with a covering of filigree tortoiseshell joined to the disc at the centre. New Ireland, South Pacific, 19th century (Staatliches Museum für Völkerkunde, Dresden)

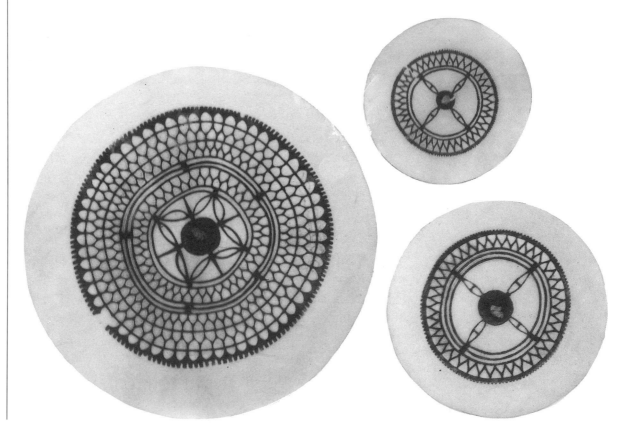

Tortoiseshell tableware, shaped after heating and polished, from the Palau Islands, West Pacific, 19th century (Staatliches Museum für Völkerkunde, Dresden)

food, would take the tortoiseshell as a by-product when they killed and cut up the turtles. But when the demand for tortoiseshell increased, the fishermen were unable to use up the meat of all the slaughtered animals. Moreover, the flesh of the Hawksbill is less popular with certain native peoples than that of the Green turtle, or is even rejected completely. So the practice grew of stripping the tortoiseshell from the live turtle by pouring boiling water over it or roasting it at a fire. With remarkable tenacity of life, the turtles survived this cruel torture and were released into the sea. But undoubtedly, within a short time, the majority of these animals died painfully from the extensive destruction of the skin and the increased susceptibility to infection that it caused.

The turtle hunters, living close to nature, were well aware of the remarkable regenerative capacity of the turtle's damaged laminae, but to expect the miracles that these fishermen believed in, was asking too much of it. Only rarely may an occasional turtle have survived. While only local people were taking tortoiseshell for their own use, the strain placed upon populations of turtles remained within acceptable limits, but when foreign demand turned tortoiseshell into a valuable export commodity, irresponsible over-exploitation of the turtles followed.

And what is turtleshell used for? Probably its earliest use was for making objects of personal adornment. There is evidence of this in the bracelets and ornamental "kapkaps" found on almost all the South Sea Islands. To make the bracelets, rectangular strips of tortoiseshell were heated and rolled up, with the edges slightly overlapping. As a decoration, encircling banderoles were engraved with various patterns. Near the centre, there are often highly stylized representations of animals that are frequently difficult to interpret. Common motifs include the crocodile, the turtle and the shark. The engraving was generally inlaid with white pigment, heightening the contrast with the dark background of tortoiseshell.

Bracelets made of tortoise-shell, shaped after heating and engraved, from the Tami Islands, South Pacific, 19th century (Staatliches Museum für Völkerkunde, Dresden)

The "kap-kap" is an ornament worn round the neck on a chain or cord. The basic element of the kap-kap is a circular disc from the shell of a mussel (*Tridacna* spec.) that has been polished completely smooth. On top of this is attached a disc of tortoiseshell worked and filed in an open filigree pattern. The tortoiseshell covering is often so delicate that it has the effect of lace. In making kap-kaps, the islanders used tortoiseshell from the Green turtle, while the material for the sturdier bracelets was obtained from the Hawksbill turtle. Kap-kaps and bracelets were used by the South Sea Islanders not only as ornamentations but also as currency.

The Dresdener Völkerkunde Museum (Dresden Museum of Ethnology) has a collection of tableware from the Palau Islands, consisting of a variety of spoons, drinking bowls, ladles and plates or trays that have been made by moulding heated tortoiseshell into a simple, elegant shape without superfluous decoration and finished by fine polishing. The material's sumptuous mottling is the only decoration on this perfectly elegant tableware from the middle of the 19th century.

The most interesting ethnographical examples of the use of tortoiseshell for personal adornment is undoubtedly that of the dance masks from the islands of the Torres Strait that were made by the inhabitants of this region between Australia and New Guinea for use in religious ceremonies.

The flat planes of the mask are made of tortoiseshell that has been heated and shaped. The mouth and eye openings were not cut or drilled but pierced through with heated tools. The malleable mass produced in this way was skilfully shaped into bulging lips and eyebrow ridges. The individual parts of brow, face and beard were then joined together. In making these masks, tortoiseshell was used primarily for the sake of its high plasticity rather than for its colour, since the typical veining is hidden under a layer of paint over the entire surface. A plume of feathers, probably from an emu or cassowary, give the head-dress its final touch. Of quite different design was the shark mask that a dancer wore on its head. Here, the beautiful marbling of the individually linked pieces of tortoiseshell is used to advantage. It reflects the markings found in many species of shark. To the fishermen of the South Seas, the shark is both a dangerous opponent and at the same time a provider of food and raw material, so it plays an important part in

Hat-shaped head mask in form of a shark, pieces of tortoiseshell heated, moulded into shape and stitched together, shark's teeth incorporated (Staatliches Museum für Völkerkunde, Dresden)

their mythology and in their songs and dances. The dances depict the ritual exorcism and symbolic slaying of the shark. The Jervis Island shark mask is an outstanding example of the highly developed folk art of Papua and its close links with nature. Even in ancient times, tortoiseshell was also in regular use as a valuable material in those parts of Europe that bordered the Mediterranean. In Italy and Spain, it really never went out of fashion, and there are examples of its use as a craft material from all stylistic epochs. From the time of the Renaissance onwards, tortoiseshell products and the material itself made their way to central and northern Europe. Here, tortoiseshell was an exotic and very valuable material and was worked only by craftsmen in the courts of the nobility. The era of French classicism at the time of Louis XIV, the Sun King, saw the climax of this development. To satisfy the monarch's intense desire for a lifestyle reflecting his dignity, a vast staff of firstrate artists and craftsmen was employed at court. A leading figure among them, as painter, interior designer, decorator and cabinetmaker, was André Charles Boulle (1642–1732). With such a combination of skills, he was well qualified to take charge of all the interior work and furnishing of the king's palaces. Constantly in search of new artistic techniques and ways of increasing the value of his work by the use of rare materials, Boulle hit upon the idea of using tortoiseshell in his pieces of furniture and other fittings. He developed a new kind of inlay work that was quite different from the classic wood veneering. The base was brass or pewter, out of

193

which decorative patterns were cut and filed. The open areas were then given a level inlay of tortoiseshell. The metal details were usually highly gilded (fire-gilding), which enhanced both the appearance and the value of the work considerably. Panels of metal and tortoiseshell inlay were used to decorate the surface of various pieces of furniture, particularly chests of drawers and cabinets. Longcase clocks or smaller console clocks with large enamelled faces and with this highly decorative treatment of the case were especially popular. The technique of metal and tortoiseshell intarsia was named after its inventor. Boulle (or Buhl) furniture and particularly Boulle clocks were still produced long after he had died. Today they are treasured exhibits in museums.

Tortoiseshell was also used in the baroque period in the production of small objets d'art. Small cosmetic boxes in silver or silver-gilt inlaid and decorated with mother-of-pearl, tortoiseshell and enamel were in great demand. Snuff boxes were often moulded

Book and two snuff boxes tortoiseshell, mother of pearl and fire-gilt brass mounting, German, 18th century (Staatliche Kunstsammlungen Dresden, Museum für Kunsthandwerk)

Console clock in boulle
technique
(tortoiseshell and metal intarsia) French, 18th century
(Staatliche Kunstsammlun-
gen Dresden, Museum für
Kunsthandwerk)

in tortoiseshell and the lid set in a narrow gilded brass mounting. Another typical example of the craft of the period is seen in covers for small books in which tortoiseshell is worked in Boulle technique. Weapons, particularly the shafts of ornate pistols and rifles, were also decorated with inlay work, and for this purpose, tortoiseshell became as fashionable as ivory. As long as boulle marquetry was restricted to the royal workshops, and as long as the courtly baroque of Louis XIV did not extend to the ascendant middle classes, the "primary producers" of tortoiseshell, the sea turtles themselves, suffered no disadvantage. But when, at the end of the 18th and the beginning of the 19th century, there was a growing demand in bourgeois circles for tortoiseshell products at a more reasonable price, the mass slaughter of marine turtles began. However elegant the tortoiseshell combs, sometimes of enormous size, may have looked in the elaborate coiffures affected by aristocratic and bourgeois ladies alike, they represented a threat on an unprecedented scale to turtles in all tropical ocean regions. Originally, the orna-mental combs came predominantly from Mediterranean countries (the "Spanish comb"). But soon the enormous demand could not be satisfied by the import of readymade goods, so workshops and manufactories were set up in Central Europe in which imported raw tortoiseshell was processed. In the Old Town of Vienna, quite close to the Cathedral of St. Stephen, just such a shop still exists, selling "the finest tortoiseshell wares, made on the premises".

The design of the tortoiseshell goods frequently reflects interesting trends in con-temporary taste. Whereas the older, late baroque combs were often made with carved and engraved decoration in the Oriental manner, very often in the style known as "chinoiserie" (European imitation of "Chinese" motifs fashionable during the baroque

196

period), the 19th century favoured the Biedermeier style with simpler decorations based on indigenous plant motifs. In this, probably the most bourgeois of all stylistic epochs, a feeling for beauty combined with utility was never lacking. Just one example is the lorgnette made to be used by a wealthy middle class citizen for reading, the handle of which is of tortoiseshell in a simple but effective and beautiful design expressive both of quality and distinction. Letter openers, manicure sets and again, numerous snuff boxes complete this brief glance at the craft of the 19th century.

In its physical characteristics, tortoiseshell is very similar to thermoplastic synthetic materials of more recent times. The invention of celluloid made it possible to produce a remarkably, indeed deceptively, convincing imitation of natural tortoiseshell. As a result, the demand for tortoiseshell decreased perceptibly, to the benefit of the turtles. On the other hand, tortoiseshell itself provided a stimulus for the development of plastics and elastomers of all kinds, and these have since become important in their own right, and essential to modern manufacturing processes. Nowadays, the use of tortoiseshell might well be restricted to the restoration of objects of real artistic and historical value, until one day perhaps, programmes of controlled breeding will develop stocks of turtles in sufficient numbers to ensure that they are no longer endangered species, and to permit once again the use, in moderation, of a beautiful natural product. But to reach that point, there is still a long way to go . . .

People for whom turtle flesh is a regular item of food have from time immemorial seen turtle-shell as a natural product that they could use for a wide variety of purposes. The shallow, concave shells of marine turtles serve the South Sea Islanders as containers in which to carry and store fruit that has been harvested, or in which to collect mussels, shrimps and other marine creatures that enrich their diet. Many native races in South Africa, such as the Bushmen, use the shells of land tortoises as portable, multi-purpose containers. In particular, they like to fashion holders for tobacco, ointments or powders that they can wear round the neck, out of beautifully marked shells of the small South

Turtle shells as containers, containers in the shape of turtles

Kawa bowl in the form of a marine turtle,
wood, carved and polished
Samoa Islands, 19th century
(Staatliches Museum für Völkerkunde, Dresden)

Personal seals with tortoises
on the signet head.
Ivory, Chinese, 19th century.
(Collection of P. E. His, Basel)

Buchu boxes made by South
African tribes
The lower opening of the turtle shell is sealed with resin
and wax, the anterior lobes of
the plastron are removed,
and leather fringes decorated
with pearls are added. The
boxes were used by the wom-
en of the Hereros and the
Bushmen, as a container for
buchu, a reddish body-dust-
ing powder obtained from
various plants. The stopper
for the portable powder box
consisted of a piece of
sheepskin or jackal skin,
which also served to apply
the powder to the skin.
Shells of land tortoises
(*Psammobates oculifera* and
Geochelone pardalis),
Namibia and South Africa,
19th century.
(Staatliches Museum für
Völkerkunde, Dresden)

African land tortoises of the genus *Psammobates*, or those of juvenile Leopard tortoises *(Geochelone pardalis)*. To do this, they first remove the front part of the plastron in order to extend the opening. Just beneath it, two holes are bored, through which a leather thong is threaded as a neck-strap for the box. Examples of such containers can be found in every ethnographical collection of old native South African artefacts. The older the collection, the more common are the shells of the Geometric tortoise *(Psammobates geometrica)*, the most beautiful and today, the rarest of the South African land tortoises. In the civilization of tropical peoples, there are many links between the use of turtle shells as natural receptacles and the fashioning of vessels in animal shape out of wood, clay and other materials.

It is a general rule that at the hand of the craftsman, the natural model undergoes considerable abstraction and alienation, so that it is not easy to associate the resulting work directly with the concrete natural object upon which it is based. The deliberate turning to the natural model such as we find in the zoomorphic representation of animal form in these vessels is, therefore, all the more remarkable. The examples illustrated, from Central Africa, the South Seas and America in pre-Columbus times, are repre- sentative of many more. The ideal background for the creation of these vessels, in ad- dition to deep feelings of identification with nature, probably has a basis in the mytho- logical and philosophical interpretation of the animals represented. The wooden Kawa bowl from the Samoa Islands in the form of a sea turtle, known as a tanoa, is a very appropriate example of such associations.

Most tanoas are much more highly stylized than the one illustrated. Usually the head and the suggestion of the turtle's limbs are absent from the drinking edge of the bowl.

Box made of rock crystal with silver mounting, French 18th century. Miniature paintings on the sides depict the capture of turtles.
(Collection of P. E. His, Basel)

Turtle with dragon head as the lid of a small box. Brass casting on wooden plinth, lacquered, Chinese, 19th century
(Collection of P. E. His, Basel)

Box, lacquerwork
Burma, 20th century
(Collection of P. E. His, Basel)

Turtle as box
Cloisonné (enamel work on
metal) with wooden plinth,
lacquered black
Chinese, 19th century
(Collection of P. E. His, Basel)

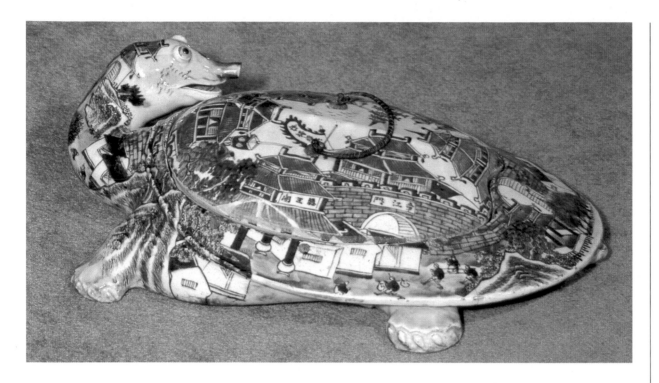

Dish with lid, in the shape of a soft-shelled turtle (*Trionyx* spec.) Lid with brass handle, porcelain with cobalt-blue underglaze painting Chinese, 18th century (Collection of P. E. His, Basel)

From the roots of the Kawa pepper, the Samoans prepare an intoxicating drink, Kawa-Kawa. In a drinking ceremony at religious festivals, it is drunk from the tanoas. In the natural religion of the islanders, animals that supply food and the raw material for craft products, as marine turtles do, play an important part. So it is logical that the turtle shell, that was in general use as a natural vessel, should serve as model for the stylized carving of the ritual drinking vessel in the shape of a turtle. Restriction of the vessel's use to ceremonial occasions was a symbolic act of cultic veneration of the highly prized sea turtles.

The ceremony rose to its climax amid the singing and dancing of the intoxicated islanders. This custom has largely died out today. The songs and dances are still performed as a tourist attraction, but the most beautiful of the Kawa bowls are now in Ethnological Museums in America and Europe.

Vessels in the form of animals became particularly fashionable in Europe during the baroque era. This time, the intellectual background was not that of the artist's identification with nature or the religious and philosophical interpretation of the animal, but that of an exaggerated desire for outward symbols of social status in aristocratic and bourgeois circles. The two early Meissen porcelain butter dishes in the form of turtles are an interesting example.

The South Seas region provides another example of man putting parts of the turtle body to practical use. On various of the islands, there are simple tools that may have served as scrapers or hoes. Attached to a wooden handle is a blade made out of a piece of that reinforced part of the carapace of a sea turtle incorporating the ribs. Blade and handle are bound together skilfully by strong natural fibres that pass through specially drilled holes. The blade is cut cleanly out of the carapace. The natural narrowing of the

Hoe or scraping implement made from the rib section of a marine turtle. The blade and the wooden handle are joined together by cording. Bismarck Archipelago, South Pacific, 19th century (Staatliches Museum für Völkerkunde, Dresden)

bone towards the edge of the shell is cleverly exploited, and the blade is finely ground and polished to produce a sharp edge. Because it is so light, this original, highly practical tool could be used in the island's plantations with ease by the women who were responsible for the field work.

Hermes' lyre

The best known musical instrument of classical antiquity is the lyre. Its stylized representation is often used in iconography as the symbol of music. Greek mythology tells how Hermes, one of the legitimate sons of Zeus, as god of herdsmen and of nature, once found a tortoise in the idyllic mountain world of his Olympian home, killed it and used its shell as the resonance body of the first lyre. The lyre was a simple stringed instrument with five to eighteen strings. It developed further into the multi-stringed Greek cithara and then into the more familiar modern zither. The lyre and cithara had already been known for a long time in the Near East, and like much in the development of classical civilization, these instruments were in fact taken over from the Orient into Graeco-Roman culture. But the use of turtle shells as the sound chests of musical instruments did not remain an exclusively Greek prerogative. Similar examples occur in other civilizations. Various Amerindian peoples make use of turtle shells without any special preparation, simply as rattles or small drums. The "sansa" or "zanze" from the Congo region has become well-known. It is a plucked-string instrument with several tuned wooden tongues that produce sound on a resonator made out of the shell of a pelomedusid turtle (*Pelusios* or *Pelomedusa*), with a wooden covering plate. In the Museum of Musical Instruments *(Instrumentenmuseum)* in the Vogtland town of Markneukirchen, one of the most famous centres of musical instrument manufacture, there is a fine example of southern

A favourite subject of paintings on Greek vases is the slaying by the impatient and quick-tempered pupil Heracles of his stern music teacher Linus. The tutor was only just able to save the precious lyre from Heracles' destructive rage. Here, a similar motif.
Greek drinking cup (scyphus) with painting by the Attic master Pistoxenos—"Linus teaches Iphicles to play the lyre", about 480 B.C. (Staatliches Museum Schwerin)

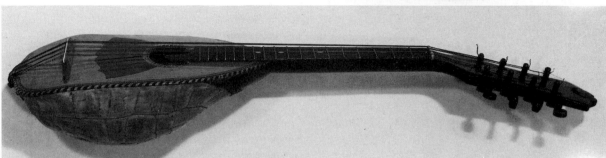

"Sansa" or "zanze", musical instrument made from a turtle shell (*Pelomedusa* or *Pelusios*) with wooden covering-plate and five wooden tongues. Congo, 19th century (Staatliches Museum für Völkerkunde, Dresden)

Mandolin, the resonance body is the shell of a European land tortoise Probably Italian, 19th century (Musikinstrumentenmuseum Markneukirchen, German Democratic Republic)

European handicraft. A mandolin, probably of Italian or Spanish origin, combines a beautiful shell of a tortoise with an elegant fingerboard to make a valuable instrument of high artistic merit. In this connection, an unwelcome example is the mass production by unscrupulous souvenir manufacturers in Morocco of primitive stringed instruments with no value whatsoever as a reflection of the cultural heritage of the country, but which entail the destructive exploitation of the endangered Iberian or Spur-thighed tortoise (*Testudo graeca*).

A discussion on the use of vernacular or scientific terms for animals would make a chapter on its own. It is an ancient practice among all peoples for common indigenous animals to be given names in the common language. If later on, vernacular names must be found for foreign animals as well, there exist various possibilities. One of the most attractive is certainly that of adopting the vernacular name by which the animal is known in its own native home. As far as turtles are concerned, this has rarely happened. Only the Matamata *(Chelus fimbriatus)* had the privilege of carrying its remarkable Indian name ("I kill") across the world, wherever naturalists and zoologists have dealings with it. The great attention currently being paid to the critically endangered species of Land tortoises on Madagascar may well be the opportunity for the "Malagasy Prow-breasted tortoise" *(Asterochelys yniphora)* to exchange its artificial vernacular name for the Malagasy name of "Angonoka". And perhaps the "Sokake" *(Asterochelys radiata)* will follow its example, although it has long been known by the attractive and appropriate vernacular name of the Radiated tortoise.

How Turtles got their name

A tradition that began with Gcsnor's Animal Books in the Middle Ages and has continued by way of Brehm and Grzimek until the present day, has provided well-established names for very many exotic animals, and so for many foreign turtles, which it would be a pity to exclude from everyday language—indeed, there is very little danger of that happening. We have Painted turtles, Snapping turtles, Starred tortoises and Spurred tortoises and many more, while rather long names are frequently contracted: turtle connoisseurs speak of "Snake-necks" and "Snappers" and leave the "turtle" out. There are, however, also some examples of linguistic confusion. Galapagos tortoises are literally „tortoise-tortoises", although nobody minds about it. Tortoises have provided the name not only of these islands but also of Tortugera, Tartaruga and names of similar construction in the Latin America area.

Various peoples have used vernacular names to distinguish between quite large groups of turtles. The ancient Greeks separated freshwater turtles as "emys" from marine turtles that were called "chelonai". In English, "turtles" and "tortoises" generally refer to aquatic and terrestrial species respectively.

As the currency of international communication, scientific names have long since achieved paramount importance. But although they have linguistic content, they should not be regarded as primarily a vehicle of this content, but as a strictly regulated code, in which linguistic description plays a merely subordinate role. The scientific names reveal much that is interesting but, at times, also confusing. Curiously, the common Algerian or Mediterranean Spur-thighed tortoise has the scientific name *Testudo graeca*, that is "Greek tortoise", while the Greek tortoise is called *Testudo hermanni*. This contradiction can be explained by the obligatory code-function of scientific nomenclature. It became known only later that when Carl von Linné, founder of the scientific system of classification gave *Testudo graeca* its name, he had on hand a specimen from northwest Africa. But for the sake of stability, the scientific name is unalterably tied to the animal known as the type specimen.

In general, scientific names have their origin in Latin or latinized Greek words. "Emys", "chelonai", "chersus" and "testudo", added to various combinations of syllables and words, all signify turtles or tortoises. Occasionally other classical words are the basis of the name.

The Greek word "pyxis", meaning "box", became the nucleus of a number of turtle's names. Rarely, popular names from the native country are latinized, such as the Indian "kachuga" for the Roofed turtles. A final philological practice is exemplified in many names, particularly specific names, rarely generic, that represent dedications to particular people who thus become the animal's patron. In this group, there are many eminent scientists from past and present, who have devoted their life to zoology, or even specifically to chelonology, such as Bell, Gray, Smith and Krefft in England, Bibron and Dumeril in France, and in America, Holbrook, Agassiz, Stejneger, Dunn, Baur, Gaige and Barbour—and this includes only those names that occur frequently—as well as Peters, Mertens and Wermuth in Germany, Steindachner and Siebenrock in Austria and many more. Thus an interest in the names of turtles also throws light upon an aspect of the scientific history of this group of animals.

Eagles seize Tortoises and then dash them on rocks

from a height, and having smashed the Tortoise's

shell they extract and eat the flesh.

It was in this way, I am told, that Aeschylus of Eleusis,

the tragic poet, met his end.

Aeschylus was seated upon a rock, meditating,

I suppose, and writing as usual.

He had no hair on his head and was bald.

Now an Eagle supposing his head to be a rock,

let the Tortoise which it was holding fall upon it.

And the missile struck the aforesaid poet

and killed him.

Appendix

Turtles within the agreement on international trade in endangered species of animals and plants in their natural habitat

Turtles in Appendix 1 (species in danger of extinction, in which trading is not permitted except under certain exceptional circumstances)

Batagur baska
Geoclemys hamiltoni
Geoemyda tricarinata (= Melanochelys tricarinata)
Kachuga tecta tecta
Morenia ocellata
Terrapene coahuila
Geochelone (= Testudo) elephantopus
(= Chelonoidis elephantopus)
Geochelone (= Testudo) geometrica
(= Psammobates geometrica)
Geochelone (= Testudo) radiata
(= Asterochelys radiata)
Geochelone (= Testudo) yniphora
(= Asterochelys yniphora)
Eretmochelys imbricata imbricata
Lepidochelys kempi
Lissemys punctata punctata
Trionyx ater
Trionyx nigricans
Trionyx gangeticus
Trionyx hurum
Pseudemydura umbrina

Turtles in Appendix 2 (endangered species in which trading is strictly controlled)

Clemmys muhlenbergi
Chersina spec. (= Chersina)
Geochelone spec.
Gopherus spec.

Homopus spec.
Kinixys spec.
Malacochersus spec.
Pyxis spec.
Testudo spec.
Caretta caretta
Chelonia mydas
Chelonia depressa
Eretmochelys imbricata bissa
Lepidochelys olivacea
Dermochelys coriacea
Podocnemis spec.
(spec.: all species of the genus in question)

The 1973 Washington Convention on Species Conservation

List of recent turtles (Order Testudines)

Preceding abbreviations indicate systematic status:
F = family, Sf = subfamily, T = tribe, G = genus
Arrangement is in accordance with the systematic classification given on p. 82

Suborder Casichelydia
1st Group within the Suborder, Cryptodira

F Cheloniidae (Marine or Sea turtles)

Sf Cheloniinae

G *Chelonia* (Green turtles)
Chelonia mydas mydas (LINNAEUS 1758), Atlantic Green turtle, Mediterranean and Atlantic
Chelonia mydas japonica (THUNBERG 1787), Pacific Green turtle, Indian Ocean and Pacific
Chelonia depressa GARMAN 1880, Australian Green turtle or Flatback, North and NW coast of Australia

G *Eretmochelys* (Hawksbill turtles)
Eretmochelys imbricata imbricata (LINNAEUS 1766), Atlantic Hawksbill, Mediterranean and Atlantic
Eretmochelys imbricata bissa (RÜPPELL 1835), Pacific Hawksbill, Indian Ocean and Pacific

Sf Carettinae

G *Caretta* (Loggerhead turtles)
Caretta caretta (LINNAEUS 1758), Loggerhead, all major oceans

G *Lepidochelys* (Ridleys)
Lepidochelys kempi (GARMAN 1880), Atlantic or Kemp's Ridley, Gulf of Mexico, Atlantic
Lepidochelys olivacea (ESCHSCHOLTZ 1829), Pacific Ridley, Atlantic, Indian Ocean and Pacific

F Dermochelydidae (Leathery turtles or Leatherbacks)

G *Dermochelys coriacea* (LINNAEUS 1766), Leatherback, all major oceans

F Dermatemydidae (Tabasco turtles)

Sf Dermatemydinae

G *Dermatemys* (Tabasco turtles)
Dermatemys mawi GRAY 1847, Tabasco turtle, South-eastern Mexico to Belize, Guatemala and Honduras

F Kinosternidae (Mud and Musk turtles)

G *Kinosternon* (Mud turtles)
Kinosternon acutum GRAY 1831, E Mexico (Campeche, Vera Cruz), Belize to Guatemala
Kinosternon alamosae BERRY and LEGLER 1980, Alamosa Mud turtle, NW Mexico (Sonora to Sinaloa)

Kinosternon angustipons LEGLER 1965, S Nicaragua, Costa Rica, W Panama
Kinosternon bauri bauri GARMAN 1891, Striped Mud turtle, Lower Florida Keys, USA
Kinosternon bauri palmarum STEJNEGER 1925, Upper Florida Keys and Florida, USA
Kinosternon creaseri HARTWEG 1934, Yucatan Mud turtle, E Mexico (Yucatan)
Kinosternon dunni SCHMIDT 1947, Dunn's Mud turtle, W Columbia
Kinosternon flavescens flavescens (AGASSIZ 1857), Yellow Mud turtle, Central and S USA, NE Mexico
Kinosternon flavescens durangoense IVERSON 1979, N Mexico (Durango)
Kinosternon flavescens spooneri SMITH 1951, Illinois Mud turtle, Central USA (Illinois, Iowa and Missouri)
Kinosternon flavescens arizonense GILMORE 1922, Southwestern Mud turtle, USA (Arizona) and NW Mexico (Sonora to Coahuila) (syn. with *K. f. stejnegeri* HARTWEG 1938)
Kinosternon herrerai STEJNEGER 1925, Herrera Mud turtle, SE Mexico (Vera Cruz)
Kinosternon hirtipes hirtipes WAGLER 1830, Mexican Mud turtle, Central Mexico (Valley of Mexico)
Kinosternon hirtipes chapalaense IVERSON 1981, Chapala Lake Mud turtle, Mexico (Ialisco and Michoacan, Lake Chapala)
Kinosternon hirtipes megacephalum IVERSON 1981, Viesca Mud turtle, Central Mexico (Coahuila)
Kinosternon hirtipes murrayi GLASS and HARTWEG 1951, Big Bend or Murray's Mud turtle, S USA (SW Texas), NW and Central Mexico (Chihuahua to Mexico)
Kinosternon hirtipes magdalense IVERSON 1981, San Juanico Mud turtle, Central Mexico (Michoacan, Magdalene valley)
Kinosternon hirtipes tarascense IVERSON 1981, Patzcuaro Mud turtle, Central Mexico (Michoacan, Lake Patzcuaro)
Kinosternon integrum (LE CONTE 1854), W and SE Mexico (Sonora to Oaxaca and Vera Cruz)
Kinosternon leucostomum (DUMERIL, D. and B. 1851), White-lipped Mud turtle, E Mexico, Belize, Guatemala, Honduras, Nicaragua, Costa Rica, Panama (syn. *K. postinguinale*)
Kinosternon leucostomum spurelli BOULENGER 1913, Spurell's Mud turtle, W Columbia
Kinosternon oaxacae BERRY and IVERSON 1980, S Oaxaca, Mexico
Kinosternon scorpioides scorpioides (LINNAEUS 1766), Scorpion Mud turtle, Columbia, Venezuela, Guiana, Surinam, Fr. Guiana, N Brazil
Kinosternon scorpioides abaxillare (BAUR 1925), Chiapas Mud turtle, S Mexico (Chiapas)
Kinosternon scorpioides albogulare DUMERIL and BOCOURT 1870, Costa Rice, Isle San Andres and Canas
Kinosternon scorpioides carajasensis DA CUNHA 1970, Brazil (Para, Serra dos Carajas)
Kinosternon scorpioides cruentatum (DUMERIL, D. and B. 1851), Red-spotted Mud turtle, S Mexico (Chiapas, Oaxaca), Guatemala, El Salvador, Honduras, Nicaragua, Costa Rica (syn. *K. albogulare* DUMERIL and BOCOURT 1870)
Kinosternon scorpioides pachyurum MÜLLER and HELLMICH 1936, Bolivia

Kinosternon scorpioides seriei FREIBERG 1936, NW Argentina

Kinosternon scorpioides panamense K. P. SCHMIDT 1946, Panama

Kinosternon sonoriense sonoriense (LE CONTE 1854), Sonoran Mud turtle, SW USA (SE California to SW Texas), N Mexico (Sonora to Durango, Chihuahua)

Kinosternon sonoriense longifemorale IVERSON 1981, Sonoyata Mud turtle, Mexico (NW Sonora)

Kinosternon subrubrum subrubrum (LACEPEDE 1788), Eastern Mud turtle, E and SE USA (Illinois to N Florida)

Kinosternon subrubrum hippocrepis GRAY 1856, Mississippi Mud turtle, SE USA (Oklahoma to E Texas, Mississippi)

Kinosternon subrubrum steindachneri SIEBENROCK 1906, Florida Mud turtle, SE USA (Florida)

G *Sternotherus* (Musk turtles)

Sternotherus carinatus (GRAY 1856), Razorback or Keel-backed Musk turtle, S USA (Oklahoma, Texas, Mississippi)

Sternotherus depressus TINKLE and WEBB 1955, Flattened Musk turtle, SE USA (N Alabama, Tennessee)

Sternotherus minor minor (AGASSIZ 1857), Loggerhead Musk turtle, SE USA (S Tennessee to Florida)

Sternotherus minor peltifer SMITH and GLASS 1947, Stripeneck Musk turtle, SE USA (E Tennessee to Mississippi and Alabama)

Sternotherus odoratus (LATREILLE 1801), Common Musk turtle, Stinkpot, S Canada to Texas and Florida

F Staurotypidae (Large-headed Mud turtles)

G *Claudius* (Large-headed Mud turtles)

Claudius angustatus COPE 1865, Narrow-bridged Mud turtle, E Mexico, Guatemala and Belize

G *Staurotypus*

Staurotypus salvini GRAY 1864, Salvini's turtle, S Mexico, Southern Guatemala and El Salvador

Staurotypus triporcatus (WIEGMANN 1828), Giant Musk turtle, SE Mexico, Northern Guatemala and Belize

F Chelydridae (Snapping turtles)

G *Chelydra* (Snapping turtles)

Chelydra serpentina serpentina (LINNAEUS 1758), Common Snapping turtle, S Canada, E USA (except Florida), E Mexico (as far as Yucatan)

Chelydra serpentina acutirostris PETERS 1862, Panama and Ecuador

Chelydra serpentina osceola STEJNEGER 1918, Florida Snapping turtle, SE USA (Florida)

Chelydra serpentina rossignoni (BOCOURT 1868), Guatemala, Honduras, El Salvador, Nicaragua, Costa Rica

G *Macroclemys* (Alligator Snappers)

Macroclemys temmincki (TROOST 1835), Alligator Snapping turtle, SE USA (Kansas, Indiana to Florida and Georgia)

F Platysternidae (Big-headed turtles)

G *Platysternon* (Big-headed turtles)

Platysternon megacephalum megacephalum GRAY 1831, S China, Hainan, Northern and Central Vietnam

Platysternon megacephalum peguense GRAY 1870, S Burma, Central N Thailand, N Laos

Platysternon megacephalum tristernalis SCHLEICH and GRUBER 1983, Yünnan, China

Platysternon megacephalum vogeli WERMUTH 1969, NW Thailand (Chiengmai)

F Carettochelydidae (Papuan turtles)

Sf Carettochelydinae

G *Carettochelys* (Papuan turtles)

Carettochelys insculpta RAMSEY 1887, Plateless River turtle or Pig Nose turtle, S Papua-New Guinea and N Australia (Northern Territory)

F Trionychidae (Soft-shelled turtles)

Sf Cyclanorbinae

G *Cyclanorbis*

Cyclanorbis elegans (GRAY 1869), Nubian Soft-shelled turtle, Central Africa (Togo to Sudan)

Cyclanorbis senegalensis (DUMERIL and BIBRON 1835), Senegal Softshell, Central Africa (Senegal to Nigeria and Sudan)

G *Cycloderma*

Cycloderma aubryi (DUMERIL 1856), Aubry's Softshell, West Africa (Gabun, Chad, Central African Republic, Zaire, Congo as far as Angola)

Cycloderma frenatum PETERS 1854, Zambesi or Bridled Softshell, Southeast Africa (Tanzania to Mozambique)

G *Lissemys* (Indian Soft Terrapins)

Lissemys punctata punctata (LACEPEDE 1788), Pakistan, N India, Bangladesh, NW Burma

Lissemys punctata granosa (SCHOEPFF 1801), India S of the Ganges, Sri Lanka

Lissemys punctata scutata (PETERS 1868), Central Burma

Sf Trionychinae

G *Chitra*

Chitra indica (GRAY 1831), River Softshell, Pakistan, N India, Bangladesh and Eastern Indochina

G *Pelochelys* (Giant Soft-shelled turtles)

Pelochelys bibroni (OWEN 1853), Giant Soft-shelled turtle, Eastern India, Indochina, S China with Hainan, Sunda Archipelago, Philippines and New Guinea

G *Trionyx* (Soft-shelled turtles)

Trionyx ater WEBB and LEGLER 1960, Black Softshell, N Mexico (Coahuila)

Trionyx cartilagineus (BODDAERT 1770), Black-Rayed Softshell, Southern Indochina, Sunda Archipelago

Trionyx euphraticus (DAUDIN 1802), Euphrates Soft-shelled turtle, Asia Minor (SE Turkey, Syria, Irak, Iran, N Israel)

Trionyx ferox (SCHNEIDER 1783), Florida Softshell, SE USA (South Carolina, Georgia and Florida)

Trionyx formosus GRAY 1869, Burmese Softshell, Burma

Trionyx gangeticus CUVIER 1825, Ganges Soft-shelled turtle, Afghanistan (Pakta), Pakistan, N India (Indus, Ganges)

Trionyx hurum GRAY 1831, Peacock Softshell, Eastern India (Ganges and Brahmaputra)

Trionyx leithi GRAY 1872, Nagpur Softshell, Central India (from Ganges southwards to Madras)

Trionyx muticus muticus LE SUER 1827, Smooth or Spineless Softshell, Mid and Central southern USA

Trionyx muticus calvatus WEBB 1959, Gulf Coast Smooth Softshell, Central southern USA, Gulf Coast (Mississippi)

Trionyx nigricans ANDERSON 1875, Temple Softshell, Bangladesh (only in Chittagong)

Trionyx sinensis sinensis WIEGMANN 1804, Chinese Softshelled turtle, China, Korea, Far East of USSR, N Vietnam, Japan, Hawaii (introduced there)

Trionyx sinensis tuberculatus CANTOR 1842, Taiwan, Hainan, Central China

Trionyx spiniferus spiniferus LE SUER 1827, Eastern Spiny Softshell, S Canada, Eastern USA

Trionyx spiniferus asper (AGASSIZ 1857), Gulf Coast Spiny Softshell, SE USA (Mississippi to North Carolina)

Trionyx spiniferus emoryi (AGASSIZ 1857), Texas Spiny Softshell, SW USA and NE Mexico

Trionyx spiniferus guadelupensis WEBB 1962, Guadelupe Spiny Softshell, S USA (S Texas)

Trionyx spiniferus hartwegi (CONANT and GOIN 1948), Western Spiny Softshell, NW USA (Montana, Minnesota, Colorado and Arkansas)

Trionyx spiniferus pallidus WEBB 1962, Pallid Spiny Softshell, S USA (Oklahoma, Texas, Louisiana)

Trionyx steindachneri SIEBENROCK 1906, Steindachner's Softshell, S China and Hainan

Trionyx swinhoei (GRAY 1873), Shanghai Softshell, S China (Shanghai)

Trionyx subplanus GEOFFROY 1809, Malayan Soft-shelled turtle, Western Indochina, Sunda Archipelago, Philippines

Trionyx triunguis (FORSKAL 1775), African or Nile Soft-shelled turtle, Africa (except NW Africa and S Africa), SW Asia (Israel)

F Testudinidae (Land tortoises, True tortoises)

G *Chersina* (African Bowsprit tortoises)

Chersina angulata (SCHWEIGGER 1812), Bowsprit tortoise, S Africa (Great Namaqualand and Cape Province)

G *Agrionemys* (Four-toed tortoises)

Agrionemys horsfieldi (GRAY 1844), Horsfield's tortoise, Soviet Central Asia, Iran, Afghanistan, N Pakistan

---

G *Asterochelys* (Radiated tortoises)

Asterochelys radiata (SHAW 1802), Radiated tortoise, SW Madagascar

Asterochelys yniphora (VAILLANT 1885), Angonoka, Central W Madagascar (Cape Sada)

G *Chelonoidis* (South American tortoises)

Chelonoidis chilensis chilensis (GRAY 1870), Argentine tortoise, Central and N Argentina, Paraguay

Chelonoidis chilensis donosobarrosi (FREIBERG 1873), S Argentina (Patagonia, La Pampas)

Chelonoidis chilensis petersi (FREIBERG 1873), N Argentina (Santiago del Estero and La Rioja)

Chelonoidis carbonaria (SPIX 1824), Coal tortoise, Red-footed tortoise, S America E of Andes from Columbia to N Argentina and Paraguay

Chelonoidis denticulata (LINNAEUS 1766), Brazilian Giant tortoise, Hercules tortoise, Jaboty tortoise, Wood tortoise, Yellow-footed tortoise, S American Forest tortoise, S America E of Andes, from Columbia to Peru, Central Brazil and Bolivia and Island of Trinidad

Chelonoidis elephantopus elephantopus (HARLAN 1827), Giant Galapagos tortoise, Galapagos, (SW Albemarle)

Chelonoidis elephantopus abingdoni (GÜNTHER 1877), Galapagos (Abingdon)

Chelonoidis elephantopus becki (ROTHSCHILD 1901), Galapagos (N Albemarle)

Chelonoidis elephantopus chathamensis (VAN DENBURGH 1907), Galapagos (Chatham)

Chelonoidis elephantopus darwini (VAN DENBURGH 1907), Galapagos (James)

Chelonoidis elephantopus ephippium (GÜNTHER 1875), Galapagos (Duncan)

Chelonoidis elephantopus guentheri (BAUR 1889), Galapagos (SE Albemarle)

Chelonoidis elephantopus hoodensis (VAN DENBURGH 1907), Galapagos (Hood)

Chelonoidis elephantopus microphyes (GÜNTHER 1875), Galapagos (N Albemarle)

Chelonoidis elephantopus nigrita (DUMERIL and BIBRON 1835), Galapagos (Indefatigable)

Chelonoidis elephantopus vandenburghi (DE SOLA 1903), Galapagos (Central Albemarle)

G *Geochelone*

Geochelone elegans elegans (SCHOEPFF 1795), Star tortoise, Indian Starred tortoise, India and Sri Lanka

Geochelone elegans platynota (BLYTH 1863), Burma tortoise, Burma

Geochelone pardalis pardalis (BELL 1828), Leopard tortoise, SW South Africa

Geochelone pardalis babcocki (LOVERIDGE 1935), Leopard tortoise, E Africa from Sudan to SE South Africa

Geochelone sulcata (MILLER 1779), African Spurred tortoise, Central Africa from Senegal to Ethiopia, Sahel zone

---

G *Gopherus* (Gopher tortoises)

Gopherus agassizi (COOPER 1863), Desert tortoise, Californian Gopher tortoise, SW USA (Nevada, California, Arizona), NW Mexico (Baja California, Sonora)

Gopherus berlandieri (AGASSIZ 1857), Texas tortoise, S USA (Texas) and NE Mexico (Coahuila, Nuevo Leon and Tamaulipas)

Gopherus flavomarginata LEGLER 1959, Mexican Gopher tortoise, N Mexico (Chihuahua, Coahuila, Durango)

Gopherus polyphemus (DAUDIN 1801), Georgia Gopher tortoise, SE USA (Louisiana, Georgia, S Carolina, Florida)

G *Homopus* (Flat tortoises)

Homopus areolatus (THUNBERG 1787), Areolated or Parrotbeak tortoise, S Africa (SE Cape Province)

Homopus boulengeri DUERDEN 1906, Boulenger's tortoise, S Africa (Karroo region to Great Namaqualand and Cape Province)

Homopus femoralis BOULENGER 1888, Karroo tortoise, S Africa (SE Cape Province)

Homopus signatus (SCHOEPFF 1801), Speckled tortoise, S Africa (SW Cape Province, Namaqualand)

G *Indotestudo* (Indian tortoises)

Indotestudo elongata elongata (BLYTH 1853), Yellow tortoise, Eastern India, all Indochina

Indotestudo elongata forsteni (SCHLEGEL and MÜLLER 1844), Sulawesi and Halmahera

Indotestudo elongata travancorica (BOULENGER 1907), Travancore tortoise, SW India (Travancore, Cochin)

G *Kinixys* (Hinged tortoises, Flexible tortoises)

Kinixys belliana belliana GRAY 1831, Bell's Eastern Hinged tortoise, Central and S Africa (Cameroon to Angola, Ethiopia to Botswana), Madagascar

Kinixys belliana mertensi LAURENT 1956, Central Africa (N Congo)

Kinixys belliana natalensis HEWITT 1935, Natal and Mozambique

Kinixys belliana nogueyi (LATASTE 1886), W Africa (Senegal to Cameroon)

Kinixys erosa (SCHWEIGGER 1812), West African or Schweigger's Hinge-backed tortoise, W Africa (Gambia to Congo)

Kinixys homeana BELL 1827, Home's Hinged tortoise, W Africa (Guinea to Congo)

G *Malacochersus* (Flexible-shelled tortoises, "Crevice" tortoises)

Malacochersus tornieri (SIEBENROCK 1903), Pancake tortoise, Tornier's tortoise, E Africa (Kenya and Tanzania)

G *Manouria*

Manouria emys emys (SCHLEGEL and MÜLLER 1844), Burmese Brown tortoise, S Indochina (S Thailand, S Burma, Sunda Archipelago)

Manouria emys nutapundi (REIMANN and WIROT 1979), Mid and NW Indochina (N Thailand, N Burma)

Manouria impressa (GÜNTHER 1882), Impressed tortoise, Mid and Southern Indochina

G *Megalochelys* (Aldabra Giant tortoises)

Megalochelys gigantea (SCHWEIGGER 1812), Seychelles Giant tortoise, Aldabra and Seychelles

G *Psammobates* (South African Land tortoises)

Psammobates geometrica (LINNAEUS 1758), Geometric tortoise, South Africa (SW of Cape Province)

Psammobates oculifera (KUHL 1820), African Serrated tortoise, South Africa (Damaraland, Namaqualand, Orange Free State, Botswana)

Psammobates tentoria tentoria (BELL 1828), African tent tortoise, SE Africa (SE of Cape Province)

Psammobates tentoria trimeni (BOULENGER 1886), Western tent tortoise, South Africa (Namaqualand)

Psammobates tentoria verroxi (SMITH 1839), Northern tent tortoise, South Africa (Great Namaqualand, Orange Free State, Cape Province)

G *Pyxis* (Spider tortoises)

Pyxis arachnoides arachnoides BELL 1827, Spider tortoise, SW Madagascar (from Tulear southwards)

Pyxis arachnoides brygooi (VUILLEMIN and DOMERGUE 1972), SW Madagascar (Morombe to Tulear)

Pyxis arachnoides matzi BOUR 1978, SE Madagascar

Pyxis planicauda (GRANDIDIER 1867), Flat-backed tortoise, W Madagascar (near Morondava)

G *Testudo* (European Land tortoises)

Testudo graeca graeca LINNAEUS 1758, Spur-thighed Mediterranean Land tortoise or Moorish tortoise, S Spain, Pityusen, NW Africa (Morocco to Libya)

Testudo graeca ibera PALLAS 1814, Eastern spur-thighed or Iberian Land tortoise, Balkan Peninsula, Caucasus countries, NW Turkey, N Iran

Testudo graeca terrestris FORSKAL 1775, Asia Minor (Anatolia, Lebanon, Syria, Israel) and NE Africa (Egypt, Libya)

Testudo graeca zarundyni NIKOLSKIJ 1896, E Iran

Testudo hermanni hermanni GMELIN 1789, Hermann's or Greek or Spur-tailed Mediterranean Land tortoise, S Italy, Balkan Peninsula

Testudo hermanni robertmertensi WERMUTH 1952, E Spain, S France, Central Italy, Corsica and Sardinia, Balearic Is.

Testudo kleinmanni LORTET 1883, Egyptian tortoise, Libya to Egypt, Sinai, S Israel

Testudo marginata SCHOEPFF 1792, Margined tortoise, Greece, Sardinia

F Emydidae (Emydid turtles, Terrapins, Pond turtles)

Sf Batagurinae (Old World Emydid turtles)

T Geoemydini

G *Cyclemys* (Malayan Pond turtles)

Cyclemys dentata (GRAY 1831), Indochina, western Indo-Austral. Archipelago, Philippines

G *Geoemyda* (Spengler's terrapins)

Geoemyda spengleri spengleri (GMELIN 1789), Indochinese serrated terrapin or Spengler's terrapin, S China, SE Indochina, Sumatra and Kalimantan

Geoemyda spengleri japonica FAN 1931, Japan (Riu-kiu Islands)

G *Heosemys* (Spined terrapins)

Heosemys depressa (ANDERSON 1875), Arakan terrapin, W Burma (Arakan)

Heosemys grandis (GRAY 1860), Giant Spined terrapin, Southern Indochina

Heosemys leytensis TAYLOR 1920, Philippines (Leyte Island)

Heosemys silvatica (HENDERSON 1912), SW India (Cochin)

Heosemys spinosa (GRAY 1831), Common spined terrapin, Indochina and Indo-Austral. Archipelago

G *Melanochelys* (Indian terrapins)

Melanochelys tricarinata (BLYTH 1856), NE India (Bangladesh)

Melanochelys trijuga trijuga (SCHWEIGGER 1812), Hard-shelled terrapin, India (Bombay, Madras, Mysore)

Melanochelys trijuga coronata (ANDERSON 1878), SW India (Travancore, Cochin)

Megalochelys trijuga edeniana (THEOBALD 1876), Burma

Megalochelys trijuga indopeninsularis (ANNANDALE 1913), E India (Chota Nagpur to Bengal)

Megalochelys trijuga parkeri (DERANIYAGALA 1939), N Sri Lanka and coastal regions

Megalochelys trijuga thermalis (LESSON 1830), Sri Lanka, mountain region

---

G *Rhinoclemmys* (American terrapins)

Rhinoclemmys annulata (GRAY 1860), from Costa Rica south to Columbia, Venezuela and Ecuador

Rhinoclemmys areolata (DUMERIL, DUMERIL and BIBRON 1851), from Mexico (Vera Cruz, Quintana Roo) southwards to northern Guatemala and Belize

Rhinoclemmys diademata (MERTENS 1954), Venezuela

Rhinoclemmys funerea (COPE 1876), Costa Rica

Rhinoclemmys melanosterna (GRAY 1851), Columbia, Ecuador and Panama

Rhinoclemmys nasuta (BOULENGER 1902), Ecuador

Rhinoclemmys pulcherrima pulcherrima (GRAY 1855), Mexican Reed or Wood turtle, W and S Mexico (Sonora to Guerrero, as far as western Oaxaca)

Rhinoclemmys pulcherrima incisa (BOCOURT 1868), S Mexico (Oaxaca, Chiapas), S Guatemala, El Salvador

Rhinoclemmys pulcherrima manni (DUNN 1930), Costa Rica

Rhinoclemmys pulcherrima rogerbarbouri (ERNST 1978), Mexico (Sonora)

Rhinoclemmys punctularia (DAUDIN 1802), French Guiana, N Brazil and Trinidad

Rhinoclemmys rubida rubida (COPE 1870), S Mexico (Oaxaca)

Rhinoclemmys rubida perixantha (MOSIMANN and RABB 1953), SW Mexico (Colima, Michoacan)

G *Pyxidea* (Indian Keelbacked terrapins)

Pyxidea mouhoti (GRAY 1862), Keelbacked terrapin, from E India (Assam) eastwards to Indochina (N Thailand, Laos, N Vietnam) and Hainan

---

G *Notochelys*

Notochelys platynota (GRAY 1834), Purple-bellied terrapin, S Indochina (S Vietnam, S Thailand, Malaysia), Sunda Islands (Sumatra, Banka, Kalimantan)

T Batagurini
1st Group:

G *Chinemys*

Chinemys kwangtungensis (POPE 1934), S China (Kwangtung) and N Vietnam

Chinemys megalocephala FANG 1934, China (Nanking Province)

Chinemys reevesi (GRAY 1831), Chinese terrapin, Reeves' turtle or Golden turtle, Central China and Japan

---

G *Cuora* (Asiatic Box turtles)

Cuora amboinensis (DAUDIN 1798), Amboina or Malayan Box turtle, S Indochina, Indo-Austral. Archipelago, Philippines

Cuora flavomarginata flavomarginata (GRAY 1863), Yellow-headed Box turtle, S China, Taiwan and Riu-Kiu Islands

Cuora flavomarginata hainanensis LI 1958, Hainan

Cuora galbinifrons BOURRET 1939, Vietnamese Box turtle, N Vietnam, S China

Cuora trifasciata (BELL 1825), Three-lined or Three-handed Box turtle, N Vietnam, S China and Hainan

Cuora yunnanensis (BOULENGER 1906), Yunnan Box turtle, S China (Yunnan)

G *Geoclemys* (Indian Black Pond turtles)

Geoclemys hamiltoni (GRAY 1831), Black Pond turtle, Pakistan and N India (as far as Bengal)

G *Hieremys* (Temple turtles)

Hieremys annandalei (BOULENGER 1903), Temple turtle, Annandale's turtle, S Indochina

---

G *Malayemys* (Malayan turtles)

Malayemys subtrijuga (SCHLEGEL and MÜLLER 1844), Malayan snail-eating turtle, S Indochina and Java

---

G *Mauremys* (Old World Pond turtles)

Mauremys caspica caspica (GMELIN 1774), Caspian turtle, Caucasus countries, SW Asia (E Turkey, Iran, Irak)

Mauremys caspica rivulata (VALENCIENNES 1833), Southern Balkan Peninsula, SW Asia (W Turkey, Syria, Israel, Crete, Cyprus)

Mauremys japonica (TEMMINCK and SCHLEGEL 1833), Japanese terrapin, S Japan

Mauremys leprosa (SCHWEIGGER 1812), Spanish turtle, Iberian Peninsula and NW Africa

Mauremys nigricans (GRAY 1834), Chinese terrapin, S China, N Vietnam, Taiwan and Hainan

---

G *Morenia*

Morenia ocellata (DUMERIL and BIBRON 1835), Indochina (Burma)

Morenia petersi (ANDERSON 1879), E India (Bengal)

G *Ocadia*

Ocadia sinensis (GRAY 1834), Green-headed turtle, S China and E Indochina (as far as Central Vietnam), Hainan and Taiwan

---

G *Sacalia*

Sacalia bealei (GRAY 1831), Ocellate Pond turtle, S China, E Indochina, Hainan

---

G *Siebenrockiella* (Black turtles)

Siebenrockiella crassicollis (GRAY 1831), Black turtle, S Indochina, Sunda Islands, Sumatra, Java and Kalimantan

---

2nd Group:
(Genera specialized as diving turtles)

G *Batagur* (Batagur turtles)

Batagur baska (GRAY 1831), Batagur turtle, NE India (Bengal), Indochina, (Burma, Thailand, S Vietnam, Malaysia), Sumatra

---

G *Callagur* (Callagur turtles)

Callagur borneoensis (SCHLEGEL and MÜLLER 1844), Painted Batagur, Malay Peninsula, Sumatra and Kalimantan

---

G *Hardella* (Diadem turtles)

Hardella thurji thurji (GRAY 1831), Diadem turtle, India (Ganges and Brahmaputra)

Hardella thurji indi (GRAY 1870), India (Indus)

G *Kachuga* (Roof turtles or Roofed terrapins)

Kachuga dhongoka (GRAY 1834), Dhongoka Roof turtle, S Nepal, NE India, eastwards to Assam and Bangladesh

Kachuga kachuga (GRAY 1831), Bengal Roof turtle, S Nepal, NE India, Bangladesh, eastwards to NW Indochina (Burma)

Kachuga smithi (GRAY 1863), Smith's Roof turtle, Pakistan, NE India, eastwards as far as Bengal

Kachuga sylhetensis (JERDON 1870), Assam Roof turtle, NE India (Assam)

Kachuga tecta tecta (GRAY 1831), Indian Roof turtle or Roofed terrapin or Dura terrapin, Pakistan, N India (Indus, Lower Ganges, Brahmaputra)

Kachuga tecta circumdata MERTENS 1969, N India (Upper Ganges and Yamuna)

Kachuga tecta tentoria (GRAY 1834), Central India (Mahanadi, Godavari and Kistna Rivers)

Kachuga trivittata (DUMERIL and BIBRON 1835), W Indochina (N Burma)

G *Orlitia* (Bornean River turtles)

Orlitia borneensis FRAY 1873, Bornean River turtle, S Indochina (Malaysia), Sumatra and Kalimantan

Sf Emydinae (American Emydine turtles)

T Nectemydina

G *Chrysemys* (Painted turtles, Cooters and Sliders)

Chrysemys picta picta (SCHNEIDER 1783), Eastern Painted turtle, S Canada, E of USA (S to Georgia and Alabama)

Chrysemys picta dorsalis AGASSIZ 1857, Southern Painted turtle, SE of USA (course of Mississippi)

Chrysemys picta marginata AGASSIZ 1857, Midland Painted turtle, SE Canada and mid USA (E to New York, S to Alabama)

Chrysemys picta belli (GRAY 1831), Western Painted turtle, S Canada, Western and Central USA except for range of *Ch. p. dorsalis*

Chrysemys concinna concinna (LE CONTE 1830), River Cooter, SE USA (Oklahoma to Virginia)

Chrysemys concinna hieroglyphica (HOLBROOK 1836), Slider or Hieroglyphic turtle, S USA (from Kansas eastwards to Kentucky, southwards to Texas and Alabama)

Chrysemys concinna mobilensis (HOLBROOK 1838), Mobile Cooter, Gulf Coast of USA (from Texas to W Florida)

Chrysemys concinna suwanniensis (CARR 1937), Suwannee Cooter, Florida (Suwannee River)

Chrysemys concinna texana (BAUR 1893), Texas Slider, S USA (Texas) and NE Mexico (Nuevo Leon)

Chrysemys floridana floridana (LE CONTE 1830), Cooter, SE USA (from Maryland through N Florida to SE Alabama)

Chrysemys floridana hoyi (AGASSIZ 1857), Missouri-Slider, S USA (from Kansas and Illinois southwards to Texas and Alabama)

Chrysemys floridana peninsularis (CARR 1938), Peninsula-Cooter, SE USA (Florida)

Chrysemys rubriventris rubriventris (LE CONTE 1830), Red-bellied turtle, E USA (from New Jersey southwards to North Carolina)

Chrysemys rubriventris alabamensis (BAUR 1893), Alabama Red-bellied turtle, SE USA (N Florida to Alabama)

Chrysemys rubriventris bangsi (BABCOCK 1937), Plymouth turtle, NE USA (Massachusetts)

Chrysemys rubriventris nelsoni (CARR 1938), Florida Red-bellied turtle, SE USA (Florida)

Chrysemys scripta scripta (SCHOEPFF 1792), Yellow-bellied turtle, Pond Slider, E and SE USA (Virginia to N Florida)

Chrysemys scripta elegans (WIED 1839), Red-eared turtle, Mid and E USA, NE Mexico

Chrysemys scripta troosti (HOLBROOK 1836), Cumberland turtle, E USA (from Kentucky to Alabama)

Chrysemys scripta gaigeae (HARTWEG 1939), Rio Grande or Big Bend turtle, S USA (Texas) and N Mexico (Coahuila and Durango)

Chrysemys scripta hiltoni (CARR 1942), Sonora Slider, NW Mexico (Sonora and Sinaloa)

Chrysemys scripta taylori (LEGLER 1960), Cuatro Ciénegas Slider, N Mexico (Coahuila, Cuatro Ciénegas)

Chrysemys scripta nebulosa VAN DENBURGH 1895, Baja California Cooter, NW Mexico (Baja California)

Chrysemys scripta cataspila (GÜNTHER 1885), Mexican Slider, NE Mexico (Nuevo Leon south to Vera Cruz)

Chrysemys scripta ornata (GRAY 1831), Ornate Slider, W Mexico (Sonora to Oaxaca)

Chrysemys scripta yaquia (LEGLER and WEBB 1970), Mexico (Sonora)

Chrysemys scripta grayi BOCOURT 1868, Gray's Slider, S Mexico (Pacific coast E of Isthmus of Tehuantepec) to Guatemala and El Salvador

Chrysemys scripta venusta (GRAY 1855), Costa Rican Slider, SE Mexico to Costa Rica

Chrysemys scripta callirostris (GRAY 1855), Jicotea, South American Slider, from Columbia eastwards to Venezuela

Chrysemys scripta dorbigni (DUMERIL and BIBRON 1835), South American Slider, NE Argentina to Uruguay

Chrysemys scripta brasiliensis (FREIBERG 1969), Brazilian Slider, S Brazil (Rio Grande do Sul)

Chrysemys terrapen terrapen (LACEPEDE 1788), Antillian or Jamaican Slider, Jamaica

Chrysemys terrapen angusta (BARBOUR and CARR 1940), Pinar del Rio Slider, Cuba (Pinar del Rio)

Chrysemys terrapen decorata (BARBOUR and CARR 1940), Haitian Slider, W Hispaniola (Haiti and Ile de Vache)

Chrysemys terrapen decussata (GRAY 1831), Cuba Slider, Cuba and Isle of Pines (syn. *Ch. t. rugosa* (SHAW 1802)

Chrysemys terrapen felis (BARBOUR 1935), Cat Island Slider, Cat Island

Chrysemys terrapen granti (BARBOUR and CARR 1941), Grand Cayman Island terrapin, Grand Cayman Island

Chrysemys terrapen malonei (BARBOUR and CARR 1938), Great Inagua terrapin, Bahamas (Great Inagua)

Chrysemys terrapen plana (BARBOUR and CARR 1940), Rio Jobabo terrapin, Cuba (W Oriente, Rio Jobabo)

Chrysemys terrapen stejnegeri (SCHMIDT 1928), Porto Rico Slider, Porto Rico, Vieques Island

Chrysemys terrapen vicina (BARBOUR and CARR 1940), San Domingo Slider, Hispaniola, San Domingo

G *Graptemys* (Map turtles or Sawbacks)

Graptemys barbouri CARR and MARCHAND 1942, Barbour's Map turtle, SE USA (inner triangle of Alabama, Georgia, Florida)

Graptemys caglei HAYNES and McKOWN 1974, Cagle's Map turtle, Guadeloupe River Map turtle, SE USA (Texas, Guadeloupe and San Antonio River)

Graptemys flavimaculata CAGLE 1954, Yellow-blotched Map turtle, SE USA (Mississippi, Pascagoula River)

Graptemys geographica (LE SUEUR 1817), Common Map turtle, from SE Canada southwards across Central USA (to Kansas, Oklahoma, Georgia)

Graptemys kohni (BAUR 1890), Mississippi Map turtle, Mid and southern USA, southwards to Gulf Coast (Texas to Alabama)

Graptemys nigrinoda nigrinoda CAGLE 1954, Black-knobbed Map turtle, SE USA (Alabama, Black Warrior River and Alabama River)

Graptemys nigrinoda delticola FOLKERTS and MOUNT 1969, Delta Map turtle, SE USA (Alabama, delta in Mobile Bay)

Graptemys oculifera (BAUR 1890), Ringed Map turtle, SE USA (Louisiana and Mississippi, Pearl River)

Graptemys pseudogeographica pseudogeographica (GRAY 1831), False Map turtle, N and Central USA (Minnesota to Illinois)

Graptemys pseudogeographica ouachitensis CAGLE 1953, Ouachita Map turtle, Mid USA (Kansas to Louisiana)

Graptemys pseudogeographica sabinensis CAGLE 1953, Sabine Map turtle, S USA (E Texas and Louisiana)

Graptemys pseudogeographica versa STEJNEGER 1925, Texas Map turtle, S USA (Central and S Texas)

Graptemys pulchra BAUR 1893, Alabama Map turtle, SE USA (Louisiana to Florida)

G *Malaclemys* (Diamondback terrapins)

Malaclemys terrapin terrapin (SCHOEPFF 1793), Northern Diamondback terrapin, NE USA (coast of Massachusetts to North Carolina)

Malaclemys terrapin centrata (LATREILLE 1802), Carolina Diamondback terrapin, E USA (coast of North Carolina to Florida)

Malaclemys terrapin littoralis HAY 1904, Texas Diamondback terrapin, S USA (Gulf Coast from Louisiana southwards to Yucatan, Mexico)

Malaclemys terrapin macrospilota HAY 1904, Ornate Diamondback terrapin, SE USA (S and W coast of Florida)

Malaclemys terrapin pileata (WIED 1865), Mississippi Diamondback terrapin, SE USA (Gulf Coast from W Florida to Louisiana)

Malaclemys terrapin rhizophorarum FOWLER 1906, Mangrove Diamondback terrapin, SE USA (Florida Keys)

Malaclemys terrapin tequesta SCHWARTZ 1955, Florida Diamondback terrapin, SE USA (E coast of Florida)

T Emydina

G *Clemmys* (American Pond turtles)

Clemmys guttata (SCHNEIDER 1792), Spotted turtle, NE and E USA (Illinois to Maine, southwards to Georgia)

Clemmys insculpta (LE CONTE 1830), Wood turtle, SE Canada (Nova Scotia) to NE USA (Virginia)

Clemmys marmorata marmorata (BAIRD and GIRARD 1852), Western or Pacific Pond turtle, SW Canada (British Columbia) to NW USA (California)

Clemmys marmorata pallida SEELIGER 1945, W coast of USA from N California to NE Mexico (Baja California)

Clemmys muhlenbergi (SCHOEPFF 1792), Muhlenberg's turtle, Bog turtle, NE USA (from New York to North Carolina)

G *Deirochelys* (Chicken turtles)

Deirochelys reticularia reticularia (LATREILLE 1801), Eastern Chicken turtle, SE USA (E Louisiana to North Carolina)

Deirochelys reticularia chrysae SCHWARTZ 1956, Florida Chicken turtle, SE USA (Florida)

Deirochelys reticularia miaria SCHWARTZ 1956, Western Chicken turtle, SE USA (Oklahoma to Louisiana and Texas)

G *Emydoidea* (American Semi-box turtles)

Emydoidea blandingi (HOLBROOK 1838), Blanding's turtle, SE Canada and Central USA (area of Great Lakes)

G *Emys* (European Pond turtles)

Emys orbicularis (LINNAEUS 1758), European Pond turtle, Europe (except Scandinavia and NE Europe) eastwards to W Asia (Lake Aral), NW Africa (Morocco to Tunisia)

G *Terrapene* (American Box turtles)

Terrapene carolina carolina (LINNAEUS 1758), Eastern Box turtle, NE USA (Maine to Georgia, westwards to Michigan, Illinois, Tennessee)

Terrapene carolina bauri TAYLOR 1895, Florida Box turtle, SE USA (Florida)

Terrapene carolina major (AGASSIZ 1857), Gulf Coast Box turtle, SE USA (Gulf Coast from W Florida to Texas)

Terrapene carolina mexicana (GRAY 1849), Mexican Box turtle, E Mexico (Nuevo Leon southwards to Vera Cruz)

Terrapene carolina triunguis (AGASSIZ 1857), Three-toed Box turtle, Central and S USA (from Missouri southwards to Texas and Alabama)

Terrapene carolina yucatana (BOULENGER 1895), Yucatan Box turtle, SE Mexico (Yucatan and Quintana Roo)

Terrapene coahuila SCHMIDT and OWENS 1944, Coahuila Box turtle, NE Mexico (Coahuila)

Terrapene nelsoni nelsoni STEJNEGER 1925, Nayarit Box turtle, NE Mexico (Nayarit)

Terrapene nelsoni klauberi BOGERT 1943, Klauber's Box turtle, NW Mexico (S Sonora)

Terrapene ornata ornata (AGASSIZ 1857), Ornate Box turtle, Central and S USA (from S Dakota and Illinois southwards to Arizona and Texas)

Terrapene ornata luteola SMITH and RAMSAY 1952, Desert Box turtle, S USA (S Texas) and NE Mexico (Coahuila to Tamaulipas)

2nd Group within the Order, Pleurodira (Side-necked turtles)

F **Pelomedusidae** (Pelomedusid turtles)

G *Erymnochelys* (Madagassian River turtles)

Erymnochelys madagascariensis (GRANDIDIER 1867), Madagascar, particularly NW

G *Pelomedusa* (Helmeted turtles)

Pelomedusa subrufa subrufa (LACEPEDE 1788), Helmeted turtle, tropical Africa and Madagascar

Pelomedusa subrufa olivacea (SCHWEIGGER 1812), NE Africa (Eritrea)

G *Pelusios* (African Mud turtles)

Pelusios adansoni adansoni (SCHWEIGGER 1812), Adanson's Mud turtle, W and Central Africa (Senegal, Mali, eastwards to Sudan)

Pelusios adansoni nanus LAURENT 1956, W Africa (Zaire southwards to Angola)

Pelusios bechuanicus bechuanicus FITZSIMONS 1932, S Africa (Angola, Namibia to Zimbabwe, Zambia and Botswana)

Pelusios bechuanicus upembae BROADLEY 1981, Zaire, Shapa Province, Upemba National Park

Pelusios carinatus LAURENT 1956, Congo Pelomedusid turtle, W Central Africa (Zaire and Congo)

Pelusios castaneus castaneus (SCHWEIGGER 1812), Brown Pelomedusid turtle, W and Central Africa, (except for area of other subspecies) Madagascar, Seychelles

Pelusios castaneus chapini LAURENT 1956, Central Africa (Lake Albert territory)

Pelusios castaneus derbianus (GRAY 1844), W Africa (from Gambia to Liberia)

Pelusios castaneus rhodesianus LAURENT 1965, Central Africa (from Zaire, Congo, southwards to Angola and Zimbabwe)

Pelusios castanoides HEWITT 1931, E Africa (Kenya to S Africa), Madagascar and Seychelles

Pelusios gabonensis (DUMERIL 1956), Gaboon turtle, W Africa (from Liberia to Gabun)

Pelusios niger (DUMERIL and BIBRON 1835), Black Pelomedusid turtle, W Africa (from Gambia to Angola)

Pelusios seychellensis (SIEBENROCK 1906), Seychelles

Pelusios sinuatus (SMITH 1838), Serrated Mud turtle, E and SE Africa (Somalia through Kenya south to Botswana)

Pelusios subniger (LACEPEDE 1788), East African Mud turtle, E Africa (Ethiopia to South Africa, Madagascar, Seychelles, Mauritius)

Pelusios williamsi williamsi LAURENT 1956, William's Pelomedusid turtle, SE Africa (Lake Victoria)

Pelusios williamsi lutescens LAURENT 1956, SE Africa (territories of Lakes Albert and Edward)

G *Peltocephalus*

Peltocephalus dumeriliana (SCHWEIGGER 1812), Dumeril's turtle, NE of S America (from Guayana, Surinam, eastwards to NE Brazil)

G *Podocnemis* (South American River turtles)

Podocnemis erythrocephala (SPIX 1824), Red-headed River turtle, NE Brazil (Rio Negro)

Podocnemis expansa (SCHWEIGGER 1812), Arrau turtle, North of S America (Orinoco and Amazon)

Podocnemis lewyana DUMERIL 1852, NW South America (Columbia and Venezuela)

Podocnemis sextuberculata CORNALIA 1848, Aiaca turtle, Northern S America (Amazon)

Podocnemis unifilis TROSCHEL 1848, Yellow-spotted Amazon turtle or Terracay turtle, Northern S America (from Venezuela eastwards to NE Brazil)

Podocnemis vogli MÜLLER 1935, Orinoco turtle, Northern South America (Venezuela, Orinoco region)

F Chelidae (Snake-necked turtles)

Sf Chelinae

G *Chelodina* (Australian Snake-necked turtles)

Chelodina expansa GRAY 1852, Giant or Broad-shell Snakeneck, E Australia (from N Queensland southwards to Victoria)

Chelodina longicollis (SHAW 1802), Common Snakeneck, E Australia (Queensland to Victoria)

Chelodina novaeguineae BOULENGER 1888, New Guinea Snakeneck, S New Guinea and NE Australia

Chelodina oblonga GRAY 1847, Oblong tortoise, SW Australia

Chelodina parkeri RHODIN and MITTERMEIER 1976, Parker's Snakeneck, SW Papua New Guinea

Chelodina rugosa OGILBY 1890, Northern Snakeneck, N Australia (Northern Territory and Queensland)

Chelodina siebenrocki WERNER 1901, Siebenrock's Snakeneck, SW Papua New Guinea

Chelodina steindachneri SIEBENROCK 1914, Western Snakeneck, NW Australia

G *Chelus* (Matamatas)

Chelus fimbriatus (SCHNEIDER 1783), Matamata, N and Central S America)

G *Elseya* (Australian Snappers)

Elseya dentata dentata (GRAY 1863), Elseya turtle or Deepshelled snapper, N and NE Australia (Northern Territory and Queensland)

Elseya dentata novaeguineae (MEYER 1874), New Guinea

Elseya latisternum (GRAY 1867), Shaw-shelled snapper, NE Australia

G *Emydura* (Australian Short-necked turtles)

Emydura australis australis (GRAY 1841), Red-faced tortoise, NW Australia

Emydura australis subglobosa (KREFFT 1876), New Guinea Painted tortoise, Papua New Guinea and West Irian (syn. *E.a.albertisi* BOULENGER 1888)

Emydura australis kreffti (GRAY 1871), Krefft's tortoise, E Australia (from Queensland southwards to New South Wales)

Emydura macquarrii (GRAY 1829), Murray's River turtle, SE Australia (New South Wales)

Emydura signata AHL 1932, Brisbane Short-necked tortoise, E Australia (SE Queensland)

G *Hydromedusa* (American Snake-necked turtles)

Hydromedusa maximiliani (MIKAN 1820), Prince Maximilian's turtle, SE Brazil

Hydromedusa tectifera COPE 1869, Cope's terrapin, Otter turtle, Argentine Snake-necked terrapin, SE Brazil, Paraguay, Uruguay and Argentina

G *Phrynops* (Toad-headed turtles)

Phrynops geoffroanus geoffroanus (SCHWEIGGER 1812), Geoffroy's Side-necked turtle, Central southern South America (Brazil and Paraguay)

Phrynops geoffroanus tuberosus (PETERS 1870), NE and E South America (from Guayana eastwards to NE Brazil, south to Bahia)

Phrynops gibbus (SCHWEIGGER 1812), Gibba turtle, NE and Central South America (Trinidad, from Guayana eastwards to NE Brazil, Amazon region)

Phrynops hilari (DUMERIL and BIBRON 1835), Frog-headed turtle, SE South America (SE Brazil, Uruguay, Paraguay, Argentina)

Phrynops hogei MERTENS 1976, Hoge's Side-necked turtle, S Brazil (Sao Paulo State)

Phrynops nasutus nasutus (SCHWEIGGER 1812), Common South American Toad-headed turtle, South America from Venezuela eastwards to Brazil, southwards to Paraguay

Phrynops nasutus dahli ZANGERL and MEDEM 1958, NW South America (Columbia)

Phrynops nasutus wermuthi MERTENS 1969, NW South America (Peru, Amazon region)

Phrynops rufipes (SPIX 1824), Red Toad-headed turtle, Northern Central Brazil

Phrynops tuberculatus tuberculatus (LUEDERWALDT 1926), E Brazil (Bahia)

Phrynops tuberculatus vanderhaegei BOUR 1973, Paraguay

Phrynops williamsi RHODIN and MITTERMEIER 1983, William's Toad-headed turtle, SE Uruguay, E middle Argentina

G *Platemys* (Flat-shelled turtles)

Platemys macrocephala RHODIN, MITTERMEIER and McMORRIS 1983, Central Bolivia and Central Brazil

Platemys pallidipectoris FREIBERG 1945, Argentina (Gran Chacos)

Platemys platycephala platycephala (SCHNEIDER 1792), Flat-shelled turtle, N South America from Peru to Surinam, N Brazil

Platemys platycephala melanonota ERNST 1983, Peru (Rio Cenepa and Rio Santiago), Ecuador (Rio Napa and Rio Curanay)

Platemys radiolata radiolata (MIKAN 1820), Central South America (Brazil from Amazon southwards to Sao Paulo)

Platemys radiolata spixi (DUMERIL and BIBRON 1835), SE South America (N Argentina and S Brazil)

G *Rheodytes* (Fitzroy turtles)

Rheodytes leucops LEGLER and CANN 1980, Fitzroy turtle, NW Australia (Fitzroy River)

Sf Pseudemydurinae

G *Pseudemydura* (Swamp tortoises)

Pseudemydura umbrina SIEBENROCK 1901, Western Swamp tortoise, SW Australia (near Perth)

Bibliography

General

BELLAIRS, A.: *The Life of Reptiles*. Univers. Nat. Hist. Series. New York, 1970.

BOJANUS, L.: *Anatome testudinis europaeae*. Vilnius, 1819–21. Reprint Ohio, 1970.

GANS, C. et al.: *Biology of the reptilia*. Academic Press, London and New York, continuously since 1969, at present 13 vols.

PORTER, K.: *Herpetology*. Philadelphia, London, Toronto, 1972.

TERENTYEV, P. V.: *Gerpetologia* (in Russian). Moscow, 1961.

Grzimeks Tierleben. Vol. *Kriechtiere*, Part *Schildkröten*. Revised by M. Mlynarski and H. Wermuth, Zürich, 1973.

Monographs

BUSTARD, R.: *Sea turtles, their natural history and conservation*. New York, 1973.

CARR, A.: *The Turtle: a natural history*. London, 1968.

GAFFNEY, E.: "Comparative cranial morphology of recent and fossil turtles," in: *Bull. American Museum Nat. Hist.* Vol. 164, 2. New York, 1979.

HARLESS, M., and H. MORLOCK: *Turtles—perspectives and research*. New York, Chichester, Brisbane, Toronto, 1979.

IVERSON, I.: *Turtles of the world*. A checklist. Kansas, 1984.

MLYNARSKI, M.: *Fossile Schildkröten. Die Neue Brehm-Bücherei 396*. Wittenberg-Lutherstadt, 1969.

MLYNARSKI, M.: "Testudines", in: *Handbuch der Paläoherpetologie*. Part 7. Stuttgart and New York, 1976.

PARSONS, J.: *The Green turtle and men*. University of Florida Press, 1962.

PRITCHARD, P.: *Living turtles of the world*. Neptune City, 1967.

PRITCHARD, P.: *Encyclopedia of turtles*. Neptune City, 1979.

WERMUTH, H., and R. MERTENS: *Schildkröten, Krokodile, Brückenechsen*. Jena, 1961.

WERMUTH, H., and R. MERTENS: "Testudines, Crocodylia, Rhynchocephalia", in: *Liste der rezenten Amphibien und Reptilien. Das Tierreich*. Instalment 110. Berlin and New York, 1977.

Faunas and studies in identification and classification

Europe:

ARNOLD, E. N., and J. A. BURTON: *A field guide to the Reptiles and Amphibians of Britain and Europe*. London 1978.

BRONGERSMA, L. D.: *European Atlantic turtles*. Leiden, 1972.

GLÄSS, H., and W. MEUSEL: *Die Süßwasserschildkröten Europas. Die Neue Brehm-Bücherei* 418. Wittenberg-Lutherstadt, 1969.

MERTENS, R., and H. WERMUTH: *Die Amphibien und Reptilien Europas*. Frankfurt/Main, 1960.

OBST, F. J., and W. MEUSEL: *Die Landschildkröten Europas. Die Neue Brehm-Bücherei* 319. Wittenberg-Lutherstadt, 1978.

SCHREIBER, E.: *Herpetologia Europaea*. Jena, 1912.

TRUTNAU, L.: *Europäische Amphibien und Reptilien*. Stuttgart, 1975.

Asia:

BANNIKOV, A.G., I.S.DAREVSKY, V.G.ISTCHENKO, A.K.RUSTAM-OV, and N.N.SCERBAK: *Opredelitel premykayushchikh i zemnovodnykh v faune SSSR.* Moscow, 1977.

BOURRET, R.: *Les tortues de l'Indochine.* Hanoi, 1941.

MAO, S.H.: *Turtles of Taiwan.* Taipel, 1971.

NUTAPHAND, WIROT: *The turtles of Thailand.* Bangkok, 1979.

POPE, C.H.: *The reptiles of China.* New York, 1933.

ROOJI, N.de: *The reptiles of the Indo-Australian Archipelago.* Vol. 1. Leiden, 1915.

SMITH, M.A.: *The Fauna of British India, Ceylon, and Burma. Reptilia and Amphibia.* 1st vol. London, 1931.

TAYLOR, E.H.: *Philippine turtles.* Manila, 1920.

Africa:

LOVERIDGE, A.: "Revision of the African terrapins of the Family Pelomedisidae." in: *Bull. Museum Cambridge, USA.* 1941.

LOVERIDGE, E., and E.E.WILLIAMS: "Revision of the African tortoises and turtles of the suborder Cryptodira", in: *Bull. Museum Cambridge, USA.* 1957.

Australia:

CANN, J.: *Tortoises of Australia.* London, Sydney, Melbourne, 1978.

COGGER, H.: *Reptiles and Amphibians of Australia.* Sydney, Wellington, London, 1975.

GOODE, J.: *Freshwater tortoises of Australia and New Guinea.* Melbourne, 1967.

America:

BEHLER, J.L., and F.W.KING: *The Audubon Society Field Guide to North American Reptiles and Amphibians.* New York, 1979.

BRUCE BURY, R.: *North American Tortoises—Conservation and Ecology.* Washington, 1982.

CARR, A.: *Handbook of turtles. The turtles of the United States, Canada, and Baja California.* Ithaca, New York, 1952.

ERNST, C.H., and R.W.BARBOUR: *Turtles of the United States.* University Press of Kentucky, 1972.

FREIBERG, M.: *Turtles of South America.* Neptune City, 1981.

OBST, F.J.: *Schmuckschildkröten. Die Neue Brehm-Bücherei 549.* Wittenberg-Lutherstadt, 1983.

POPE, Ch. H.: *Turtles of the United States and Canada.* New York and London, 1939.

SMITH, H.M., and R.B.SMITH: *Synopsis of the herpetofauna of Mexico.* Vol VI: *Guide to Mexican turtles.* North Bennington, 1979.

Terrariatology

FRITZSCHE, J.: *Das praktische Terrarienbuch.* Radebeul, 1980.

KLINGELHÖFFER, W., and C. SCHERPNER: *Terrarienkunde.* Vol. 4: *Schlangen, Schildkröten, Panzerechsen.* Stuttgart, 1959.

KREFFT, P.: *Das Terrarium.* Berlin, 1926.

KREFFT, G.: *Schildkröten.* Brunswick, 1949.

NIETZKE, G.: *Die Terrarientiere.* Stuttgart, 1969 and 1972.

OBST, F.J.: *Schildkröten, AT-Ratgeber-Reihe* 12. Leipzig, Jena and Berlin, 1980.

OBST, F.J., K.RICHTER, and U.JACOB: *Lexikon der Terraristik und Herpetologie.* Leipzig, 1983.

STETTLER, P.H.: *Handbuch der Terrarienkunde.* Stuttgart, 1978.

WILKE, H.: *Schildkröten.* Munich, 1980.

In addition to this necessarily restricted selection from the literature, we would particularly recommend a number of books providing a more general survey of amphibians and reptiles, in which turtles are dealt with in considerable detail.

Acknowledgements

For support of all kinds that I have received during more than three decades devoted to a study of amphibians and reptiles, and in particular of chelonians, I am greatly indebted to a large number of people. Whether it was in the provision of live or preserved specimens, or of rare works in the literature, in the use of foreign archives, collections and libraries, the preparation or procurement of photographs, some of them unique—all have made a substantial contribution to my work and finally to the writing of this book. But undoubtedly the greatest benefit is that these activities and contacts have gained for me a valuable circle of friends, many of whom are named below. In drawing up a list, there is a danger that some individuals may be overlooked. If there are any of these, I hope they will forgive me and nevertheless be assured of my gratitude for the help they have shown me. I would like particularly to mention the following: Prof. Dr. H. Ambrosius, Leipzig, Karl Marx University; Dr. P. Arnold, Dresden, Münzkabinett der Staatl. Kunstsammlungen; Dr. T. Baackmann, Gladbeck (Federal Republic of Germany); D. Ballasina, Tervuren (Belgium); A. Bautin, Dushanbe (USSR); E. Blättler, Lucerne; Dipl.-Ing. K. H. Bochow, Weimar; Dr. W. Böhme, Bonn, Museum Alexander Koenig; J. Cann, Phillip Bay, Australia; H. Budde, Ammansegg (Switzerland); Prof. Dr. I. S. Darevsky, Leningrad, Zoological Institute of the Academy of Sciences; M. Drescher, Eberswalde (German Democratic Republic); Dr. W. E. Engelmann, Leipzig, Zoological Garden; M. Förster, Dresden and Leipzig; Dr. J. Franzen, Frankfurt/Main, Senckenberg Museum; Prof. W. Frair, New York; R. Friedel, Leipzig; J. Fritzsche, Dresden; J. Furrer, Seon (Switzerland); L. Gärtner, Dresden; Dr. T. Harrison (†), Sarawak; H. Heinemann, Helbra (German Democratic Republic); Dr. J. Hemmerling, Leipzig; Dr. R. Hertel, Dresden, Staatliches Museum für Tierkunde; P. E. His, Basel; G. Hoffmann, Dresden and Radeberg; R. Honegger, Zürich, Zoological Garden; H. Jes, Cologne, Aquarium of Cologne; H.-V. Karl, Erfurt and Weimar; P. and R. Kisser, Uhldingen, House of Reptiles; J. Klages, Zürich; Dr. G. Kuchling, Vienna; Dr. M. Lambert, London; B. Langerwerf, Waspik (Netherlands); J. Langula, Erfurt; Dipl.-Ing. D. Losansky, Frankfurt/Oder; Dr. F. Luttenberger, Vienna, Tierpark Schönbrunn; Meeresmuseum Stralsund; W. Meusel, Karl-Marx-Stadt; Prof. Dr. M. Mlynarski, Cracow, Zoological Institute of the Academy; A. Nöllert, Holzendorf (German Democratic Republic); J. Opitz, Frankfurt/Oder; N. L. Orlov, Leningrad;

Dipl.-Ing. I. Pauler, Vienna and Frankfurt/Main; R. Pawley, Brookfield (USA), Brookfield Zoo; M. Peltier, Olten (Switzerland); Prof. Dr. G. Peters, Berlin, Zoologisches Museum; Dr. H. G. Petzold (†), Berlin, Tierpark; G. Praedicow, Erfurt; Dipl.-Biol. M. Reimann, Braunweiler (Federal Republic of Germany); Dr. N. Reinheckel, Dresden, Staatliche Kunstsammlungen; J. Rotter, Wittinsburg (Switzerland); H.-W. Rudloff, Wittenberg-Lutherstadt; K. Rudloff, Berlin, Tierpark; Prof. Dr. W. Sachsse, Mainz, Institut für Genetik der Universität Mainz; S. Schaarschmidt, Hamburg; E. Sochurek, Vienna; Staatliches Museum für Völkerkunde Dresden; O. Stemmler, Basel; P. H. Stettler, Bern; N. Thang, Ho-Chi-Minh-City; Dr. U. Thieme, Wittenberg-Lutherstadt; Dipl.-Biol. L. Trutnau, Altrich (Federal Republic of Germany); H. Trieth, Bern; G. Uhlig, Zeitz (German Democratic Republic); Dr. H. Ullrich, Berlin; Ch. Unternährer-Stocker, Basel; H. and W. Weissinger, Sankt Andrä-Wördern (Austria); H. Winkler, Rostock; C. J. Winkelmann, Rosmalen (Netherlands); K. Ziegan, Berlin (West).

Equally I wish to thank the publishing house of EDITION LEIPZIG, who made the publication of this book possible, Herrn Wolfgang Leuck who made the drawings with skill and expertise, Herrn Matthias Weis who prepared the maps and Frau Traudl Schneehagen who designed the book with imagination and sympathy. I am particularly indebted to my friend M. Förster, who prepared a large number of technical photographs especially for the book. My colleague Frau B. Heger and my wife provided valuable assistance in the preparation of the manuscript. Further thanks are due to Mrs. Furness for her excellent translation of the German text into English. My thanks finally go to my family who were able to share my interests through the years.

Sources of illustrations

Author's archives: 19 (top), 144 (bottom left), 202, 203 (bottom)
Bochow, K.-H., Weimar: 18
Cann, J., Phillip Bay: *60* (top left; bottom), *61*, *62* (3 ×)
Förster, M., Leipzig: 58 (top left and right), *64*, *89*, *96* (bottom), 98 (top), *129*, 132 (2 ×), 133 (3 ×), 134 (2 ×), 135 (2 ×), 136, 137, 138 (top; centre left and right), *152*, 175, *177*, 178, 181, *188*, 190, 191, 192, 193, *194*, *195*, 196, 197 (bottom), 198, 201 (bottom), 203 (top)
Franzen, J., Frankfurt (Main): 95 (bottom)
Furrer, J., Seon: *103* (top)
Goode, J., Frankston: *60* (top right), *147* (2 ×)
Harrison, T., Sarawak: 10, 11 (3 ×), 14
Heusser, H., Zurich: 130 (top left and right), 131 (top left and right)
Höflinger, E., Basel: 197 (top), *199* (2 ×), *200* (2 ×), *201* (top)
Honegger, R., Zurich: 19 (bottom), 21, 22 (3 ×), 23 (top right), 90 (bottom), 98 (bottom), 100 (2 ×), *104*, *140* (top), *141*, 142 (top)
Klages, J., Zurich: *15*, 148, 149
Lambert, M. R. K., London: 23 (bottom)

Moll, E., Charleston: *56*, *57* (2 ×)
Obst, F. J., Dresden: *50* (bottom), *52* (4 ×), *53* (bottom), *54* (3 ×), *55*, *93* (bottom), *97*, *99*, *101* (3 ×), *103* (bottom), 138 (bottom), *140* (bottom), *141*, 146 (centre; bottom right), *151*, endpaper
Patchett, Perth: *50* (top)
Pauler, J., Vienna: *51*
Peabody Museum, Yale: 94 (bottom)
Peltier, M., Olten: 94 (top), 95 (top), *150*
Pritchard, P., Aitland: 20
Rudloff, K., Tierpark Berlin: 58 (centre left and right; bottom), 59, 63, 90 (top), 91, *93* (top), *96* (top), 130 (bottom), 131 (bottom), 139, *143*, 144 (bottom right), 145
Schaarschmidt, S., Hamburg: *9*, *12*, *13* (2 ×), 14 (top), *16*, *17*, *24*
Sochurek, E., Vienna: 102 (right), 146 (top)
Thieme, U., Wittenberg Lutherstadt: 144 (top)
Trutnau, L., Altrich: *49*, 53 (top), *102* (left), *184*, *187*
Zimmermann, J., Wittenberg Lutherstadt: *92*
Zoological Society, New York: 150 (bottom)

Index of popular names of those turtles and tortoises mentioned in the book.

Numbers in *italics* refer to illustrations.
g = genus, t = tribe, sf = subfamily, f = family, og = ordergroup
supf = superfamily, so = suborder, o = order

Index of scientific names of those turtles and tortoises mentioned in the book.

Numbers in *italics* refer to illustrations.
g = genus, t = tribe, sf = subfamily, f = family, supf = superfamily, sg = subgroup, og = ordergroup, so = suborder,
o = order